Rethinking Writing

Rethinking Writing

PESHE C. KURILOFF
University of Pennsylvania

ST. MARTIN'S PRESS   NEW YORK

Senior Editor: Mark Gallaher
Associate Editor: Kim Richardson
Project Editor: Joyce Hinnefeld
Production Supervisor: Christine Pearson
Text Design: Leon Bolognese
Graphics: G&H Soho
Cover Design: Tom McKeveny

Library of Congress Catalog Card Number: 88-60555

Manufactured in the United States of America.
32109
fedcba

For information, write:
St. Martin's Press, Inc.
175 Fifth Avenue
New York, NY 10010

ISBN: 0-312-00274-2

ACKNOWLEDGMENTS

Erma Bombeck, "Motherhood: The Second Oldest Profession." Reprinted by permission of
The Aaron M. Priest Literary Agency, Inc.
One hundred words from "Living Like Weasels," from *Teaching a Stone to Talk* by Annie
Dillard. Copyright © 1982 by Annie Dillard. Reprinted by permission of Harper &
Row, Publishers, Inc.
Excerpt from "Tradition and the Individual Talent," from *Selected Essays* by T. S. Eliot, ©
1950 by Harcourt, Brace, Jovanovich, Inc., renewed 1978 by Esme Valerie Eliot,
reprinted by permission of Harcourt, Brace, Jovanovich, Inc., and Methuen and Co.
"Were Dinosaurs Dumb?" Reprinted from *The Panda's Thumb, More Reflections in Natural
History*, by Stephen Jay Gould, by permission of W. W. Norton & Co., Inc., copyright
© 1980 by Stephen Jay Gould.
From "When America Entered the 20th Century," by Irving Howe, September 28, 1986,
Book Review. Copyright © 1986 by the New York Times Company. Reprinted by
permission.
Three hundred fifty words from "Letter from Birmingham Jail," from *Why We Can't Wait* by
Martin Luther King, Jr. Copyright © 1963, 1964 by Martin Luther King, Jr. Reprinted
by permission of Harper & Row, Publishers, Inc.
Maxine Hong Kingston, "No Name Woman," from *Woman Warrior*, © Alfred A. Knopf,
1976. Reprinted by permission of Alfred A. Knopf, Inc.

Acknowledgments and copyrights are continued at the back of the book on page 230, which
constitutes an extension of the copyright page.

PREFACE

Although it is primarily about writing, *Rethinking Writing* is also about reading and thinking. It is intended to help advanced students become more competent, independent writers by showing them how to read constructively, think creatively, and write effectively for a variety of purposes and audiences. Culled from nine years of teaching advanced nonfiction writing at the University of Pennsylvania, the advice offered here has worked for many of my students. I hope it will work for yours.

The approach taken in this book assumes that students have control over the mechanics of writing—grammar, punctuation, spelling, sentence and paragraph structures, basic forms, and the rudiments of good style. *Rethinking Writing* picks up where many freshman composition textbooks leave off. It follows a process approach to writing, emphasizing the importance of writing in stages and of learning in the course of writing. It also assumes, however, that students and their instructors care about the written text that students produce. Consequently, it does not take the product of writing for granted. The process students go through when they write must lead to a satisfactory product.

There are numerous approaches to teaching writing, many of which ignore the primary role the individual writer plays in creating the text and the role specific readers play in determining its value. In my experience, no particular way of writing works for all writers or communicates with all readers. Writers have to know themselves, their goals, and their audiences in order to write effectively. As a result, *Rethinking Writing* encourages students to trust themselves and to gear what they write to specific audiences.

Rethinking Writing also presents writing as a social act that takes place between people. It suggests that all writers want to communicate with readers and that the rewards of writing come from successfully communicating with a chosen audience. Because writing acquires significance primarily through the interaction between writer and reader, this book offers no absolute definition of good writing. Good writing elicits the response the writer seeks from specific readers.

The structure of this book suggests a model for learning writing that has proven useful for many students. Chapter 3, "Revising Writing," comes after "Writing for Readers," because many student writers need to come to terms with their audiences in order to revise efficiently. Chapter 5, "Writers and Their Ideas," comes relatively late in the book because creative thinking is not a prerequisite for good writing. Once students have internalized a model for the writing process, have developed reader awareness, and have practiced revising, they can more easily let their creativity emerge. Chapter 6, "The Writer's Personality," comes last because students often more readily master voice when other features of writing are under control.

Chapter 4, "The Conventions of Writing," introduces the concept of communities of writers and readers. Students—even advanced undergraduates—are often unaware that, like other kinds of communities, discourse communities have customs that members must observe if they want to belong. If writers want readers to accept them as psychologists, as mechanical engineers, or as attorneys, they must write like other members of that community, sharing the same language and following the same rules for presentation. By reviewing conventions in three different disciplines, *Rethinking Writing* demonstrates how conventions govern writing and how students, as they enter new fields or undertake new writing tasks, can begin to identify the conventions they need to observe in their writing.

Rethinking Writing can be used effectively in a writing course or in a writing-intensive course. If students are in a class with other writers, many of the activities suggested to help them consider their readers can be carried out with classmates. If such ready-made readers are not available, however, students can still learn what they need to know. They might be encouraged to form a writers' group and do some of their work together. Instructors in writing-intensive courses could help students by volunteering to read drafts or providing alternative readers. Much of what students need to learn about writing can be best taught through response. Students can read this text on their own, but their learning will be greatly enhanced by teachers who are willing to act as knowledgeable and responsive readers.

Although the rules for writing change from community to community, certain aspects of writing are consistent across communities, and it is those aspects this book emphasizes. Rather than trying to teach students how to write for specific occasions, *Rethinking Writing* asks them to learn principles of writing that they can apply in any context. A great deal can be learned about familiar subjects by thinking about them in a new way. My goal in this book is to offer students a new perspective on writing. I believe that the process of rethinking has value in itself, but I also believe that the rethinking required of students reading this book will lead them to write more effectively.

Acknowledgments

As is usually the case, *Rethinking Writing* represents a group, rather than an individual, accomplishment. I would like to acknowledge my editor at St. Martin's, Nancy Perry, for arousing my interest in this book and for setting a high standard. My gratitude goes also to Kim Richardson, associate editor, for helping me get permission to print the Chagall painting. I am grateful also to Roberto Kison for his permission to use his paper on Henry James and to Alan Scheiner, the writer of the social science research paper, and Leanna Lamola, the writer of the lab report. Thom Larson and Nina Stoyan also deserve thanks for helping me understand science writing. I want to thank two good friends, Susan Viguers and Rona Heifetz, for reading the manuscript and offering useful advice, and thanks go to Neal Hebert for keeping the office running so I could stay home and write. My family—my husband, Peter, and my children, Aaron, Gabriel, and Shoshana—deserve great credit for living with me during this period and for their faith in my capacity to do whatever needed to be done.

A number of instructors in a variety of fields served as reviewers of *Rethinking Writing*. I would like to express my appreciation for the comments and suggestions of Chris Anson of the University of Minnesota (Communications and Composition); Christine Cetrulo of the University of Kentucky (English); Lee Edgerton of the University of Kentucky (Agricultural Sciences); Anne Herrington of the University of Massachusetts (English); David Jolliffe of the University of Illinois, Chicago (English); Lorraine Morgan of Stanford University (Human Biology); Laura Otten of LaSalle University (Sociology and Criminal Justice); Linda Peterson of Yale University (English); Kate Ronald of the University of Nebraska, Lincoln (English); Ronald Schroeder of the University of Mississippi (English); Margot Soven of La Salle University (English); Jane Stanbrough of the University of California, Davis (English); Herman Stelzner of the University of Massachusetts (Communications); Margaret Stempien of Indiana University of Pennsylvania (Mathematics); David E. Stock of Washington State University (Mechanical Engineering); Douglas Thayer of Brigham Young University (Humanities); Bob Whitney of Millsaps College (English); and Mike Williamson of Indiana University of Pennsylvania (English).

Finally, I want to acknowledge all the students I have taught over the last ten years at the University of Pennsylvania, especially Writing Advisors. With remarkable persistence, they have struggled to teach me to teach them how to write. If this book works, it is because of them.

PESHE C. KURILOFF

CONTENTS

Chapter 2
Writing for Readers 45

Chapter 3
Revising Writing 71

Chapter 4
The Conventions of Writing *109*

Chapter 5
Writers and Their Ideas *161*

Chapter 6
The Writer's Personality *193*

Appendix
Some Information about Using and Documenting Sources *223*

Rethinking Writing

Introduction

Although you are probably reading this book in a course and writing under the direction of an instructor, this book is addressed to you the writer. It assumes that you have had enough experience writing to know that no one can simply tell you how to write well. You probably learned to write competently in secondary school, and you learned the requirements of college writing as a freshman. No amount of instruction alone will make you a writer, however. You have to develop a writer's consciousness, and the aim of this book is to help you do so.

Becoming a Self-Conscious Writer

The discussion that follows is intended for serious student writers who look forward to writing beyond their college years. If you have achieved a level of competence but still feel interested in learning more about writing, this book will provide some direction. However, the advice provided here will only be useful if you want to become a writer—not necessarily a professional writer, but a skilled writer in your chosen field. How do you know if that description applies to you? First, consider the following questions:

1. *Do you identify with the word* writer? If you do, you're off to a good start. If not, can you imagine yourself someday being a writer or a person who writes as part of your professional or personal responsibilities? You don't have to live in a garret or make your living from writing to be a writer. You do have to feel that writing is important, that it's worth taking time to write well, and that writing well is something you want to do.
2. *Do you find yourself outgrowing the prescriptions of your secondary-school teachers and your freshman textbooks?* Did you notice that the

1

way you were taught to write in secondary school didn't always work well in freshman composition? As your writing skills develop, for example, you may no longer need to write an outline or structure your papers on the model of the five-paragraph theme. Yet, you have no procedures to replace those you learned at an earlier stage. If you would like to learn new procedures more appropriate to your stage of development, you're probably open to becoming a writer.

3. *Do you find that the demands made on your thinking require you to change your writing?* As you are confronted with difficult conceptual tasks, capturing your thinking in writing often becomes more of a challenge. Even book reports may require more thought and more conscious effort to write than they used to. If you find yourself needing to approach your writing differently in order to bring it up to a level consistent with your thinking, you're probably ready to take on the responsibilities of a writer.

4. *As you write in different disciplines, do you find that you have to write differently?* As you move from discipline to discipline, you will probably notice that each field has its own way of writing. Sometimes, the differences are easy to identify, but at other times you may have difficulty understanding what's required. You can make these transitions more smoothly if you learn what distinguishes writing in various disciplines. If you're starting to notice those differences, you're probably starting to think like a writer.

5. *Do you find that you care more about your writing now, especially about communicating effectively with your readers?* For much of your life, you may have written exclusively for teachers, without ever considering whether they enjoyed what you wrote or found it interesting. Perhaps now you're starting to think more about who reads your writing and what effect it has on them. If so, you're acting more like a writer.

6. *As you gain experience writing, do you want to work more on your style, increase your versatility, and make your writing more interesting?* These are definitive signs of a burgeoning writer. As your goals change from meeting someone else's expectations exclusively to meeting your own, you will need to rely more and more on your own judgment and taste. If you're becoming more self-conscious about your writing and want to do more with it, you're on the way to becoming a writer.

Learning Self-Reliance

Stepping out on your own entails some risk, and you have to begin by trusting yourself. You may make some mistakes, and for a while your writing may seem to get worse, not better, as you try to achieve more complex goals. Don't lose heart. Success will come with practice and determination.

Perhaps like many writers you rely on intuition to guide your writing. You may believe in inspiration and prepare to write by invoking the muse or putting yourself in a receptive mood so that ideas will come to you. Often this process involves rituals, such as retreating to a special place or playing special music. Some writers fear that if they neglect those rituals, they will lose their power.

Although inspiration can seem like a gift to a struggling writer, you have to recognize inspiration and know how to use it. As Louis Pasteur eloquently put it, "Chance favors only the prepared mind," and it might be added that inspiration visits only the prepared writer. If you believe in yourself instead of the muse, you dispel the mystery that often surrounds writing. You can use your ability to think constructively, make decisions, and solve problems to empower you as a writer.

Just as you can become a skilled mechanic or musician through practice, you can also become a skilled writer. You begin with simpler tasks, under supervision, and then move on to more demanding ones. First, you perfect the book report and the basic research paper. You practice introducing ideas, developing them, giving examples, summarizing, and drawing conclusions. You work on the thesis statement, sorting through your thoughts and bringing them together into a single, unifying idea. These types of skills are mandatory for any writer, and anyone can learn them with practice.

This all sounds deceptively simple. Although it's not simple, it's not impossible either. If you have good resources for writing, good language skills, a good vocabulary, some experience with writing, and the desire to write well, you have much of what you need to become self-reliant and to succeed.

Getting to Know Yourself as a Writer

In addition to having basic skills, you also need to know yourself. What are your strengths and weaknesses as a thinker and as a writer? Do you have good ideas but have trouble expressing them? Do you write fluently but get bored by what you write? Do you find that you never understand what you're writing until you write the conclusion? Looking at yourself from the outside, how are you like and unlike other writers? What do you do that's unique? How might someone else describe the way you write?

To encourage self-awareness, begin by raising to consciousness everything you do in the process of writing. Try to include as much detail as possible. Concentrate on identifying individual quirks that might help you understand your attitude toward writing. Don't evaluate what you do. Just write everything down. Your list might start like this:

> read
> take notes
> read over my notes and organize them
> talk with my roommates about my paper
> clear my desk
> make a pot of coffee
> tell myself it doesn't matter what I write now—I can always change
>   it later
> write my introduction first
> promise myself I'll quit at midnight no matter what

Think for a minute about each item on your list, and make a note about why you do each thing. For example, what function does reading serve? It provides you with information, but it also prompts your thinking about your subject. That's why sometimes it's helpful to read even when you're in the middle of writing. Why do you clear your desk? Maybe you need to put aside distractions and create space that your thinking and writing can fill. As you work, do you fill that space with evidence of your effort, like pages of notes, books open to relevant pages, and empty coffee cups? Perhaps the litter you produce contributes to your sense of accomplishment. Assume that every activity you perform in the process of writing serves a purpose, and try to figure out what the purpose is. You will probably discover that many of the rituals you perform unconsciously serve you well. If you thought them through consciously, they might serve you even better.

Now make a list of everything that makes you feel good in the process of writing and another list of everything you dislike. How many of the good feelings can you count on every time you write? Can you think of ways of ensuring that you have more good experiences and fewer negative ones? For example, you might make sure you feel good about finishing a paper by allowing yourself enough time to read it over and make final changes. You might eliminate the feeling of panic that emerges when your ideas seem out of control by generating a thesis and having a plan before you start drafting. Even though you've developed habits that you've depended on for years, think about changing the way you write. Try to approach writing flexibly, and remain open to suggestions that make sense to you and do not undermine your identity as a writer.

Finally, note what you do that works and what doesn't work. Then gradually, one step at a time, stop doing what doesn't work and see if you can build on what does. If outlining works, fine; if it doesn't, don't waste your time. Find another way of organizing your thinking that feels more comfortable. Ways of coming up with alternatives are discussed later in this book (see Chapter 5). Do arranging and rearranging your notes help you get your thoughts in order? If so, would taking notes on file cards instead of notebook paper make your notes easier to sort? Might it help to move either to different color notecards or to different size paper as your thinking progresses so that you can easily identify what notes belong to what stage of thinking?

By the time you've gone over all the items on your lists, you should know yourself as a writer better than you did before. Armed with increased self-knowledge, you can take steps to make writing an easier and more routinely successful process than it may be for you now. Try out the techniques recommended in the pages ahead, and adapt the suggested strategies to suit your needs. Read this book with a combination of receptiveness and healthy skepticism. Remember that you are the authority on your writing.

Making Informed Choices

Should you say *I* or *we* when you refer to yourself in a paper? Should you present the events you plan to analyze in chronological order or begin with the most important ones? The writing process abounds with such choices. How do you know what to choose?

Unfortunately, until a choice has been made and acted upon, no one knows for sure whether it will work. As a result, learning about writing frequently means learning from your mistakes. Familiarity with choices other writers have made combined with experience in trying out different possibilities yourself will help prevent some mistakes; but you will never learn anything new about writing if you don't take risks. The point is not to avoid mistakes, but to make more wise, even exciting, choices and thereby increase your mastery over writing.

One way to increase your chances of choosing wisely is to recognize when choices exist. If you don't realize that you could use *I* instead of *we*, you give up an opportunity to make an informed choice. Using *we* may work out well, but perhaps *I* would work even better. How will you ever know if you don't think about it and maybe try it both ways? In addition, how will you know what to choose the next time? If you don't consciously make choices each time you write, you lose the benefit of your experience.

To begin increasing your self-consciousness about your choices, stop and think about what you're doing the next time you write a paper. Go ahead and write the way you usually do. Then look back at what you've written and identify each time you had a choice to make, whether you made that choice implicitly or explicitly. Look at the form of your paper, what you put in the beginning, middle, and end. Look at what you chose to say about your subject. Look at what you used for evidence to support your point of view. Look at your tone.

For each decision that you made, generate several alternatives. How else could you have approached your subject? What other beginning might you have chosen? What other examples could you have used? What else might you have included? Could you have sounded less formal? More specifically, should you have started a new paragraph every time you did? Could some of your paragraphs be divided and some combined?

If you think consciously about every choice you make in writing, you can easily become overwhelmed, but it's important to acknowledge the large number and variety of choices that exist. Writing is a complicated activity, and it makes demands on you at all levels, on your conscious mind and on your unconscious. As you acquire skill and experience, you naturally tend to relegate more choices to your unconscious, to allow yourself to make those decisions (such as when to begin a new paragraph) automatically. That's fine, as long as you don't forget that those choices are being made and that you can remake them if you choose. When you lose sight of your role in decision making, you surrender control of your writing to forces outside your conscious mind. For someone who wants to gain rather than surrender control of writing, it's probably wiser to err in the direction of consciously making too many decisions rather than too few. You can always give up some decisions once you have in perspective the spectrum of decisions you need to make.

What information do you need to choose wisely? Of course that varies from choice to choice and task to task. We'll examine some of your options in later chapters of this book.

Learning through Writing

Most writers are learners by nature. They enjoy writing because they enjoy discovering new ideas and communicating with themselves and other people about those ideas. New ideas motivate them to write.

As a writer, seek out opportunities to learn through reading, listening, observing, discussing, and writing. By taking an active, receptive stance toward all your experiences, you provide a fertile ground in which ideas can breed. Some of these ideas will never take shape in writing, but others will lend themselves to written form. As you gain experience, you will find that more and more ideas shape themselves in your mind as the substance of writing. You may realize, for example, that you're not just thinking about whether scarce resources should go to perfecting organ transplants or to basic biological research, you're mentally writing an argument for one side or the other. If you can't decide on a position, you might write out a debate on the question.

Because learning takes place differently in different disciplines, the writing that represents what you learn looks different when you're writing a biology paper than it does when you're writing a history paper. By the same token, annual reports to stockholders and articles in *Psychology Today* are written differently. Some of these differences occur because of differences in audience, but many relate to differences in the way learning takes place and, consequently, in the way ideas must be presented in order for readers to understand them. Because coming to terms with these differences is crucial for any writer, we will talk more about them later in this book (see Chapter 4).

Writing records what you learn, but it also promotes learning. One of the rewards of writing is the learning that occurs in the process. When you're finished, you understand your subject and your thinking about that subject in a way you didn't before. That knowledge becomes a part of you and stays with you while other ideas come and go. Should you forget what you thought, you can always read what you wrote and in this way recall your thinking—a process which is highly unreliable without a written record.

To get the most enjoyment from writing, greet new ideas and experiences enthusiastically. Welcome the opportunity to learn that writing offers. Learn in order to stimulate your writing, and write to solidify your learning. Good writers are almost always active, eager learners.

Rethinking Writing

In addition to the thinking you do about subjects for writing, you will need to think more about writing itself. Any time you take on a new role as a writer, write in a new discipline, or tackle a more complex writing assignment, you need to think a little differently about writing. As you develop more advanced categories for sorting and connecting knowledge and information, you need to develop ways of incorporating those categories in writing. A thesis about Einstein's theory of relativity probably can't be covered in a five-paragraph theme. Your ideas about writing have to expand to accommodate your more expansive thinking.

How does that rethinking occur? Sometimes you know intuitively that writing in a new field or for a new purpose requires a change in how or what you write. Other times you only realize once you've tried to write that your usual procedures don't work. At such times, or when you want to go further with your writing but aren't sure how to proceed, stop and rethink. Some questions to ask, along with possible answers, will follow in the upcoming chapters, but recognizing the need for rethinking will help you more than most of the specific suggestions. In the end you'll have to work out your own strategies for achieving your own goals, but this book may point you in the right direction.

This Introduction in Brief

Rethinking Writing will help you become a more self-conscious writer. To accomplish that goal:

1. Learn to be self-reliant as a writer.
2. Get to know yourself as a writer.
3. Make informed choices about writing.
4. Learn through writing.
5. Rethink how, why, and what you write.

Lovers under Lilies, by Marc Chagall

1

Creating Models for Writing

"Writing is like diving deep under water and then slowly working your way to the surface."

"Writing is like plodding through mud up to your knees."

"Writing is like chasing a butterfly or trying to find a single star in the Milky Way."

"Writing is like putting together a puzzle with five hundred pieces. Everything has a place if you can just make it fit together."

"Writing is like a quest for the perfect idea."

What do these images of writing have in common? They reveal that for many people writing involves a struggle or a difficult journey, often including obstacles that must be overcome before a destination is reached. Some people view writing as an attempt to capture or reach an ideal, others as an effort to create something whole out of pieces. For almost everyone, though, writing is a process, an activity that occurs over time. Writing is not an explosion, not a light going on in the dark, not an epiphany, not a flash of brilliance. Writing moves along, across space, through time, until it stops being writing and is written.

Like most people, you probably know good writing when you read it. Standards may vary, but you recognize writing that influences you, that has authority, that is correct, clear, and effective. You may even have a favorite writer whose prose you admire and try to emulate. Unfortunately, even a very clear image of the writing you would like to produce doesn't necessarily help you produce it. Keeping a goal in mind helps you know where you're going, but it doesn't always help you get there. How do you go about writing the prose you want to produce?

In this chapter we'll try to answer that question by looking at writing as an activity that takes place over time, that occurs both in our heads and through the physical act of writing words down, and that divides itself into stages that can be identified and characterized. We will discuss the *process* of writing, rather than its end product, almost exclusively, and we will acknowledge the varied processes that can lead to successful outcomes.

Some of this description may seem familiar to you; other parts may seem foreign, or even alien. Try hard to put yourself in the position of the writer described in the example later in this chapter. Even if you can't identify with everything the writer does, try to understand how the writer works. A similar process, if not this one, might work for you.

Approaching Writing in Stages

The process of thinking through, organizing, and writing a paper on almost any subject requires that you use an impressive assortment of cognitive skills. You may have to learn new information or ideas, relate them to each other or to ideas you already know, make inferences, synthesize, analyze, order, create new meaning, and communicate your thinking to others. As a result, it's easy to be overwhelmed.

Writing becomes easier to control if you don't try to do too much at once. Instead, approach it in stages. You were probably taught in high school to produce a research paper by reading and taking notes, outlining, writing, and editing. Some people adhere permanently to this method of producing a paper because they find it helps them break writing down into a series of manageable tasks. Others find that, as greater demands are made on their thinking, this model becomes too rigid. Many people reject outlining as a necessary condition for writing, preferring to write first and outline later, if at all. Lots of writers find this method of writing inadequate for their needs. They write and rewrite several times before they consider a paper adequately written. A simple four-step model does not reflect the way many writers work.

Because writing is not a linear activity, it can't be adequately represented by a few discrete steps. Many writers experience writing like any other artistic process. The writing doesn't simply get produced; it develops as the writer's ideas about it change. Some people see their writing emerging like a developing photograph, a vague image that gradually acquires shape, color, texture, and reality as a result of transformations that occur over time. For some, writing emerges from a process of gradual enlightenment: after a long period of grappling in the dark, they see how it fits together, what it all means.

If the simple four-step model of writing doesn't work in all situations, however, neither does the artistic process model. It's important to realize that writing is a creative process, but it can also be described, understood, and repeated. Beginning with an assignment or initial idea, a writer thinks through to a broad understanding of the subject and then narrows the subject through planning, drafting, and revising into a specific piece of writing. This process can be represented by a diamond-shaped pattern (see Figure 1-1). In this diagram, the starting point opens up to reveal myriad possibilities that must be focused on a specific end point. Good writing demands an expansive phase, when ideas are explored and the outcome is open-ended, followed by a formative phase, when through planning, drafting, and revising, an image of an outcome takes shape and becomes the goal the writer intends to reach.

In actuality, these different phases inevitably overlap, interact, and repeat each other. As a result, the diagram becomes a less-than-perfect diamond, one that can be redrawn to accommodate the variety of processes an individual writer might follow (see Figure 1-2). Ultimately, however, the writer prevails in creating order out of disorder, imposing form on formlessness, and finding meaning in seemingly random events, bits of information, or unconnected ideas and images.

All this sounds vague because it *is* vague; no single process or set of stages can accurately describe all writing. Still, a clear message comes through. Look for a series of stages to describe your own writing process, identifying whatever specific stages you find useful. Do not try to produce writing all at once. Take your time and do it right. The example that follows offers one model for conceptualizing writing. If it doesn't work well for you, you can create your own model. We'll discuss some strategies for alternative working models at the end of the chapter.

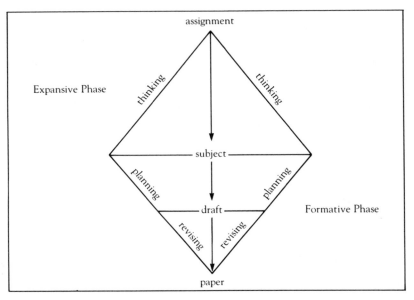

Figure 1-1

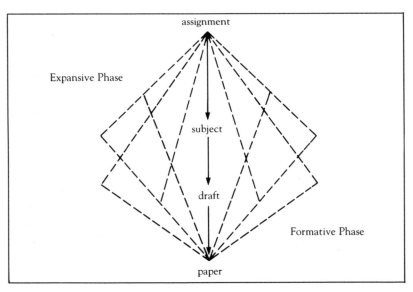

Figure 1-2

The Process of Writing: One Model

When trying to master any activity, it helps to have an image or model in your mind of how that process should go. For example, any experienced bread baker knows that making bread involves a mixing stage, a kneading stage, a stage when the dough rises, and a baking stage. For different types of bread, different ingredients are mixed together, and some breads have to rise twice. A few breads don't require kneading at all. Most bread baking, however, conforms at least loosely to the four-stage model. Knowing this helps bakers approach making new breads with some confidence. A baker may not know exactly how to make a new bread, but he or she knows generally about bread making. The same is true for writing.

Like all models, the one for writing that follows may seem artificial. It may not adequately represent the way you write. It is not, however, intended to be definitive, but suggestive. If, as you read, you can see how you might use a particular activity or create a similar stage in your writing process, write down what you're thinking. If a suggested stage makes no sense to you, try to figure out why. How do you accomplish the same goal differently? How might you incorporate the same procedure at a different stage? Use the model given as a guide to help you develop your own model.

Thinking Creatively

Good writing relies on good thinking, which is inherently creative. You can't write unless you have ideas. How do you get ideas? Some people naturally excel at this aspect of writing but have difficulty structuring their ideas in sentences and paragraphs. Even if creative thinking is one of your strengths, however, you can still learn to do it better (see Chapter 5).

When considering a writing assignment or when choosing a subject, too many people gravitate toward the obvious. Remember that the first thing that comes to your mind probably comes to many people's minds. Unless you want to sound like everyone else, you have to go beyond your first response. Record your idea, but don't stop there, especially if the idea fails to excite you. Keep thinking until you've exhausted your ideas on this subject and on as many related subjects as you can bring to mind. Allow your thoughts to range broadly around the subject so that you can choose what interests you to write about, and so that you can interest your readers.

The writing process begins not when you start writing, but when you start thinking about writing. Before you can project goals you want to reach in an actual paper, you have to think your way through to a question, an assertion or thesis, or a central idea which makes your subject manageable for the type of paper you intend to write. The process of choosing a subject, developing a central idea, or identifying a thesis represents a critical stage because so much follows from it. If you can't generate energy and commitment at this point, you're going to have a long uphill climb ahead of you. You can't afford to sit back and wait for stimulating ideas to enter your consciousness. You have to go after ideas, attack and subdue them when necessary, or sometimes let them carry you away. The richer your thinking at this early stage of writing, the more likely you are to make an informed choice of subject or approach to your subject. The more your subject excites you, the more likely you are to want to write well.

Thinking about a Paper. To concretize the model of writing being presented, let's work through an example. Assume that you are taking a course on twentieth-century art and that you have been assigned to write a three- to five-page paper. Your instructor asks you to visit the Marc Chagall exhibit at the Museum of Art, describe the exhibit, and draw some conclusions about Chagall's work from what you see. You have not yet studied Chagall, but you have learned about some of his contemporaries and are by now familiar with the period. How do you begin thinking about this assignment?

You could employ several possible strategies to help you think about the assignment. You could begin by reading about Chagall's life and style, so you know what to expect. The exhibit might give you some of that information, but reading ahead of time will help you know what to look for. That way, when you finally see the paintings, you'll already have some ideas about them on which you can build. You want to find out, if you can, what characterizes Chagall's style. Is he associated with any school or movement? Did his painting change over time? How did his background influence his art? Sometimes instructors discourage students from reading about an artist or writer before forming their own opinions. If that's the case, you might want to view the exhibit, then read, and then observe again. If your instructor absolutely forbids reading about Chagall at all while you're writing, you could review what you have read about the period and Chagall's contemporaries. What concerned artists at that time? What were they trying to accomplish? How did they define the relationship between art and life? Such thinking forms a base on which to construct your view of Chagall and helps you think about angles you could use to develop your paper.

When you actually look at the paintings, you need to observe them as a writer as well as a student of art. In other words, you need to look for their artistic qualities, but you also need to look at them as the subject of writing. You're going to write about these paintings later; what are you going to say? To prepare to write, first pay attention to your own reactions. What strikes you about what you see? How does it make you feel? What does it remind you of or make you think about? Do you think Chagall intended you to respond in this way? You could formulate some of these questions before you go, so you can interview yourself afterwards, but some may only occur to you as you observe and experience the works of art, so be sure to bring along a pad and pencil. If you trust your memory, you can wait until you get home to write down your thoughts, but you risk losing some of your most pertinent observations if you don't record them immediately.

Creating a Context for Writing

Writing, like speaking, is an act of communication that occurs between people. It also occurs for a reason, whether the reason is one that you choose or one that is thrust upon you. Your audience and your purpose create a context for writing and influence the decisions you make about your writing from beginning to end. Whether you're choosing a title or selecting examples, you need to keep your audience and your purpose firmly in mind. Consequently, it's helpful to think about them early in the process.

When you're used to writing exclusively for instructors, your sense of audience may be limited. It's important to remind yourself that other audiences exist and that now or at some point in the future you will have to address them. In addition, some people write to prove a point, to provide information, to entertain, to explain, or to persuade, as well as to fulfill an assignment. As you become a more independent writer, you will want to exercise more of your options.

Audiences and purposes motivate writers in addition to helping them make decisions. If you care about your audience and believe in your reason for writing, you are more likely to want to write well. You can't always write for the reasons and to the audience of your choice, but you can make the best of the context you're assigned. Look first at the context as it's given. What does the assignment require you to do? Is an audience implied, or can you choose your audience? If you're not happy with the parameters you're given, investigate changing them. If you wrote for a different audience than the one given—for people like yourself instead of experts, for example—might that be acceptable to your instructor? Don't be afraid to ask. As part of the writing process, create the most comfortable context for writing you can.

Creating a Context for Writing about Chagall. After you see the exhibit, your head is full of images from Chagall paintings. You see figures floating in air: violin players, green cows, and red roosters, all of which defy gravity and tease your imagination. You remember broad strokes of rainbow colors, huge bouquets of flowers, and lovers tenderly embracing. There were a few scenes of violence and destruction—villages burning, war—but they impress you less than the strange gaiety of Chagall's world. You don't know what to make of it or where to begin thinking about writing.

At this stage, thinking about your audience and your purpose in writing can help you clarify your ideas. What would you like to do with the material you have? What type of writing would you most enjoy? Does that fit in with the assignment? What about this material excites you? How might you convey that excitement to readers? After some discussion with yourself, you think you'd like to write a review. You've often read reviews in the paper but have never written one yourself, and you think it might be fun. The assignment also lends itself to that treatment. If you write a review for the campus newspaper, you could write for your fellow students, an audience with whom you are comfortable. In that context, you feel more like an authority and approach the task with greater confidence.

Your professor has no objections to your plan, so you proceed to think about the exhibit with your newly identified audience in mind. How might other students react to the exhibit? Would they be as excited as you are? What would students not enrolled in the course gain from seeing the exhibit? How much background would they need in order to appreciate what you want to say about the paintings? Should you give them much background in the review, or do you think it wiser to concentrate on a description of the exhibit or some of the individual works? All these questions and many more start nagging at you.

On the long walk back from the museum (which you decide to take to think about what you've seen and because it's a nice day), you concentrate on the questions you have. Your mind is too full of ideas to focus yet, and you let your thinker-self converse with your writer-self:

T: Besides describing the exhibit, what else do I want to do in the review?
W: I want to convey my enthusiasm, and I want to say a little about Chagall if I can.
T: Should I recommend the exhibit?

W: Absolutely. That's totally appropriate.
T: What would encourage my readers to go?
W: I have to make it sound worthwhile and also fun. I can't sound
   too intellectual.

With the help of a dialogue, the decisions you need to make begin to
present themselves one by one. Gradually, you work your way down your
list until you've narrowed your options and have some sense of what you
want to do.

All of this strategic thinking, note-taking, questioning, and hypothesiz-
ing constitutes preparation for the physical act of writing. You are already
aware of an attitude toward the exhibit that you want to communicate,
and you may be ready to compile a list of points you want to make in your
paper. After some further consideration, maybe some reading, and some
discussion with friends who may or may not have seen the exhibit, you feel
ready to organize your paper.

Planning: Imposing Order on Thinking

The planning process is the design phase of writing. At this point it's
helpful to have an image, preferably a visual representation, of the work
you intend to create. Experiment with different designs, organizing and
reorganizing your ideas until you achieve a workable image. The design
might be a drawing of the parts of the paper as you envision them fitting
together, a diagram of your argument or line of thinking, an arrangement
of notecards on the floor, anything that will help you envision the paper in
its finished form.

This image is in no way final; it serves as a tentative statement of your
intention. You may change details or even the whole concept before you
finish the paper. Yet you have to start somewhere, and starting with even a
tentative plan helps you feel confident, helps point you in the right direction, and helps guide you through the labyrinth of decisions you will have
to make as you work your way toward the paper you want to write.

You can also think about planning as creating a map or set of directions
that can guide you to your destination. Mark out a route on a piece of
paper using main points as major destinations, and examples or minor
points as places to stop in between. If there is more than one way you
could get from one point to another, indicate both possibilities; you can
choose the best one when you see the whole picture. The process of
mapping puts less emphasis on the form of your final product and more on

how you're going to get there. You can map out your route without deciding how the whole will eventually take shape. Many writers find that
approach more realistic, since complete images do not occur to them until
they are farther along in the writing process.

For obvious reasons, planning progresses more smoothly when you
know what you're writing about. Researching, reading, and thinking before planning make it much easier to impose order on your ideas. Confidence about command of your material often translates into confidence
about your ability to write that material, and difficulties about getting
started often reflect insecurity about the subject matter. Further reading
and thinking frequently cure the most serious cases of resistance and
writer's block. At the very least, good preparation and control over your
ideas maximize your chances of starting smoothly.

There are essentially two approaches to planning that most writers use:
either they produce a written plan before they write out their ideas (direct
planning), or they begin to write first as a way of clarifying their thinking
(indirect planning), and then produce a plan or go right to drafting. We'll
look at direct planning first.

PLANNING DIRECTLY

Planning strategies vary widely from writer to writer. Some writers plan
exclusively in their heads, constructing elaborate thought diagrams and
visualizing exactly how a paper will look when it eventually appears on the
page. Sometimes much of the composing process has already occurred in
the writer's head, so that phrases, sentences, and paragraphs leap onto the
page when the writer finally decides the time has come to write them
down. Most writers plan on paper, producing everything from detailed
outlines to elaborate diagrams or drawings. No matter what form it takes, a
plan should remind you of what you were thinking when you created it so
you don't have to rethink from scratch. Plans also provide you with reference points, so that you merely need to check the plan to see how far
you've come and where you have to go. Having that reference can be a
godsend when you get bogged down in some complicated portion of your
argument, analysis, or description. Although you may choose to modify a
plan as you write, keeping the plan beside you provides you with an
overview of the paper that helps you modify your strategy wisely, in a
fashion consistent with your overall intention, rather than merely on the
basis of the preceding paragraph or most recent flash of insight. Whether
you stick to it or not, a plan forces on you a view of the whole that is

difficult to achieve if you just begin drafting without anything to guide you.

Like writing itself, planning is not a linear process. Plans are formed recursively, as you think forwards and backwards, trying out your ideas to see how they fit together, checking for holes, changing the beginning to fit the end, shaping your thinking until it emerges in a form you recognize as a form and believe you can translate into a piece of writing. Since plans are always changing and evolving, any description of planning procedures may sound more tentative than you would like. The following advice may help you, however, to imagine an inherently disorganized process in a more constructive way:

1. Start planning by writing down the points you want to make in the approximate order in which you plan to cover them. Use outline form, note form, diagram form, list form, or whatever form you like.
2. From this group of points, determine your central idea. It could be an assertion (This is true. She is the best candidate.), or a question (How do moths become butterflies?). Write that at the top of the page.
3. Once you identify the central idea, evaluate the order of your main points and make changes. Try to find the order that will contribute most to the clarity of your central idea and will enable you to progress smoothly through the paper.
4. Indicate with arrows or notes in the margins how points connect with each other. (These will become your transitions later.)
5. Reevaluate the order based on how successful you were at making connections.
6. Rethink your connections based on any changes you have made in the order.
7. Find appropriate material for a beginning and an ending.
8. Then rearrange the middle so that it follows from the beginning and leads to the ending.
9. Fill in your plan with as much detail as you can. Note any examples you want to use or any special device (such as diagrams or anecdotes) you want to use to convey your ideas.
10. Try writing from the plan you have constructed. If you can't work from it, rethink it.

PLANNING INDIRECTLY

Even though so much can be said in favor of making a plan before you begin drafting, you still might prefer to leap into the void and think your

ideas through in writing. Such an approach can be particularly successful if
you find yourself stuck at the planning stage, and no vision of what you
want to create emerges. Simply start writing and continue until you have
all your ideas on your subject down on paper. This may take a few pages or
many, depending on the complexity of your thinking and the difficulty of
the writing task. Just try to get through all the points you want to make in
some sketchy fashion. Don't worry about details; you can go back and fill
in after you have a clearer sense of the paper overall. Leave spaces where
you know you will want to add material and move ahead to the next main
point. If you're not sure where to go next, make a note to yourself and just
move on to the next point that occurs to you.

Although composing without a plan can feel quite risky, it can also be
exciting. By jumping in, you may discover the energy required to work
your way through to a vision of the whole paper you are trying to write.
The holes in your thinking often become painfully obvious as you have
difficulty making transitions or reaching conclusions. At the same time,
the connections between ideas may be easier to realize as you relate them
to each other in sentences and paragraphs rather than by just placing them
above or below each other on a list. The product of this process often
serves the function of an outline or can easily become an outline or
another form of plan. Just go through what you've written, extract your
central idea, highlight the main points, and proceed with your plan. If you
have trouble figuring out which ideas are the main ones, trying to outline
can help you interpret what you're trying to say.

Indirect planning may result in a more workable plan than you would
have produced by trying to plan directly, but it can also feel like more
work. Even if indirect planning is more work, don't be tempted to try to
use the writing you produce through the process of indirect planning as a
complete draft or a finished paper. What you learn from the planning
process will help you write a better draft, but it won't substitute for it.
Trying to kill two birds with one stone by planning and drafting simultaneously only works for short pieces of writing or when your thinking is
exceptionally clear from the start. If you're not careful, you can easily end
up more muddled over your draft than you were before you began writing.

Used effectively, both direct and indirect planning can produce successful results. Which strategy you choose could depend on your mood, how
much control you have over your subject, the complexity of the subject, or
the nature of the writing activity. Feel free to use the two approaches
separately or in any combination that works. Unlike required outlines in

secondary school, plans are designed for writers, not teachers. If you can write from it, it's a good plan.

Remember that planning procedures, like all aspects of the writing process, vary from writer to writer, from activity to activity, and from discipline to discipline. Short, rule-governed tasks such as lab reports do not require the extensive planning that a senior thesis, or even a term paper, demands. The human mind can only hold so much information effectively at one time, so the longer and more complicated the writing task, the more you will need to plan. Even short papers, however, often require considerable planning, because you often have to exclude much of what you know and that complicates decision making. Determining what goes into and what comes out of a short assignment can be more challenging than planning a long paper where, to develop your subject fully, you'll have to include everything you know.

Many methods of planning exist. Realistically, you may never use the same method of planning twice. In order for planning to help, rather than hinder, your thinking, it has to fit both your personal style and the intellectual discipline of the field in which you are writing. What works for the Chagall paper might get in the way of planning a technical report where you might simply want to target information for specific, predetermined sections. Past experience, knowledge of the most common planning procedures recommended by teachers and writers, and ingenuity will help you discover the best methods for planning your writing. If you still get stuck, schedule a conference with an instructor or have lunch with a friend or classmate to discuss your ideas. Sometimes attempting to explain your ideas to another person can help you better understand what you're thinking.

Planning the Chagall Paper. You begin planning by structuring the questions you've been asking yourself more methodically. You know for whom you're writing and why; now you have to decide what you want to say. What about the exhibit stands out in your mind? What did you like best about Chagall? Which was your favorite painting? Why did you like that one best?

After concentrating on recalling the paintings, maybe with the help of a few postcards you purchased or a catalog, you write down the following words: subjects, colors, view of reality. These are the aspects of Chagall's paintings that most intrigue you, especially his view of reality as reflected in the unusual way objects and people in his paintings seem to float in air. These topics satisfy you because you find them interesting and because, from the reading you've done, you know they're important. You feel confident that your instructor will approve of your choices.

At this point, you could take the assignment at face value and start writing through these three topics until you've exhausted them or, more likely, used up your space. However, that would really be doing yourself an injustice. Remember, you're writing a review, and reviewing requires you to take a position, not just to describe. What point do you want to make about each of these topics? As a writer, what insight do you have to offer your readers?

After scrutinizing your list some more and doing more thinking, something occurs to you. Chagall expresses his view of reality in all the choices he makes in his paintings—in his use of color and in his choice of subjects as well as in his arrangement. Not only that, but his paintings blend a mundane view of the world with pure fantasy in his portrayal of ordinary life and events. Clearly he's asking us to see life as dreamlike or as fantastic. You take the painting of the lovers with flowers springing from their heads as a prototype, and you begin to design your paper around this central idea. You check your notes and recall several other paintings that will illustrate this point very well. You make another list, this time of just the three paintings you have chosen to help you illustrate your point, adding some reminders to yourself about how you want to use each painting, what you want to say about it, and how the three relate to each other. Then you number them, putting them in the order you think will most help you get your central idea across to your readers. At this point, your plan looks something like the following:

```
Chagall asks us to view life as a dream.


1.  Lovers under Lilies
          lovers, a favorite subject
          typical colors: describe, muted surround-
            ings
          composition: flowers seem to spring
                        from his head
                        town in background
                        arm encircling her bare
                        breasts
          feeling: joyful, spontaneous
```

2. The Fiddler

    appears often in Chagall's work, some-
        times violin by itself, represents art-
        ist?
    darker colors: browns, white, two-
                        tone fiddle, green
                        face
                        area of black, dark-
                            ness vs. white
    figure dominates; houses behind, under-
        neath; figure seems to be floating above
        earth, stares out of painting
    feeling: mellow, haunting

3. Wedding Candles

    lots of details: animals and human fig-
        ures, animal head on human figure
        (winged, goat-headed figure with wine
        glass)
        lovers at bottom, reclining on cock?
        chandelier with burning candles casts
        light over bride and groom, man playing
        green cello
    left half blue (again), dark; right side
        light, orange in background
    feeling: somber, eerie, disturbing?

You've left a lot of holes in this plan, but it gives you a sense of basic structure. You know in essence what you want to cover in each painting, and you can see how they will reinforce each other. Should you present them in the order in which Chagall painted them? You think not, since you're not making any statement about his development as a painter. You'll leave the order as is and progress from the simplest to the most detailed, since the details help to make your point about Chagall's view of reality.

Finally, since it's spring (remember your walk back from the exhibit), you decide that spring and fantasy go together, so you will use that to encourage readers to visit the Chagall exhibit now. That can be your introduction. What about your conclusion? You're not really sure. Perhaps you should relate Chagall's view of reality to that expressed by other painters of his generation. After all, this is a paper for a course, even if you're supposed to write it as a review, and you have that information in your lecture notes. You'll probably conclude with that.

As a plan emerges, you begin to feel enthusiastic about writing. You feel tentative at first, but as you flesh out your plan, your confidence builds. The urge to procrastinate is being overcome by the urge to express yourself. You want to see how this idea will work itself out and whether you can make your writing conform to the image you have constructed of the review in your head. You might try rehearsing a paragraph or two, just to test yourself and your readiness to write. You could draft the introduction or maybe experiment with your presentation of one of the paintings. When you start to feel impatient with the preliminaries and you just want to begin writing, then write.

Writing a Draft: Making Your Ideas Connect

After a while the planning process exhausts itself. You need a detailed plan to work from, but too much detail can make the plan seem too important—that is, the plan should serve as a means to an end, not an end in itself. Knowing when to stop planning and begin drafting requires judgment and self-knowledge. As a rule of thumb, it's probably better to plan less and draft more than to obsess over planning.

During the drafting process you compose your ideas, forming them into sentences and paragraphs that relate to one another and to your central idea. Strictly speaking, whether or not you're telling a story, you must link your ideas together somehow and create a whole piece of writing out of the sequence of points recorded in your plan. Many people recognize the importance of *flow* in writing. This is when flow comes into play. Each sentence must have its own integrity, but it must also follow from the one before and lead into the one after. Each paragraph must contribute to the evolving form your paper will take when it reaches completion.

Writing at this stage requires self-discipline, so scheduling, pacing, and goal setting become increasingly important. After several hours, you may lose your ability to concentrate and need to take a break or quit for the day. If this happens, use any leftover available time for less demanding writing activities such as reviewing notes, typing or recopying text, doing some more thinking, or talking with a friend about progress made or not made. Pace yourself to get the most out of your time. Take structured breaks, designed to serve as transitions between sections or as rewards for having finished a difficult passage. If you stop too many times, the text may tend to sound choppy. If you write for long periods of time without reaching any set goals, you can easily become frustrated. Try to draft a specific section of text at a single sitting or in a given space of time, and then reward yourself with a break. If you feel isolated, use your breaks to review your writing with a friend. Support from a sympathetic listener/reader will help send you back to work refreshed.

The energy required for drafting often comes from an urge to get everything you have to say down on paper. This is an urge you should respect and use. Following your plan may prove more difficult than you expected, but it will still provide you with a lot of ideas to express. Even if your plan breaks down, don't just discard it. If you think a point needs inserting, write a note to yourself and come back later. It's easy to waste a lot of time and energy on tangents and lose the continuity of your thinking. If you can capture at least a sense of how the whole piece of writing will take shape, you can fill in the details later.

You don't need to start at the beginning, although it may be easier. You can certainly skip the introduction, if that proves hard to write, and go right to the body of the paper. Some people write the ending first, which gives them a target to aim for, especially if their purpose is to report results. Don't feel bound to any particular order. Keep your mind set on incorporating your thinking in writing and producing a workable draft. Don't distract yourself by worrying about issues such as sentence structure and word choice that don't matter at this stage. You may eliminate that word, or a whole paragraph or section that's giving you trouble, when you revise. Concentrate on the progression of your ideas and on capturing them in written form.

Drafting the Chagall Paper. Going back to the hypothetical, carefully planned Chagall paper, how does the drafting process go? How do you use your plan as a guide to help you compose? You have an image of what you want to write, but at this point you need to turn images, feelings, and thoughts into sentences and paragraphs.

After some consideration, you decide to begin at the beginning. You start there because you want to connect Chagall's painting to the season, which you had targeted for the introduction, before you describe the paintings. Besides, writing about the paintings should be easier than writing the introduction—you have pictures of them to look at and notes to base your observations on—and you want to get the harder part out of the way first.

The introduction goes smoothly after all. You take a light journalistic tone:

> If the onset of spring has left you restless,
> why not consider an outing to the Museum of Art,
> currently featuring an exhibit by one of the mas-
> ters of artistic fantasy, Marc Chagall. Full of
> flowers, as well as some harsher views of man and
> nature, Chagall's paintings lead us away from our
> private meditations into a colorful, whimsical,
> and provocative vision that the artist invites us
> to share. Drawing on our natural curiosity, Cha-
> gall uses simple people in ordinary settings to
> engage us in speculations relating to God, order,
> science, and knowledge. Without even realizing
> it's happening, we find ourselves lost in
> thoughts Chagall has elicited, deep in consider-
> ation of subjects he has chosen, a perfect way to
> forget work and celebrate the new season.

Having finished the first paragraph, you pause and consider. You're not entirely satisfied with the language in this paragraph, but you like the direction. You've connected Chagall and spring, and you've introduced your central idea about Chagall's dreamlike view of reality. You've also begun to discuss the effect of his art on viewers. You weren't counting on that, but it seems to work. You can always rephrase this part later, so you decide not to worry about the details. The question is: should you go straight to the paintings or give some background here? Your plan is vague on this point. It would make sense to follow the introduction with some examples from the paintings, but you could also say a little bit about Chagall's life and how he came to express himself in the way he did. After some debate, you decide to go on to the paintings and return to Chagall's life later. You put the first painting in front of you.

One by one, you describe the three paintings. You don't try to include every detail of the paintings, just their unique characteristics, the ones that you want to emphasize and that help prove your point about Chagall's view of reality. For example, about the first painting you write:

```
The painting of the lovers has flowers
springing from the man's head as he gazes into
the woman's eyes, his arm encircling her bare
breasts. They look intently at each other, poised
to kiss.
```

Maybe they're actually standing beneath flowering bushes, but that doesn't seem right. The flowers seem almost like a headdress for the man, and that's what intrigues you.

```
There is a house in the upper left-hand corner
and outlines of houses that suggest a town in the
background. A small, full, golden moon shines
above the house in the corner. The painting both
excites and satisfies. The message, conveyed by
blue and green tones with shades of yellow and
red slipping into violet, feels warm.
```

You read over what you've written and then look at the painting to see if your description is accurate. Nothing major bothers you. Noticing the round shape of the moon, you change the word *full*, which suggests a stage rather than a shape, to *round*.

You go through the same process with each of the paintings, choosing the details you wanted to emphasize, eliminating others, and coming back each time to Chagall's extraordinary ability to convey depth and sense through apparent visual nonsense. You realize as you write on that that's the point you keep coming back to, the central idea of the paper. You direct each of your examples toward substantiating that claim, toward revealing Chagall as a self-conscious interpreter of reality rather than an imitator of reality. You can't just accept his vision. You have to question it and question its significance.

The end seems to write itself because you have learned so much from writing about the paintings. You briefly discuss the role of the artist as interpreter of reality, mentioning a few other names, then draw the whole piece together by playing up the usefulness of Chagall's view of reality in the contemporary world. You use the phrase, *escape into reality*, instead of *escape from reality* and are pleased by the notion. You feel good as you finish the draft, because you have expressed your own ideas and they are consistent with, but not exactly the same as, views you have read. The paper says something, you are sure of that, and it's pretty much what you set out to say. You put it away for a while and go meet a friend for dinner. You promised yourself you'd finish a draft and you did. You deserve a break.

In this initial drafting stage, thinking dictates much of the writing. You can't worry too much about the niceties of language when you've got ideas pressing to be articulated. Getting those ideas down on paper remains your first priority. If you can express them well, so much the better; but you concern yourself first with making sure that you capture the gist of your thinking in your writing. Although your ideas change as you write, you rely on your plan to help you stay on track. You could easily have gone on much longer about each of the paintings, but the point was not to interpret the paintings exhaustively. Having executed your plan, you feel you have reached your goal. When you come back to the paper, you will evaluate what you have accomplished and review it from other perspectives.

Revising Writing: Achieving Perspective

Because revising is the heart of writing, a whole chapter is devoted to revising techniques later in this book (see Chapter 3). For now, let's look at the role the revising stage plays in the writing process. Revising requires you literally to see again what you have written, often to see it differently than you did when you composed it. Remember the little cards in cereal boxes that presented two different images, depending on how you held the picture? If you looked at it one way, it was a face; if you looked at it another way, it was a cat. Revising works a little like that. It demands that you see your paper from different perspectives, recognizing how it appears now, but also imagining it as it might appear if you changed it.

At other times, revising proceeds differently, and you might think about it as similar to the process of finding a pattern in a seemingly chaotic image like an inkblot. You stare and stare and see nothing but black and white areas on paper and then suddenly you perceive a cow in a pasture. When you revise, you highlight the image of the cow. That is, you bring your thinking and your intended meaning into focus so that the image is clear to both you and your readers.

REVISING ON YOUR OWN

In order to revise successfully, you have to distance yourself enough from your work to achieve perspective. Leaving a draft for a while and coming back to it helps you achieve the needed distance. When you come back to your work, you will see it from a fresh perspective, with a reader's—not just a writer's—eyes. You learn a lot about your writing that way. Sometimes the disorganization, lack of continuity, or faulty sentence structure in your writing will surprise you. Sometimes you will be pleasantly surprised by how well a piece reads. What matters, however, is the element of surprise. Seeing your work differently than you did when you first wrote it helps renew your motivation and generate the energy required to revise the paper.

Begin revising by reviewing your context for writing. Keeping your audience and purpose firmly in mind, ask yourself the following questions:

1. Is this really what I want to say?
2. Could I have approached this subject more effectively from a different angle?
3. Have I thought through this paper enough? Do I completely understand what I'm trying to do? Do I have it under control?
4. Have I paid attention to my audience? Are their needs and expectations met?

If the answers to these major questions don't satisfy you, start your work there. Perhaps the angle you chose doesn't really work, or you're still not sure exactly what you want to do with your paper. Before you rewrite anything, stop and think. Look over your plan and compare what you've done with your draft with what you intended to do. Try to pinpoint what bothers you. If you can't figure out what's wrong, ask an instructor, a classmate, or a friend to help you.

Realizing the extent of the work still to be done shouldn't overwhelm or discourage you. Always expect to rewrite. In addition to your own needs, you have an additional factor to consider at this stage—your readers. The first time around you focused on matching your words with your vision. Now you need to consider your readers' understanding.

You can't count on people reading carefully, especially when other material is vying for their attention. Consequently, at a certain point you have to make your readers' needs at least as important as your own. However pleasing a metaphor might sound to you, if it doesn't enlighten the reader, it has to go. If you like, you can put it in a folder of metaphors for future use, just so you don't feel the effort of thinking it up was wasted. Whatever you do with it, it doesn't belong in the text if it doesn't serve its purpose.

The revising process often brings to light structural and organizational problems, inadequate explication of ideas, and phrasing that is difficult to follow. Some of these problems will leap to your attention when you read over a draft after some time has elapsed. Reading the paper out loud can help you look at the writing more objectively. To identify problems that don't readily assert themselves, try projecting an image of an ideal reader in your head. How does the paper appear from that reader's perspective? Specifically, how would the reader answer the following questions:

> What is the central idea of this paper? Is it clearly expressed?
> Does the paper read well? Does each point follow logically from the previous one? Are the transitions smooth?
> What expectations are raised in the introduction? Are they met?
> Does the ending convey a sense of resolution or conclusion?
> Are all ideas clearly expressed?

This may seem like a great deal of effort, especially for a short paper, letter, or report. When asking these questions becomes a habit, however, and you internalize the procedure, the expectation that you will eventually have to answer them will guide your writing from the beginning. As a result, the need for consciously asking yourself questions diminishes. Asking questions like these also helps you gain insight into decisions you may have made unconsciously. Raising these decisions to consciousness creates the opportunity for you to choose differently, an opportunity that didn't exist until you realized a decision had been made.

Revising the Chagall Paper. When you finished drafting the Chagall paper, you felt pretty good about it. All the ideas you had planned to express went into it, as well as a few you hadn't thought of until the writing process brought them to mind. Since you haven't looked at the draft since yesterday, you pick it up and scan it quickly. You make your points all right, but now you're not sure about the flow. The paper doesn't read as smoothly as you would like it to. You're not confident that your readers will enjoy it. At this point, you assess your time. The paper isn't due for another day. You relax a little and start reading the draft aloud.

As you read, you're aware of viewing your writing for the first time from a reader's perspective. The phrases you wrote just a day ago sound somewhat unfamiliar when you hear them now. A few of them sound better than you expected, but you stumble over others, like "the fine points that surround the fiddler, which are hard to decipher in the dark." A couple of times you lose track of your line of reasoning. You wonder what "and so the painter uses the spontaneity of flowers to draw us into his vision of reality" means. Particularly when you move from painting to painting, you aren't sure why you put them in the order in which they appear. You remember that there was a reason, but it isn't clear from what you've written. Just starting with "In *The Fiddler* Chagall surrounds the central figure with lots of detail" doesn't explain why you're presenting that painting next. You're pleased with your ending; it has a lot of authority and clearly summarizes what you learned. The introduction, however, seems weak. You wonder if the ending should really be the beginning. But then how would you end?

You attack the problem of the introduction first. There's no question that the conclusion, with a few minor alterations, could serve as the introduction and that it would get the paper off to a stronger start. You hesitate. You might be making a lot of work for yourself. Is it worth it? You decide to plunge in. You cross out the introduction and move the conclusion to the front, cutting it down a bit, eliminating sentences such as the following one that summarizes your argument:

```
Chagall does not, then, take us out of the real-
ity we know; he reinterprets reality in a way
that alters our perspective on it.
```

Then you add a few sentences that preview your point about Chagall as a creator of dreams and fantasies:

```
Marc Chagall lures us into a world of dreamlike
wakefulness, where, suspended in time and space,
we sense rather than see the world we know.
```

You read it over and decide that this approach has more punch. It is definitely more consistent with your central idea than was your original discussion of Chagall and spring. You've vastly improved the opening and increased the likelihood that readers will want to read on.

The new beginning necessitates some attention to the transition between the first paragraph and the second. You look at the second paragraph carefully:

> One painting after another in this striking collection evokes a startling dreamlike vision of events. Some of the details are familiar, but the overall effect is strange, even disturbing, at times. We don't recognize the real world in the world on the canvas. Yet we have a sense that we've seen these images before, or at least that the feeling they create is not strange.

There's something wrong, but you're not sure what. What are you trying to say? You think about the sentences for a few minutes and read them over several times. Finally, you realize that they just repeat what you say in the first paragraph about Chagall's reality and postpone the meatier part of the paper, the actual examination of the paintings. With some regret (cutting is always painful), you take out the second paragraph and go right to your examples.

Checking your plan, you remember that you put your description of the painting of the lovers first because the way Chagall uses fantasy is easier to explain through that painting than through the others. You clarify that point in the next paragraph and then add a couple of sentences at the beginning of your discussion of each painting so that readers can follow what you're doing. You want them to understand how each painting supports your central idea, and transitions are crucial for helping readers make connections. They also greatly contribute to flow. Reading over the new transitions, you realize that the paper fits together much better now. The paragraphs follow each other smoothly, and you don't have to reread the first sentences of a paragraph to figure out why it comes next. Satisfied with what you've accomplished so far, you turn your attention to the ending.

The ending poses more of a problem. Because you've said everything you wanted to say, a formal conclusion will seem superfluous or redundant, especially since this is a short paper. The most effective way to conclude would be simply to finish what you're saying and stop writing. Your goal is to leave your readers satisfied and with a sense of completeness, to ease them back into the atmosphere beyond the paper. In this case, you can't just stop at the end of the discussion of the last painting. You have to pull the paper together somehow. You think back to your original beginning, to the point about Chagall and spring. When you wrote that, you were trying to influence your readers to visit the exhibit by associating it with spring. Now you realize that, since you dropped that introduction, you never really accomplished that goal. With a sense of relief and satisfaction, you write a paragraph that summarizes the positive feelings Chagall engenders in the attentive viewer, inviting the reader to share those positive feelings by going to see the exhibit. At this point the paper seems complete and, since you have almost run out of time, you decide to consider it revised to the best of your ability. You've made your point, and you believe your readers will both understand and accept it.

REVISING WITH FEEDBACK

The ability to distance yourself from your work is an acquired skill and one of the most essential writing skills to cultivate. Yet no matter how skillful you are at reading your own work critically, there is no substitute for a real reader. Even though you may feel reluctant to share unfinished work, feedback from an interested reader will enhance the revising process considerably.

In the case of your Chagall paper, let's assume that the weakness of the introduction and the problems with the transitions do not leap out at you. Instead, your sense of satisfaction at having written a paper you like and which you feel expresses your ideas dominates your responses. Because you don't want to leave success to chance, however, you seek out a friend down the hall before you revise the paper. You ask the friend to read through the paper and tell you whether, based on your description, the exhibit sounds worth visiting. (See Chapter 3 for more specific suggestions about soliciting and using feedback.)

Although flattery feels good, and you'd like to go out rather than work today, you know this paper isn't finished. You don't want to intimidate your reader into simply making a few insignificant comments and patting you on the back. You're going to revise the paper no matter what she says, and you want to make that clear to her. You want guidance from your reader about how to make those revisions.

Your reader responds positively to the paper at first, explaining that the exhibit sounds worthwhile and that she would definitely like to go. You breathe a sigh of relief. You have accomplished your main purpose. Now for the details. Under questioning, your reader reveals that she doesn't really understand what you mean by Chagall's view of reality and how he expresses it in his paintings. The paintings sound strange and interesting to her, but she doesn't follow your explanation. Why do the flowers springing from the lover's head suggest a dreamlike view of reality? Are you trying to argue that Chagall's paintings represent dreams?

As you discuss the paper with her, your sense of what you need to change becomes clearer. You've accomplished your goal (she wants to see the exhibit), but you haven't really made your point about Chagall. Obviously, you need to go into greater detail when you describe the paintings, but you're disturbed by the fact that the descriptions of the paintings don't seem to substantiate your claim about Chagall's view of reality. You realize that the individual paragraphs make sense, but the connections need work. Perhaps you're not orienting the reader properly or using the right evidence to back up your conclusions. You thank your reader and approach the revising process with a renewed sense of purpose.

As you review the paper, you begin to see what you've taken for granted and that you need to clarify not your commentary on the paintings, but the conclusions you draw from it. You need to explain more carefully how you got from your interpretation of the paintings to your view of Chagall. Without too much surprise, you realize that you yourself weren't really clear about that until you'd finished drafting the paper. Consequently, some of your most crucial connections don't appear until your last paragraph. You had a feeling that was a problem. You need to move your last paragraph forward and use the paintings as evidence for your point of view, rather than describing the paintings and then hoping your reader will draw the same conclusions you do. You need to take a more authoritative stance toward the material and toward your reader. Your readers, who know little or nothing about Chagall, need more guidance from you. With these new insights and the motivation they create, revising seems manageable, and you approach the process with greater confidence.

REVISING AS RETHINKING WHAT YOU'VE LEARNED

No matter how clear a vision you start with, you learn about your subject as you write. (If you don't learn, you're probably not thinking deeply enough about your subject.) As you convert your thoughts into sentences and paragraphs, you impose order on your thinking, which helps you recognize what you know and what you don't know. Until you feel sure about what you know, it's difficult to communicate that knowledge to others. Once you have a draft, use what you learned while drafting to help you revise. Ideas that you expressed tentatively while drafting, because you weren't sure about them, can be revised into assertions once you feel more confident about what you know. As you read through a draft, be alert for sentences, like the following, that don't seem to go anywhere: "The significance of this design is hard to assess because the pattern is difficult to determine. It could express the artist's fear of death or it could point the way to rebirth and renewal." Anytime you feel as if you're moving in a circle instead of straight ahead, you probably didn't fully understand what you were trying to say. When you think about it again, after completing a draft, you may understand it better. If you don't, you may have to do some more reading or ask your instructor for help.

In composing your paper on Chagall, you wrote the following paragraph:

> Chagall uses muted colors in his painting of the lovers: lots of blue, as is typical of much of his work, as well as pale reds, yellows, green, and even white. These colors tend to blend together in the flowers springing from the young man's head. His side of the painting is crowded with the flowers, while you notice mostly her creamy-colored bare breasts. The contrast is evident.

As you're revising, this passage catches your attention. It conveys information, but that information doesn't lead to any conclusion. What is the point? Is it simply that there is contrast? What exactly do you mean? Each sentence expresses an independent thought. You can see how you made the leap from thought to thought, but you can't remember why. The paragraph seems to focus on color, but in the end you're not sure whether you mean that the contrast refers to color or to the overall presentation of the man and the woman.

Whenever you read a paragraph you've written and can't immediately determine why you wrote it or what you're saying, you're probably still learning about your subject. In this case, figuring out the effect of Chagall's composition could take some effort. Thinking about the problem by describing the painting in writing is a useful way to learn. It may not result in the most forceful writing at the moment, but it will help you clarify your thinking and improve your writing later.

After reading over your description and thinking more about Chagall's intention, you rewrite the paragraph above:

```
    Chagall's lovers face each other, and each
contributes a specific tone to the embrace. He
brings spontaneity and joy with his bouquet of
color and texture; she, approaching him bare-
breasted, brings softness, purity, and sensual-
ity. The blue surroundings, the community at a
distance help set them apart. They exist in this
world, yet they really only belong to each other.
```

At this point you have a definite idea to communicate, a point of view toward the painting which comes across clearly. The writing is self-assured and directed. You know from the first sentence what the last sentence in the paragraph is likely to be. Reading this paragraph gives you confidence in your ideas. It convinces you that you know what you're talking about.

Finishing Writing

Finally, and only finally, do you concern yourself with the correctness and elegance of what you've written. Not everyone is a great speller or a master of English grammar and usage, but anyone can use a dictionary and a style book, and now is the time. You may have made minor changes and looked up words as you went along, but you aren't finished until you have taken care of all the details. You don't want to embarrass yourself and destroy your credibility by making careless mistakes.

In addition, this is the time to review words and phrases that never really satisfied you, but for which you couldn't think of an alternative. You might look at a thesaurus to stimulate your thinking or ask someone for suggestions if a suitable substitute still doesn't come to mind. You have completed the most taxing part of the writing process, and since fussing over words and phrases now won't interfere with your concentration, use whatever time you have left by being as picky as you like.

Other details to attend to include sentences and phrases that might strike your readers as awkward. When you read the sentence aloud, if it doesn't make sense or if you have to read it several times to understand it, change it. Don't spend inordinate amounts of time switching words around, since your taste may not correspond with that of your readers. But do rid your prose of sentences that don't read well or say what you want them to say. In some instances and with some audiences, this work takes on critical importance, since one careless misspelling or ungrammatical sentence can completely undermine your authority. Readers do not respect writers who don't bother to finish their work.

If you're familiar with language and have experience using it, finishing writing is much easier. If you don't know the language well, you can learn it by writing and reading. The more you write, the more experience you gain with words, sentence and paragraph structures, punctuation, grammatical structures, and language usage, and the more expertise you develop. The more you read, the more you expose yourself to the varieties of language experts consider correct, as well as to exceptions to the rules. By reading broadly, you acquaint yourself with language used in ways you have never encountered before. By reading attentively you learn the intricacies of language, such as when a carefully chosen semicolon markedly alters the meaning of a sentence—revealing an author's strategy—and when it's nothing more than a convenience.

Even if you know language very well, specific editing strategies will help you discover which finishing touches a particular piece of writing requires. Rereading will help you pinpoint problems. Read at least once for sight (misspellings, punctuation errors), once for meaning (beginnings and endings, transitions, length of paragraphs), and once for sound (awkward sentences, sentence rhythms, word choice). If you don't discriminate well visually, read aloud and listen for mistakes. Then ask a friend who's a good speller to check your spelling or use a word processing program with a spelling and style checker to locate errors. Weigh your own preferences against your readers' needs and tastes, and be willing to sacrifice pet expressions if they don't advance your writing. Because you need to be alert to notice small problems, don't try to finish a paper when you're sleep-deprived and seeing double anyway. Save enough time to allow you to edit when you're feeling refreshed and can examine your work objectively. Then scrutinize it until you're convinced it's technically *perfect*.

Finishing the Chagall Paper. After all the care you put into revising the Chagall paper, finishing the paper presents no problems. You read it out loud, sentence by sentence, stopping sometimes to read a sentence over several times, and then make adjustments. Reading aloud helps a great deal with punctuation. It's easier to sense where commas do and don't belong when a sentence is read aloud. Reading aloud also calls attention to a missing question mark or to two sentences that have been run together, because the sentences don't sound right when read aloud.

You keep a style book next to you for easy reference, but you only need it twice, to check the rules for using dashes and to make sure that a question mark you've placed outside the quotation marks belongs there. You feel in control of everything else, but just to be safe, you run the paper through a spelling checker. You're glad you did, because the computer picks up not only one misspelling but several typos. Finally, your paper is finished. You go to bed, feeling good about "a job well done."

Alternative Models for Writing

If this model for writing doesn't work for you, what alternatives do you have? Are there other ways of conceptualizing writing that would make it more accessible? Even at its best, the model presented here would only work well in certain situations. It was designed with a basic college term paper in mind. For a different type of writing, you might proceed quite differently. Not only might you change the order of the stages, you might also skip some stages and add new ones.

If you were writing in a form that is highly structured—a lab report, for example—you could begin by becoming familiar with the form of the report. You would want to know not only how, but also why, a report is written, and what information belongs in which sections. You could define this as a researching stage, although you are also attempting to understand the context which is given to you. Once you are familiar with lab report format and know what questions you have to answer, you would conduct an experiment. Planning in this context might take the form of note-taking, since a plan is implicit in the assignment. The process of deciding what to put in the report and where to put it could become its own decision-making or interpreting stage, and then drafting and revising would follow. If the report were well thought out during the decision-making stage, revising and finishing might be combined, since you would be working with smaller and more self-contained units of writing. The model might be developed as follows:

1. Understanding the context for writing
2. Conducting the experiment
3. Taking notes
4. Analyzing and organizing material
5. Drafting
6. Revising and finishing

A model for writing news stories for a newspaper could be simpler. Since news stories also follow a strict format (they conventionally take the shape of an inverted pyramid), many decisions are made for you, and you don't have to think about your subject in the way you do when you have more autonomy as a writer. You would begin by gathering information (who, what, where, when), then organize it according to importance and record it in short paragraphs, starting with general information and getting more specific as you go along. On the other hand, if you were writing a dissertation or book, you would need a more complex model to guide you through the writing process. You might even go through several writing cycles, thinking about, drafting, and revising one section before you move on to the next and then finally tackling the whole.

The simpler the writing task, the less need there is for a detailed model of writing. When you have the freedom to select your own form and to write for purposes you identify and for audiences you choose, the task becomes much more complex. Not only must you think in more complex terms about your subject, but you must also think about writing, and the intellectual demands this thinking about writing makes on you may be the more challenging ones. You can help yourself meet this challenge by choosing or devising a model for writing before you begin the process. Experience will help you recognize the best way to proceed. If you practice with less demanding tasks and keep a record of models that work for you, you will have resources to use when a difficult piece of writing taxes your inventiveness as a writer.

This Chapter in Brief

Create a model for writing to guide you through the writing process and to assist you in successfully completing difficult writing tasks. Identify stages that fit your way of thinking, make writing easier to control, and ensure a satisfactory outcome. The following stages are recommended:

thinking, creating a context for writing, planning, revising, and finishing. Feel free, however, to develop your own stages. As you design your model, use this advice:

1. Think before you write as well as while you're writing.
2. Engage freely in writing to help you learn about your subject and yourself, but learn your subject before you try to teach it to others.
3. Write for real readers and for reasons you can identify.
4. Rehearse your ideas in your head or on paper before you begin drafting.
5. Plan.
6. Assume you will write everything several times and try to accomplish specific goals in each draft.
7. Use trusted readers to help you direct your revision.
8. Revise carefully and thoroughly until you're satisfied that you have accomplished your purpose.
9. Edit your writing; don't give up until it's finished.

Nearly Everybody Reads the Bulletin, by Ben Shahn

2

Writing for Readers

For whom was the following paragraph written?

> Mental phenomena are to be regarded as the result of the interplay of forces pressing respectively toward and away from motility. The organism is in contact with the outside world at the beginning and at the end of its reaction processes, which start with the perception of stimuli and end with motor or glandular discharge.

Obviously it was not written for a general audience. It presumes that readers know something about the subject and have an interest in it, since the writer does nothing to explain or to create interest. Coming across a paragraph like this one, lay people would feel as if they'd stumbled in the wrong door. Clearly, this writing was not meant for them to read.

It was, however, intended for someone to read, someone with the appropriate background and interest. Like all writers, the writer of this paragraph had an audience in mind. A piece of writing that does not work for all audiences is not necessarily bad. Writing is only good or bad to the extent that it communicates what the writer has chosen to say to the intended audience. As far as we know, this paragraph does that.

Developing Reader Awareness

All writing involves interaction between a writer and readers. The words you write down don't communicate what you want to say by themselves. They acquire meaning only as they are read and interpreted by readers. By the same token, the quality of your writing is not inherent in your prose. If readers respond favorably or are influenced by what you say, they describe your writing as "good." If readers don't believe you or respond negatively to what you've written, your writing is "bad." In order to produce writing readers evaluate as good you must be sensitive to the needs and interests of your audience.

Let's look at a simple example. How does a letter from a student to his mother become, by some objective standard, a good letter? The only person who can really make that judgment is the person for whom the letter is intended, the mother. Her son may say to himself, "This is a good letter," when he rereads it before mailing it, but he won't know if he's right until he hears from his mother again. He believes that the letter is good because he knows his mother and thinks he can predict her responses. If he's wrong, if he gets an angry phone call instead of the pat on the back he expects, he'll have to reevaluate the letter. It won't seem as good as it did originally if the letter doesn't do what he wants it to do.

The interaction between writer and reader involved in personal letter writing seems straightforward. We all think of such letters as a means of carrying on a relationship, and sensitivity to the reader's needs is obviously important. Outside of our personal correspondence, however, we frequently take our relationships with readers for granted, focusing on what we're trying to say rather than on the connection we're trying to make with another person. Some textbook writing can serve as the prototype for such impersonal writing. Authors sometimes place the requirements of the subject matter and their own interpretations of their subjects above a reader's need to be treated considerately by the person communicating the material. As a result, such writing often gets in the way of learning and alienates all but a few readers who share the writer's assumptions and interest in the material.

We can readily find examples of writing that ignores the reader in everyday business writing. In an effort to communicate information as efficiently as possible, business writers often ride roughshod over the reader's sensibilities. The discourteous "Dear Sir," when the reader is a woman, is a case in point. The business writer who threatens: "If we do not hear from you within five (5) days, we will assume that you have defaulted on your loan and will pursue legal action against you," when it's summer and the reader is gone on a month-long vacation, shows no awareness of the reader's circumstances. The writer presumes that the reader is at home and has received previous correspondence, which is incorrect. The letter interprets the reader's failure to pay an installment on time in the worst possible light and assumes that the reader has bad intentions rather than, for example, a poor memory. Upon returning from vacation, the reader of such a letter is likely to feel insulted and enraged. Rather than simply paying the amount owed, the reader might prefer to switch banks in response to the writer's insensitivity.

Contrast this with the concern for the institution's relationship with the reader exhibited by the following letter:

Dear Ms. Clark,

   Recently we reminded you that your mortgage account was overdue, but we still haven't heard from you. Perhaps you never received our reminder, or you have been out of town. Maybe you mailed your payment, and we never received it.

   Would you please check your records and let me know whether you sent your payment or when you plan to send it, if it is not already in the mail? I would appreciate it if you could call me at 848-9687 as soon as possible, so that we can clear up the status of your account.

                                        Many thanks for your cooperation.

This letter states the facts and presumes nothing. It is written by an individual person to an individual person, acknowledging the relationship between them. It still sounds businesslike and to the point, but the writer does not accuse or threaten the reader. At this stage of the relationship, while the writer still knows relatively little about the reader, the writer shows sensitivity to the reader's circumstances and concern for the future of their relationship. Both types of letters would probably bring about results, but the more personal one would certainly create a better feeling on the reader's part.

   Friendly gestures toward the reader occur in much good writing, although we often don't notice them as we read. Writers who are sensitive to their readers, however, will strive to communicate their concern, some

more explicitly than others. For example, even when writing on economics, a subject most people perceive as notoriously impersonal, John Kenneth Galbraith takes pains to consider his readers. Here is an excerpt from
Galbraith's classic economics text, *The Affluent Society*:

> Such was the legacy of ideas in the great central tradition of eco-
> nomic thought. Behind the facade of hope and optimism there re-
> mained the haunting fear of poverty, inequality, and insecurity. Partly
> latent, partly in the suppressed background of conviction, these doubts
> could easily be aroused by such an occurrence as the Great Depression.
>
> But the reader will surely ask if there was not a more confident
> stream of ideas—one more completely purged of all traces of the Ri-
> cardian gloom. The question will occur especially to Americans: surely
> in the American tradition there must have been a more consistently
> optimistic current. Here there must have been some who rejected
> doubt—who reflected an indigenous and abounding confidence. Per-
> haps among those who neither read nor wrote there was such confi-
> dence. But those who gave voice to the American ideas were far from
> confident.

Because this subject can be difficult, Galbraith's sensitivity to his readers' experience and his effort to direct us toward an appropriate line of
questioning inspire especially grateful feelings. Whether or not we feel like
experts approaching the text, we feel informed and respected by the author
as we read. Obviously, he loves his subject and wants us at least to understand it, if not come to love it, as he does. He also has strong feelings
about his audience. He interrupts his train of thought about the Great
Depression at the end of the first paragraph to address a question he
imagines readers will have as a result of what he has just said. The continuity of his presentation is important, but his readers' interests are equally
important. Even in textbook writing, which assumes a captive audience,
good writers choose strategies that demonstrate their concern for their
readers. All successful writers take steps to ensure that what they intend to
communicate is received by their readers. Like any other form of social
interaction, communication in writing takes place between individuals,
not just speakers of a common language.

Becoming an Aware Reader

Few readers engrossed in a piece of writing pause to consider what the
writer intends for them. Even if you do think about it, you may not reach

any conclusions. You know a story is affecting you, but you're not sure why and you're less sure whether or not you're responding the way the writer intended you to respond. You can learn a great deal about writing from reading the work of other writers attentively, however.

Like writing, reading well demands skills that take practice to acquire. You may know perfectly well how to follow a plot or glean information from a text, but to learn about writing you have to be able to identify with the writer. What strategy does a writer employ to influence readers? How does a writer express or establish tone? You want to recognize not just what writers say to their readers, but what they do to them. As a reader, does writing excite you, make you cry, make you furious, make you want to impeach your governor? Let's look at how a writer influences readers and how, by reading, you can do the same.

Exposing the Writer's Intention

The most effective way to learn from reading is to trust yourself as a reader. To understand what a writer is doing, examine your responses to the text first. If you feel excited, curious, angry, or frustrated, consider why you feel that way. Is that what the writer wants? Try to trace your response to a sentence or paragraph in the text. When a writer says, "Thousands of people die needlessly every year as a result of mistakes made by hospital personnel," does that make you angry? Why? Consider the word *needlessly*. If the writer omitted that word or used the word *unexpectedly* instead, would that alter your response to the sentence? What if *decisions* was used instead of *mistakes*? Against whom is your anger directed? Are you angry at nurses and doctors? At technicians or hospital administrators? Did the writer want you to respond with anger? Did the writer try to direct your anger toward specific culprits? How can you tell?

No matter how carefully you read, you can't always be sure you're understanding the writer's intention correctly. Even so, you can learn a lot about how writers influence readers by trying to think like the writer. Instead of receiving a text passively, make it explain itself to you. Make the writer accountable for every decision, even those made unconsciously or unintentionally.

For practice, let's read the following text together, thinking as writers, and examine our responses. Your responses may not always match those described; writing often affects different readers differently. For the sake of discussion, though, try to identify with the "we" in the example. Even if you don't agree with the interpretation, you can still understand the process of reading. When reading on your own, always trust your responses and seek out a source for them in the text. Your response may be idiosyncratic, but a good writer will allow for that. Tracing your responses to their source in the text will teach you what the writer is trying to do.

We begin with the first paragraph of an essay by Annie Dillard called "Living Like Weasels," from her collection titled *Teaching a Stone to Talk*.

> A weasel is wild. Who knows what he thinks? He sleeps in his underground den, his tail draped over his nose. Sometimes he lives in his den for two days without leaving. Outside, he stalks rabbits, mice, muskrats, and birds, killing more bodies than he can eat warm, and often dragging the carcasses home. Obedient to instinct, he bites his prey at the neck, either splitting the jugular vein at the throat or crunching the brain at the base of the skull, and he does not let go. One naturalist refused to kill a weasel who was socketed into his hand deeply as a rattlesnake. The man could in no way pry the tiny weasel off, and he had to walk half a mile to water, the weasel dangling from his palm, and soak him off like a stubborn label.

Start with your personal responses and then we'll look at the passage together. How do you respond to this paragraph? How does it make you feel? What words or phrases stand out for you? Why? Consider the phrase "obedient to instinct." Why does Dillard begin the sentence with that phrase? How does the image of a weasel being soaked off someone's palm "like a stubborn label" strike you? Can you picture it? Why did the writer choose that image, and why did she use it to end the paragraph?

Stepping back for a minute, let's consider the text more objectively. What can we say about it? Although this text discusses weasels and their habits, we know that it does not claim to be scientific. It does not present itself in the objective, matter-of-fact tone we expect of science. On the other hand, if we look up weasels in a reference book on mammals, such as *Mammals of the World* by Ernest P. Walker, we find the following:

> The subgenus *Mustela* includes about ten species of weasels with an aggregate range the same as that of the genus. . . . The species M. *rixosa* is the smallest living carnivore. In summer weasels are generally brown above and whitish or yellowish below; in winter they usually become white in the northern and temperate regions. The winter pelage is used for the ermine coat.
> Weasels are generally solitary and tend to be nocturnal, although they may be active day or night. Some species that climb well pursue chipmunks and squirrels in trees. . . .

Unlike the writer of this passage, Dillard doesn't use scientific words, such as *species* and *carnivore,* and she treats her subject as an individual rather than a member of a group. She is describing "a" weasel, not "the" weasel. "Who knows what he thinks?" brings us to the weasel's level and treats him as any other individual, as a person. The portrayal of the weasel as a thinking animal invites comparison with humans, which the writer follows through more specifically in the rest of the essay. As a result of the attention the writer focuses on the weasel's character and, by suggestion, on how that character might hold up in a person, the weasel lives for us in this paragraph in a way we would never expect in a scientific article— which of course would be written for a different purpose. This paragraph makes weasels seem interesting to anyone interested in animal and human nature. Arousing our interest is presumably part of Dillard's intention.

The writer of this paragraph certainly knows her weasel, but she doesn't assert her authority in a way that makes us feel inadequate or ignorant. On the contrary, she piques our curiosity by combining a factual description of how the weasel kills its prey with an anecdote about an incident between a man and a weasel. The anecdote both illustrates and interprets the facts, lending them a dimension bare facts on the page rarely acquire. The man and the weasel seem a match for each other in this brief scenario, and, anxious to discover whether one or the other will emerge superior, we want to turn the page and read on.

Already, by the end of the first paragraph, we have begun to think. If we consider the interaction between writer and reader occurring at this point, we might well conclude that the writer intended us to reflect on this subject, that she consciously chose the combination of fact and story that we have noted to engage our interest. We might also suspect that she wants us to begin comparing ourselves to weasels, to learn from them about living our lives, a suspicion confirmed a few pages later:

> I don't think I can learn from a wild animal how to live in particular— shall I suck warm blood, hold my tail high, walk with my footprints precisely over the prints of my hands?—but I might learn something of mindlessness, something of the purity of living in the physical senses and the dignity of living without bias or motive. The weasel lives in necessity and we live in choice, hating necessity and dying at the last ignobly in its talons. I would like to live as I should, as the weasel lives as he should. . . .

And finally, Dillard invites us to share her conclusions:

> I think it would be well, and proper, and obedient, and pure, to grasp your one necessity and not let it go, to dangle from it limp wherever it takes you. Then even death, where you're going no matter how you live, cannot you part.

How do we react to these conclusions? Because we are so well prepared, we certainly understand what she means. We may not agree with Dillard's philosophy, but she has raised our consciousness about animal behavior and human behavior and lured us into thinking about how we live our lives. Presumably, inducing such self-examination was what she intended.

Our responses to this text (and to all texts) do not occur by chance, on the basis, for example, of whether we identify ourselves as "woodsy" types or the kind of people who would enjoy reading about the odd behaviors of animals. The writer doesn't just say, "Here's some information about weasels. Take it or leave it." Our responses are sought by a conscientious writer who has a plan and who takes pains to attract and involve us, whatever our previous affiliation with weasels. As thoughtful and conscientious readers, we sense this communication from the writer, appreciate it, and respond accordingly.

Evaluating the Writer's Intention

After you read a text closely, examine your responses, and understand the writer's intention, you can evaluate what the writer is trying to do and how well the writer does it. You do not have to label a piece of writing as good or bad to appreciate the writer's technique. The following questions will help you evaluate what the writer has done:

> What is the writer's attitude toward readers?
> How is that attitude revealed in the text?
> How does the writer want readers to respond?
> What techniques does the writer use to influence readers?
> Do these techniques work? Do they facilitate communication with the reader, or do they intrude or interfere?

Such questions encourage you to move beyond evaluations based on simple likes or dislikes to a more respectful, as well as more educated, appreciation of the writer's choices. Examine the text carefully for clues left by the writer that will help you answer these questions as accurately as possible. Consider the whole piece of writing—its paragraphs, sentences, and words, and how they fit together. Examine the writing's structure and how the writer develops a point of view. Keep asking yourself: What is the writer doing? How and why is the writer doing this?

To help you learn as much as you can from reading, you can think about the particular piece of writing you're reading in comparison to other pieces. For example, comparing Dillard's treatment of weasels to other writings on weasels will help you appreciate the choices the author has made that create this text as a unique piece of writing. Who else writes about weasels? You could find the technical information Dillard provides about weasels in *The Audubon Society Field Guide to North American Mammals:*

> It feeds almost entirely on meadow mice, chasing them over their runways, pouncing on them, and killing them with a swift bite at the base of the skull; it also takes an occasional shrew or mole. Despite the legend, weasels do not suck blood; this notion probably arose from the fact that a weasel's snout is often bloodied when it bites its prey.

How does Dillard's presentation differ from that of the *Audubon Guide*? It's hard to get attached to an animal solely from the description in the *Audubon Guide*. If Dillard's goal is to make you feel closer to weasels, does her strategy work? How else might she have accomplished the same purpose?

Sometimes a piece of writing will remind you of something else you've read, or a writer will remind you of another writer. Dillard's culling of nature for clues that explain human behavior might remind you of Henry David Thoreau (if you are familiar with Thoreau). A passage from Thoreau's *Walden* can serve as an example:

> Sometimes I heard the foxes as they ranged over the snowcrust, in moonlight nights, in search of a partridge or other game, barking raggedly and demoniacally like forest dogs, as if laboring with some anxiety, or seeking expression, struggling for light and to be dogs outright and run freely in the streets; for if we take the ages into our account, may there not be a civilization going on among brutes as well as men? They seemed to me to be rudimental, burrowing men, still standing on their defence, awaiting their transformation. Sometimes one came near to my window, attracted by my light, barked a vulpine curse at me, and then retreated.

How does Thoreau's writing compare to Dillard's? Dillard uses more concrete description in much of her essay and leaves philosophical implications for her conclusion. She seems to learn about humanity from her interaction with weasels, while Thoreau tries to understand animals by making them like humans. For modern readers, Dillard's style seems more accessible, and her language is more familiar. Dillard seems to appreciate weasels more than Thoreau appreciates foxes, although both seem ultimately more concerned with humanity. Which writer affects you more strongly? Which writer would you choose to emulate? From whom can you learn more?

Comparisons with other writers, genres, techniques, and styles help prompt your critical faculties. When comparisons do not occur to you, imagine some. That is, compare the tone, the language, and the approach the author has taken to others the author might have chosen and examine the imagined consequences. What if Dillard had not used weasels at all but had just reflected on human behavior? What if she had offered fewer particulars about weasels? If she had started out differently, making her purpose—the analogy she intended to draw between the behaviors of weasels and people—more explicit from the start, would that have improved her essay? Would you have gotten more or less out of it? Such speculation reveals the variety of strategies for influencing readers which are available to the writer, strategies you might want to use in your own writing.

Reading Your Own Writing

Reading and responding to someone else's work always seems easier than reading your own writing. Advice to fellow writers may pour from your lips, but when you try to respond to what you've written, you can't think of any constructive comments. Why? Because reading a paper someone else has written requires you to play only one role, that of intelligent and caring reader. In order to read your own work, however, you have to distance yourself from the words you have so carefully selected and switch from proud writer to critical reader. A well-trained internal reader is a precious resource to a writer. It can give you invaluable information about your writing, help you to understand your intention, and guide you in your revision.

Recognizing Your Internal Reader

The first reader with whom you have to communicate is yourself. Almost from the beginning of the composing process, listen for two internal voices exchanging ideas, one representing your concerns as a writer and one representing your judgment as a reader. When a voice inside you responds to a paragraph you have just spent hours struggling over—saying, "That's not good. It doesn't make a point. All the sentences say the same thing. Besides, that's not what you wanted to write anyway"—your internal reader has spoken.

Your internal reader doesn't always set out to find fault. It can be remarkably—even blindly—supportive at times. When the voice remarks, "Hey, that's good. That's really good," even when you have your doubts as a writer, you know you've got a friend there, whether you want one or not.

Internal readers play a major role in the writing process, but, unfortunately, they're not always as useful as they could be. For one thing, they are not always reliable. At one o'clock in the morning, when you're confronting a 9:00 A.M. deadline and could really benefit from a little perspective, your internal reader may have retired for the night. On the other hand, it has a nasty tendency to intrude on your thinking just as you've finished a beautiful run of paragraphs. No matter how loudly you protest, your reader insists on telling you that what you've just written will never do; this means that even if you do leave it in, you no longer believe in it.

How can you ensure that your internal reader works with you instead of against you? Your internal reader is only as helpful as you train it to be. It does the best job it can under the circumstances you provide, and even internal readers deserve a good night's sleep once in a while. If you want a dependable, conscientious, even talented, internal reader, you have to nurture this part of yourself.

Using Your Internal Reader Profitably

To make the best use of your critical reading skills, allow some time to pass before you begin reading a paper you have just written. This will help you forget your earlier state of mind and put some distance between you and your work. When you go back to it, try to read it much as you would read anyone's writing. As you review your writing with a reader's eye, examine your responses as a reader and try to identify your intentions as a writer. Don't be surprised if your purpose seems clearer from this perspective than it did when you wrote the paper. Read carefully, and think about each paragraph and how it affects you. Indicate your response with a note or a symbol in the margin—perhaps a happy face if a paragraph does what you want it to do, a question mark if you have doubts about its effectiveness, a star if you can tell it's unclear. Trust your responses, and take time to record them. You can't re-create the experience of a first reading later.

Once you have identified your intentions, evaluate them. You're not looking for reassurance. You want to understand your writing and experience it the way a reader would. Although you cannot always think like the audience you are seeking to reach, you can still learn from your responses. Try as much as possible to identify with your intended readers. How might they react to your writing? Would they understand your intentions? Would they respond the way you want them to?

For example, in an attempt to describe a family tradition for readers unfamiliar with the practice, you write:

> The breaking of oplatki is always done on
> Christmas Eve before the main meal in the eve-
> ning. There is usually a large crowd because all
> of the relatives from my mother's side gather to-
> gether this night to celebrate Christmas.
>
> Oplatki is a thin waferlike food shaped like
> a rectangle and sometimes stamped with a nativity
> scene. It is usually white but can be tinted
> pink. Each person receives a portion of oplatki.
> After prayers are said, the breaking begins. Each
> person goes to every relative and breaks off a
> piece of his oplatki. In turn, that relative
> breaks off a piece of the other person's. Later
> it is eaten. After this the two people show some
> sign of affection toward each other with a kiss
> or hug. This goes on until everyone has given a
> piece of oplatki to everyone else.

Reading over these paragraphs, you realize that even though you already know what you're talking about, you still find the description a little hard to follow. Would a reader with no background be able to picture the scene? Probably not. Why would the oplatki be tinted pink? You never explain that. You say that each person goes to every relative, but you mean that each person exchanges pieces with every other person there. They don't have to be relatives. In addition, when you say, "Later it is eaten," you aren't sure your readers will understand that people eat their pieces right after they break them off. Your confusion and doubt set off alarms in your writer-self. These paragraphs obviously need to be revised if you want to communicate effectively with your readers.

Comparing your writing to work you have read—written by yourself, your peers, or professionals—can also help you as a reader. Don't allow negative comparisons between your work and that of well-known writers to intimidate you, but at the same time don't hesitate to use writing you admire as a basis of comparison. How would your favorite author have treated the same subject? As you read your writing, ask yourself how you might have done this differently. Are there techniques you can imagine that might work better for your readers?

As you read, write down any ideas you have for revising, but don't act on them yet. The reading process doesn't tell you what to do; it helps you understand what you have done and what you might want to do differently. If you're not satisfied with your accomplishment, pass that information on to your writer-self as you begin revising. Wait until you begin revising to decide what changes to make, based on what you have learned from reading. When you approach your paper from a writer's perspective again, your options will be clearer. Your sensibility as a reader should not dictate your choices as a writer.

Writing for Other Readers

Most of the time when you write, a clearly defined audience exists. Before you begin writing, identify your audience. Find out as much as you can about those people before you ask for their attention. Getting to know your readers and understanding their interests and their needs will greatly improve your chances of interacting with them successfully.

The guidelines that follow are designed to facilitate writing for a variety of different audiences. Although most of your writing thus far may have been written primarily for teachers, teachers represent only a small proportion of the readers you may write for in the future. As time goes on, you will have more and more opportunities to write for audiences other than your teachers, and these readers, who have no reason to perceive you as a learner, will expect you to take positions and try to influence them with writing that is clear and effective.

Identifying As Specific an Audience As Possible

In the absence of a clearly defined audience, you may find yourself writing to a general readership. Although some writers excel at seeming to write to no one in particular, good writing almost always addresses a specific audience. You can never persuade parents of teenage children to vote to lower the drinking age when studies show that the death rate among teenagers declines significantly in states with higher drinking ages. The argument that if you're old enough to serve in the army and vote, you're old enough to drink, just won't work. On the other hand, the latter argument is very popular among eighteen-year-olds. If you're going to convince readers that your views are correct, you have to know your audience.

Every publication is designed for specific readers. They might be members of the same profession or the same gender, or they might share the same hobbies—such as fishing or skiing—or the same interests. Even readers of a community or city newspaper have geography in common as well as concerns about the city or community in which they live. They read local publications to gain information about their own communities. As a result, the *New York Times* publishes only a limited amount of material concerning Philadelphia, a nearby northeastern city, and practically nothing about Grand Forks, North Dakota. Similarly, the *Grand Forks Herald* is likely to include far more information about farming than about goings-on in New York City. Although the readership for some publications can be quite broad (middle-class Americans, for example), few publications attempt to appeal to more than a single group of readers.

Good writing addresses the interests of its intended audience. Consequently, the more you know about who your readers are, the more likely you are to communicate with them effectively. Even among a narrow set of readers, such as students at the same college, diversity of experience will lead to more divergent interests and attitudes than you might expect. Even students at the same college who are from the same part of the country and share the same background will not have the same opinions on, say, the advisability of casual sex or intermarriage. If you write on those subjects, with the whole student body as your audience, what can you say that will influence all of them, or even a few of them? How much do you even know about other students' views on these subjects, particularly students unlike yourself? Before you try to get their attention, you'd better inform yourself.

When the audience for an assignment is not specified or when you want to practice writing for readers, targeting your writing for a particular audience will greatly enhance its effectiveness. Even when narrowing your audience means writing two articles instead of one, you're better off. Writing one aimed toward parents as readers and one toward their teenage children, or writing one version of a research report for the professor and one reporting on your survey for a student audience, will increase the likelihood of communicating effectively with your readers. It's much more gratifying to write two successful pieces than one that tries to reach too broad an audience and, consequently, misses everyone. Look for publications, such as campus or local newspapers or journals of student opinion, with whose readership you can readily identify. Beginning with more discreet writing tasks—pieces geared toward limited but actual groups of readers—will give you practice and provide the experience you need to tackle more complicated assignments for larger audiences later.

Taking Advantage of Your Authority

By its nature, writing—whether a book, article, essay, or letter—possesses its own authority. Most people, at least in Western culture, respect the written word. Simply committing your ideas to writing encourages readers to take them more seriously than they would if you spoke them.

As a result of this phenomenon, ineffective writers don't simply lack authority; they have to throw it away. They do not take advantage of the authority their status as writers confers on them. In fact, they actively invite readers to disbelieve or dismiss them. They whine: "The causes of the Civil War are very complex, and I couldn't possibly explain them all in a paper with a five-page limit. . . ." They act pompous: "Thus we see how the average citizen can be exploited by men with evil and merciless motives. In the words of a universally recognized authority, 'Let my people go.' " They disclaim responsibility: "I present this report at the insistence of the Board of Directors who, for reasons of their own, moved the deadline up two months and allowed very little time for its preparation." They make excuses: "If more information were available on this subject, I could provide a more informative summary." Or they show little command of the forms of writing: "Beyond that, there are a host of invented holidays that we think have as their emotional drive elements that fit well with the beliefs and attitudes that accompany champagne." We know we could do just as well or better than these writers. How can they expect us to take them seriously?

Laying claim to authority does not mean, however, grabbing your readers by the throat or hitting them over the head with a mallet. Writing that is clear, correct, and to the point, writing in which the ideas are well and appropriately stated, writing that interests, informs, amuses, moves, or even surprises the reader, has its own authority and requires no further embellishment to command the attention of readers. It speaks its own authority in its own, everyday voice, as in the following passage from a student paper:

```
A locally based program to create better
housing has one other major positive effect. It
empowers local residents and, when successful,
gives them tangible proof that they can actually
exercise a degree of control over their environ-
ment and lives. When the city moves in to build
or rehabilitate a house or apartment building,
usually only housing is improved. When local
groups work together, the community is improved
as well.
```

Such plain words, clearly and confidently spoken and conveying material of substance and of interest to readers, establish the authority of the writer without further ado. They assert themselves without seeming intrusive or overly aggressive. They don't ask for approval, and they don't apologize for taking up the reader's time. They just make their point and invite readers to read on.

Asserting Your Point of View

Although not all writing advocates a specific position, most writing seeks to influence readers—to make them laugh, cry, believe, act, or respond, to name a few possibilities. Whatever you write, readers assume that you have a reason for writing, a well thought-out point of view on the subject, and the desire to persuade them that your point of view has merit. Because readers expect you to work at influencing them, writing that refuses to assert itself disappoints or even angers them. Don't be misled into thinking that readers who want to draw their own conclusions want you to skip conclusions. A well-reasoned essay will allow readers to draw their own conclusions, but those conclusions will be the ones the writer wants them to draw. Unless readers have never considered the subject before and are simply seeking information, they will expect the writer, after reviewing the pros and cons of financing an education with student loans, for example, to find one side or the other more persuasive. Since you've done the research and thinking they haven't had time to do, they look to you for direction. A clear, "Yes, borrow the money. You may accumulate substantial debts, but if you're entering a high-paying profession, such as law or medicine, these debts will prove relatively insignificant and will even provide some tax advantages when you begin working," gives readers a position to which they can react. By testing their own views against the writer's, they form new opinions or confirm their old ones. In either case, they have something to react to, something that engages their interests and leaves them feeling that the effort of reading was worth it.

With the ability to influence comes responsibility, and responsibility can be burdensome. This can be a problem especially when your own views aren't fully formed. For example, you may feel totally confident about your view on abortion but less secure about the evolution of social democracy in Jacksonian America. Whenever you write, however, you have a responsibility to your readers to think out your positions carefully and to write as convincingly as possible.

Earning the Readers' Trust

Whenever you want to persuade readers to adopt your point of view, you have to make them trust you. In order for them to trust you, you have to seem credible. You can establish your credibility in a variety of ways. One way is to demonstrate your knowledge of the subject, as the writer of the following passage does:

```
     If any part of Hume's inquiry is tenuous, it
is his linking of sympathy to the principle of
utility. Sometimes the moral decisions we make
have no direct correspondence to utility, and any
relation that does exist seems merely incidental.
Not all of our judgments abide by the principle
of maximized good. For instance, if breaking a
promise would result in slightly more overall
```

good in the world than keeping it, most of us
would still keep the promise. A utilitarian might
argue that keeping the promise results in greater
good because it maintains faith in the ritual of
pact-making-and-keeping, but this is not how we
actually think of the situation. In other words,
our intuitive perception of rightness seems to
overlap rather than correspond to utility. Utility may be but one cog in the regulative machinery of moral sense.

A second approach is to draw on your experience. If you have been places
or done things that have resulted in knowledge to which your readers don't
have access, they'll be much more likely to believe you. Consider the
following excerpt:

My sister-in-law had been raised and was living in strict accordance with Moslem tradition. I
was American and, even though I was then married
to her husband's younger brother, had lived with
him in the Hashemite Kingdom of Jordan for the
last eighteen months, and in one small room in
his family's home in Amman for the past nine, I
held fast to those ways which separated me
from . . . most of the other women around me.

On the other hand, if you emphasize how you are like your readers
rather than more knowledgeable or more experienced than they are, they
may identify with you, no matter what your background. If they can
identify with you as a fellow parent, a fellow student, a fellow worker, or a
fellow concerned citizen, they are much more likely to be receptive to
what you have to say. For example, in an article titled "Quantum Physics'
World: Now You See It, Now You Don't" (*Smithsonian*, August 1987)
James Trefil heightens his readers' receptiveness to his writing by helping
them understand the lot of a theoretical physicist:

Some people have it easy. When their kids ask them what they do at work, they can give a simple, direct answer: "I put out fires" or "I fix people" or "I do arbitrage." As a theoretical physicist, I never had this luxury.

Especially when you're writing for readers who are your peers, treat them as your equals. There's no need to defer—"I'm sure you know more about this than I do"—or to talk down—"This technique may be unfamiliar to many of you who haven't had much experience at peeling potatoes, so I'll explain it carefully, step-by-step." Speak in a natural voice to your readers, as if you were engaging them in conversation. You'll be far more successful if you avoid intimidating or overwhelming your readers. Invite them, instead, to move from where they are to a position you have opened up for them.

Some readers will trust you more readily if you show them that you understand their point of view. This strategy works especially well when your readers have strong opinions on a subject. If, for example, you're advocating gay rights for an audience of homophobic persons, you're much more likely to get their attention if you first demonstrate respect for their fears about homosexuality before trying to influence them to give up those fears. By acknowledging the negative attitude toward homosexuality expressed in the Bible and responding to the question of AIDS and its relationship to the gay community, you are more likely to create a receptive audience for your own views when they later emerge in your paper. If you try instead to dismiss or ignore the feelings and concerns of your readers, they will just as readily ignore or dismiss you. If you reveal your own bias in the title or first paragraph of an essay, those who disagree with you won't bother to read further. Of course, this is not a problem if you're writing for people who agree with you. If, however, you want to reach a wider audience that includes readers with opposing views, then you need to show the same consideration for their side of the argument that you ask them to show for yours.

To earn the trust of some readers, you may have to take personal risks. If you're dealing with risky subjects, subjects likely to make your readers anxious or disturb them, you may need to take risks yourself before your readers will trust you. For example, if you're writing about the death of a parent, you will have much more credibility with readers if you reveal that you have been through this experience yourself. Your willingness to share your experience with your readers earns their trust. Most readers will respect you for having gone to the trouble of putting your ideas in writing, and in most cases no matter what they believe, they will at least hear you out.

Understanding Your Readers' Expectations

To write successfully for any specific group of readers, you must first understand their expectations. Although they are not always explicit, professors, for example, usually have definite expectations for student writing. How do you go about meeting their expectations?

Most professors have two general goals when they assign writing. Either they think writing a paper will teach you about the subject by requiring you to synthesize or to use new ideas, or they want to ensure that you'll do the reading and thinking they expect you to do for their courses. If a paper is designed to serve the same function as a test, then what you need to do is know the material and present it convincingly. Most term papers, however, demand more of writers.

In order to understand your professor's expectations, begin by asking yourself why you have been given this assignment. What does the professor expect you to do to complete it? What skills does the assignment require you to use? Why are those skills important? Is there an audience implicit in the assignment, or are you supposed to write for the professor? How does the professor expect the final product to look? Even though you can't be sure your answers are right, responding to such questions helps you to identify with your professors. If you can identify and understand their goals, you will find it easier to satisfy their expectations. The need to satisfy someone else's expectations can make writing less rewarding than it should be, but such situations occur frequently in college and in professional life. If you can respond to these situations as challenges to your creative problem-solving ability, you may find meeting your readers' needs more gratifying.

Writing for someone you don't know makes it harder to write well. In the case of a college course, a simple meeting during office hours can help you understand your professor's expectations. If you have questions about the assignment itself, don't hesitate to ask what the professor has in mind. If you can choose your topic, ask what interesting topics students have chosen in the past. If you're not sure about what you need to produce, ask to see some models. Reading a good student paper from another year will help make any instructions the professor gives more concrete.

Writing for someone who knows more about the subject than you do makes decision making more difficult. Raise the question of audience when you talk with the professor. To whom does he or she expect you to write? Many professors do not require you to write for them as audience. Is there a suitable audience, other than the professor, for this paper? Might you write to an audience of your peers, intelligent adults who are not experts on the subject? The expectations of such an audience would certainly be easier for you to understand. Inventing an alternative audience of, for example, newspaper or magazine readers for a particular assignment can work well for the writer. Be careful about writing a paper for an alternative audience, however, because such a choice could offend a professor if it is not expected.

For the sake of your writing, it's more satisfying to write for readers with whom you would enjoy conversation on the subject of your assignment. For the sake of your grade point average, however, and to succeed at communicating with different audiences, it's a good idea to conform to your readers' expectations. Some readers, particularly in more quantitative fields where readers are looking for straightforward right and wrong answers, do not welcome papers that might be labeled "creative." An example of writing in a quantitative field would be a paper dealing with economic forecasting, written to an imaginary audience of business people or members of the Chamber of Commerce.

Because readers' expectations vary, it's a good idea to check out a project with prospective readers before getting too far into it. For example, after discussing a paper on economic forecasting with your professor (your actual reader), you might discuss your ideas with a businessperson you know (an imaginary reader). Many people assume that a paper that is fun to write, such as one that is addressed to an imaginary, nonacademic audience, requires less command of the subject than a conventional academic paper. Since papers that address themselves more to lifelike situations and less to an academic exchange of ideas often require greater command of the subject matter, however, you should be wary of this assumption.

Making Your Readers' Interests Your Own

Sooner or later you will probably have to write for audiences of professional readers: committee members, boards of directors, officers of funding agencies, directors of admissions, editorial boards, and employers, to name a few. Graduate school and fellowship application essays are written for such readers, as are requests from student organizations to administrators or faculty, and letters requesting summer jobs or permanent employment after graduation.

Professional readers read your writing with a variety of motives. In many cases they have approached you first, inviting applications or proposals or requesting reports. If you want to write successfully for professional readers, you have to make their interests your own. How do you know what they want?

Whenever you can get to know professional readers on the phone or in person, you gain an advantage. Writing to someone with whom you have spoken over the phone instead of to a name or title will make you feel more at ease (and will probably make that person feel better disposed toward you). Feel free to ask for more specifics about what professional readers have in mind. The more you know about the criteria they use to evaluate applications, recommendations, proposals, or reports, the more confident you can be of producing writing that fits their criteria. Ask as well about the formats they prefer. You could present your experience, your intentions, or your findings in a variety of lights; in this case, present it the way your readers want.

Since experience will teach you whom to contact and what questions to ask in order to write successfully for professional readers, advice from someone with experience can be a great boon. If you can't find someone to advise you, read any published criteria between the lines, as well as line by line, and then call the appropriate person with questions. If you know people who have been through the same process before, discuss the task with them, especially if they had favorable outcomes. Don't neglect tone (Always formal or informal? Is it acceptable to use *I* when you're talking about yourself?) and methods of documentation (Footnotes at the back or references in parentheses in the text?). In writing for professional readers, the details can make all the difference. Writing a ten-page proposal full of rich detail about your project can ruin your chances of obtaining funding when harried readers want a maximum of five concise pages and refuse to read even a paragraph more.

Approach your task pragmatically. Don't worry about whether the required style or form inhibits your freedom of expression. Concentrate on fulfilling the requirements of the task. In addition, don't assume you have to tell the whole story. Answer the questions, say what you have to say, and say less rather than more. The goals you are seeking to achieve are concrete and measurable—you hope to get a job, be admitted to a graduate program, or obtain funding for your research—and you need to use concrete means to achieve them. Try to make your primary interests match those of your readers (to the extent that you can determine them) and to satisfy your readers' expectations at the expense of any other interests you might have as a writer.

Writing Like a Professional

When you write for professional readers, you need to cast yourself in the role of a professional writer. As a professional writer, your end may sometimes be more important than your means. For example, when your end is publication, does it really matter whether you write in the first person or third person? If the editor says third person, isn't it better to follow the editor's advice?

The readers who control access to publication fall into the category of professional readers. You may write an article blasting the professionalism of college students for your peers, but the audience who must accept the article for publication in their newspaper, magazine, or journal are in the role of professional readers. Consequently, before you have an opportunity to address the readers with whom you want to communicate, you must first interact with the professional readers.

Once again, the more you know about these readers, about their interests and concerns, the more likely you are to succeed. Read their journals, magazines, newspapers, and become familiar with their editorial policies, the type of writing they publish, and the audience they target. Look in the front or back of the publication for editorial guidelines. Try to see your work with their professional eyes, measuring it against articles they have published and determining not simply whether it's good enough but whether it fits. Are you addressing the same audience? Are you following the correct format? Is your subject similar to the subjects of previously published articles? And if it doesn't fit this publication, might it fit another? If the editors refuse to publish it, are they wrong, or were you wrong to send it to them in the first place? No matter how much we may wish that good writing, like a good diamond, would sparkle before any reader's eyes, this does not prove to be the case. Writing must find the right context and the right audience in order for its merits to emerge.

Enhancing Writing for Readers

Developing Self-Awareness

In spite of your good intentions, writing for readers can be complicated. In setting out to get to know your readers, you can neglect to understand yourself as well. On the way to writing a convincing essay on the subject of cults, for example, you might too readily assume that your readers are like yourself. You might take for granted that most people's

lives these days do not center around organized religion and that, consequently, they will have little sympathy with cults. Such assumptions,
however, ignore the reality of countless Catholics, Jews, Muslims, and
others whose religions play a central role in their lives and who understand
the attraction of cults much more thoroughly than you do. As a result of
your self-centeredness, you would have overlooked the experiences of a
number of your potential readers and, as a result, possibly defeated your
purpose in writing.

Limitations imposed on you by age, gender, religion, ethnic
background—everything that at the same time contributes to your
uniqueness—can inhibit your ability to relate to readers. You unthink-
ingly reduce your readership or, worse, alienate important readers by
failing to realize that a joking reference to the "over-forty elderly" may
offend readers who are over forty. Even when you're writing for people
much like yourself, you can't take too much for granted. The more you
see your readers as different from yourself—as individuals with unique
experiences, assumptions, blocks, and biases of their own—the more
effectively you will be able to communicate with them.

Before you get to know your reader, then, get to know yourself. Every
time you write anything even mildly controversial, identify your assumptions first. How were your opinions formed? What experiences have led
you to them? How do your beliefs compare with those of your readers? Put
yourself in your readers' shoes and try to understand their perspectives.
Might you feel differently than you do if you had had their experiences
instead of your own?

Developing Reader Awareness

Writers with good basic skills will still fail to communicate with
readers they don't understand. Consequently, the greatest danger for you
as a well-intentioned writer is thinking you understand your readers when
you actually don't. Whenever you feel tempted to skip the stage of
identifying your audience, step back and think. Even if you're writing to
your mother, how well do you know her? Well enough to ignore her
interests? It's often the people you know best whose interests as readers
you can most easily misunderstand.

The more you know about all kinds of readers, the greater your resources as a writer. Although living in foreign countries or unfamiliar
cultures, seeking out exotic experiences, and cultivating new acquain-
tances will not necessarily help you write better business letters, such

adventures won't hurt either. If you let them, all human encounters provide information about readers you know or might come to know. Keep a writer's notebook and make yourself a student of your potential readers. No amount of skill or of beautifully descriptive language, and no number of well-shaped sentences or paragraphs, can overcome a writer's failure to understand readers. If your readers don't interest you enough to make you want to know them, then you certainly won't interest them, and you might as well stop writing.

This Chapter in Brief

Your relationship with your readers should always be a high priority. It's easier to identify with your readers if you practice being a reader yourself. Your roles as reader and writer are closely connected. To enhance your chances of communicating effectively with your chosen audience:

1. Write to be read by readers.
2. Read critically, as a writer. Learn something about writing from everything you read.
3. Write for yourself as a reader first and then for other readers.
4. Get to know yourself; examine your ideas, values, beliefs, and interests. Ask yourself how they influence your writing and make sure they do it no harm.
5. Write for as specific an audience as you can.
6. Get to know your readers; try to understand their ideas, values, beliefs, and interests.
7. Always approach writing as a transaction between you and others. Never allow yourself to get so carried away by your subject or purpose that you neglect your audience.
8. Remember that good writing does not declare itself for all to see. Readers determine what's good and what isn't.

Typewriter, by Fumio Yoshimura

3

Revising Writing

Revising, not composing, is the heart of the writing process. Almost anyone can produce an adequate, workable draft, but not everyone knows how to turn such drafts into well-written, finished writing. Although the quality of a draft makes some difference, even your most problematic drafts can become good pieces of writing if you're willing to work on them. You won't want to work that hard at everything you write. Shorter, rule-bound assignments should be dispatched more quickly and with less fanfare. Writing that matters to you, however, requires and deserves revision. In this chapter we will look at how the transformation from draft to revision takes place.

What prompts you to revise? Your own response to your writing or feedback from another reader generally stimulates the urge to make changes. When a reader fails to understand your writing, you recognize the need to clarify what you've written. You might also revise in order to develop or condense your thinking, to be more comprehensive or more specific, to focus more on a particular audience, or to improve your writing stylistically. When you care deeply about the outcome of your writing, when you think a good paper might get published, win an award, help you get into the graduate program of your choice, achieve funding, or lead to a job or a career, you will work harder at it. Whatever your reason, the impetus almost

always stems from feedback you give yourself or feedback you have received from readers.

A good revision requires a highly motivated writer. If you don't expect
to work hard at revising, and you aren't convinced that the effort will pay
off, then revising can easily degenerate into an editing session, and the
opportunity to confront the larger, more significant issues in your writing
will evaporate. Seize revising as your chance to perfect your always imper-
fect draft. Try at least once to make your communication as accurate, as
elegant, and as successful as it can possibly be. The level of accomplishment you can achieve may well surprise you.

Giving Yourself Feedback

When you read over a draft of a paper, don't expect that problems will
assert themselves. Poor style will not necessarily look poor as your eyes
glance over the page, and not even errors in syntax or spelling will always
be apparent. The visual approach to revision has its merits, but it finally
proves inadequate as a method of revising. The problems that need addressing when you revise require a broader type of vision.

Before you make any changes in the text, you need to acquire a sense
of the whole piece of writing. Depending on the state of the draft, several
rereadings may be necessary before a complete picture emerges and you can
evaluate what you've written. To glean as much information as possible,
read your paper slowly out loud, alerting yourself to both strengths and
weaknesses. Use all your resources—your intelligence, your feelings, your
intuition—to give you the most complete experience of your prose. Don't
censor your responses. Make a note of everything you think and feel.
Don't try to interpret your responses yet. Respond in one reading and
interpret your responses later.

To interpret your responses, compare them with those you intended
your readers to have. If you don't respond the way you had hoped your
readers would, why don't you? Some responses are relatively easy to interpret. For example, if you lose track of your central idea as you read, or if by
the time you get to the end you've forgotten what the central idea was,
then you know continuity is a problem. Other responses require more
initiative to understand and use effectively. If you don't have a sense of
accomplishment, of a problem raised and solved, of a thesis articulated and
proven, of a place or process fully described, then you know you haven't

achieved your purpose. Feedback related to your overall purpose requires your attention first.

Knowing how to read your writing so that you achieve the perspective you need to revise successfully requires considerable skill and practice. The questions that follow will help guide you in giving yourself feedback.

What Have I Done and What Do I Still Need to Do?

The first step in the revision process is an obvious one—recognizing the need to revise. Instead of waiting for teachers or other readers to identify that need for you, always assume you will revise to some extent. Then the question becomes not whether to revise but what to revise.

To answer that question, you must first understand what you've written. Begin by focusing your attention on this question: What have I done? What you have said is important, too, but your primary concern is with your purpose, with what you have tried to do. Until you have a sense of your accomplishment so far, elements of the text that need revising will not be clear to you. How does the text you created compare to the one you intended to create? The text isn't necessarily bad because it isn't exactly what you intended, but you might want to bring it closer to your original idea. Do you want to change your goals at this point? If not, then how far are you from the paper you intended to write?

Your ability to read well plays a crucial role at this stage of the revising process. In the same way that you might try to identify the writer's intention in someone else's writing, you must examine your own intentions. Let's take a paragraph from a fictitious children's fairy tale to create a model for the way your reading should instruct your revising. We'll look at the text first as readers.

```
        Two bunnies lived happily in a hole. One
day, however, they got themselves into a lot of
trouble. One of the bunnies had a penchant for
being very naughty and had several times found
himself in trouble with the police. The police
knew this bunny's predilections and were always
on the lookout for him. On this particular day,
he took his friends by the ears and insisted that
```

```
they go steal some food from a neighbor's garden.
His friend, although basically passive in nature,
was easy to lead astray. Off they went together
to engage in a morning of thievery and gluttony.
They had just finished pigging out on carrots,
which were their favorite food, when the farmer
appeared and shot at them, and they ran for their
lives. This all happened once upon a time, but
they never forgot about it as long as they lived.
```

This paragraph is fun to read, but we're not sure what to make of it. What does it mean? What are we supposed to think about it? It seems to want to tell a story but never actually develops a plot. It offers bits of information that don't seem to add up to a point. Does the fact that the bunny was known to the police have any relevance to the story? Is the reader supposed to learn something from this story? Are we supposed to discover, for example, that crime doesn't pay? This story sounds a bit like the tale of Peter Rabbit, but the author has obviously embellished the particulars. What are we supposed to conclude from that? Why, also, does the writer add the "once upon a time" at the end, as if it were an afterthought, instead of placing it at the beginning where it belongs? That seems strange.

The confusion we experience as readers leads us to raise questions like these and to identify problems inherent in the text. Reading this paragraph is frustrating. The story is misshapen; it begins where it should end and ends where it should begin, and the middle makes no sense. Since we have no context for interpreting what the writer was trying to do, we tend to conclude the worst. We assume the writer was not skillful enough to make this idea into a successful piece of writing.

Try, however, to identify with the writer. From that perspective, the writing seems quite different. For the sake of discussion, let's say that you are the writer and that you were responding to an assignment for a course in children's literature that asked you to update a traditional children's story and place it in the context of contemporary culture. You thought that making Peter Rabbit a juvenile delinquent and adding an accomplice in place of Benjamin Bunny would help to make the story more relevant to today's urban youth. You inserted the traditional beginning at the end of the paragraph, because you thought that contemporary readers would respond better to a more "realistic" approach. You didn't want them to realize until the end that you intended the story to read like a modern fable.

By reading the paragraph in this way, you can see how you might have thought about the task and how you could go about rethinking it. Let's assume that you recognized problems in the text, that you questioned the suitability of tacking "once upon a time" onto the end of the paragraph, and that you felt some concern about whether the characterization of Peter Rabbit as a juvenile delinquent actually worked. You weren't sure, however, how to change your text to make it do what you wanted it to do.

Because you feel uneasy about this paragraph, you allow plenty of time to revise it. Before you make any changes, however, you try to describe what you've done and how that compares to what you set out to do. You have outlined a story that presents elements of the original story of Peter Rabbit, except that Peter has taken on a modern, urban identity. By making Peter's character more realistic, you have turned the story more explicitly into a fable. That is, what you have written is clearly not a simple animal story. Though you have tried to change the context for the story, to create a different cultural environment, you haven't followed through. You have continued to locate the story in the country, while this new Peter definitely belongs in the city. The story needs more coherence, a more consistent treatment of the subject, and clearer organization to succeed in accomplishing your goals.

With these considerations in mind, you might revise the paragraph like this:

```
    Once upon a time in a suburb of New York
there lived a rabbit named Peter who was well
known to the local rabbit police. Being a vegetar-
ian by instinct, Peter had an insatiable craving
for homegrown veggies and was frequently caught
stealing from his neighbor's garden. Finally, out
of desperation, the frustrated gardener greeted
Peter one morning with a .45 pistol pointed right
at his twitching nose. This cured Peter once and
for all of stealing the fruits of someone else's
labor.
```

Although this paragraph remains far from perfect, your intention comes across much more clearly. You chose to jettison the second bunny, since it seemed an unnecessary distraction from the main point, and you made the urban context more explicit and consistent. Most important, you have created some movement from the beginning to the end, and the paragraph makes its point. You have even strengthened the implied comparison between this version of the story and the original story of Peter Rabbit.

Through the process of clarifying your intention and identifying strengths and weaknesses in your writing, you moved from an exploratory stance toward your work to a more assertive mode. Once you had something down in front of you to work with, you began to see where you were having trouble. Once you could see what you had done, you could more easily decide what you still needed to do.

What Was My Central Idea and What Should It Be?

Sometimes your intention needs to be rethought, not just clarified. Approach revising in this way when you don't have a clear sense of accomplishment. When reading over your draft leaves you feeling unsure about what you were trying to do, go back to the beginning and rethink your answers to the questions about audience and purpose that you answered before you began to write. Reconsider your central idea. Perhaps it wasn't a great idea to begin with. Don't just try to patch up your writing when something major is obviously missing.

Let's look at another paragraph, an introduction to a paper written for a course in management. Again, try to identify with the writer.

> When studying biographies of great histori-
> cal figures, an interesting question is always
> whether history makes men or men make history. It
> is indisputable that Andrew Carnegie belonged to
> an elite fraternity of the richest and most power-
> ful businessmen of the late nineteenth century.
> An objective assessment of Carnegie's accomplish-
> ments shows that Carnegie made his own way; he
> recognized the opportunities that industrializa-

```
tion presented and maximized their usefulness
through innovation and hard work, building one of
the greatest corporations of his time.
```

Reading this through as the writer, you feel a little uncertain about your central idea. You imply in this first paragraph that Andrew Carnegie made history, but you don't actually say that until your conclusion, several pages later, where you write, "Andrew Carnegie helped to shape the history of the late nineteenth century and to build one of the greatest fortunes ever amassed until that time." Reading that statement, you wonder about the significance of "making history." How exactly does amassing a fortune constitute shaping history? Do you believe Carnegie was so successful that he became a model for other industrialists, or that his methods set a standard for the Industrial Revolution? Did Carnegie help create the Industrial Revolution, or did he just influence its course or character? What do you really want to say?

With these questions in mind, you rethink what you were trying to do. You realize that you don't really want to argue the general point that men make history. Instead, you just want to assert that Andrew Carnegie made his mark on American history by proving himself one of the most creative and successful businessmen of the Industrial Revolution. You can use the Industrial Revolution as background without getting into the larger historical question. Thinking along these lines, you rewrite the introductory paragraph to conform with your redefined intention:

```
    By the end of the nineteenth century in
America, the economic climate, the growth of
technology, and the availability of labor cre-
ated conditions conducive to the rise of the
large corporation. Yet only a few men were capa-
ble of taking advantage of those conditions. An-
drew Carnegie recognized the opportunities indus-
trialization created and exploited them to their
fullest. His reliance on cost-control methods,
his love of innovation, and his brilliant busi-
ness sense made him one of the great industrial-
ists of his time.
```

The problem you experienced initially resulted from your effort to place
your thesis about Carnegie in a larger context. When you realized that the
larger context only obscured your purpose and that you did not intend to
pursue your ideas at the level of historical argument or to focus on the
question about men and history, you were able to concentrate on documenting Carnegie's achievement as a businessman, the revised central
idea of your paper.

Have I Met the Needs of My Audience?

Frequently, problems with a text develop when writers don't understand their audiences or how to reach them. While drafting, you naturally
focus on your need to express your ideas. As part of revising, however, you
need to refocus on your readers' needs. If you prepared to write thoroughly,
you know for whom you're writing and have some sense of their needs. At
this stage, you want to compare how you intended to take those needs into
consideration with what you actually did in your draft.

Let's assume that you are given an assignment in a course on health
and public policy which asks you to compare several articles on obesity and
draw conclusions for a general audience. The title of the paper is "Obesity:
Genetic or Environmental Disorder?" You begin with:

        Goldblatt, Moore and Stunkard (1965), using
    data taken from a home survey of Midtown Manhat-
    tan, concluded that social environment ("milieu")
    often determined which people were obese. Al-
    though different ethnic groups involved in the
    study were examined, different prevalences of obe-
    sity were ascribed to social and cultural prac-
    tices rather than different genetic inheritance.
    Garn and Bailey (1976) arrived at similar ideas
    through a comparative study of adoptees, their
    adoptive parents, and nonbiological siblings.
    They found genetically unrelated family members,
    such as adoptees and spouses, to be similar in
    patterns of obesity to the rest of their family,

thus making a strong case for environment as the
primary influence in obesity. Biron, Mongeau and
Bertrand (1977), also studying adoptees, observed
no "intrafamiliar environmental factors [that]
play[ed] a significant role in the parent–child
and child–child resemblance of body weight." They
also went on to suggest that their study might
provide limited support for the argument that genetic factors have a greater role in determining
obesity than environmental ones, but refuse to
conclude that there is a definite relationship.

Reading over the paragraph, you determine that you seem in control of the
data, you know where you're going to take it, and the style seems appropriate for the subject. But who is the audience? Although this subject might
interest the audience of general readers specified in the assignment, the
form and style you have chosen exclude them. You jump into the subject,
assuming that your readers are familiar with the data and your manner of
presentation. Your title reveals that you intend to discuss whether genetic
or environmental factors cause obesity, but you offer no context for that
discussion in the first paragraph. A knowledgeable reader would probably
require no context, but a nonspecialist—the audience for your paper—
needs more information in order to follow your train of thought.

You quickly realize that you unconsciously wrote this paper for the
professor teaching the course (a reasonable automatic response). How
might you change it to address an audience of general readers? At this early
point in the paper, readers primarily need to understand the question
raised in the title and its significance so that they can prepare themselves
to make sense of the data. Taking these factors into consideration, you
begin by stating the question:

For many years, researchers have attempted
to determine whether genetic or environmental factors have more influence on who we become, particularly in relation to our intelligence, our
personalities, and our health. Recently, a number

```
        of medical researchers have studied this question
        as it bears on the issue of obesity. Do people
        become obese because the genes they inherit from
        their parents predispose them to obesity, or do
        social pressures in their environment lead them
        to overeat? Unfortunately, the studies carried
        out in this area so far do not agree.
```

Although this paragraph still may not engage readers who shy away from science, it doesn't warn them off either. You've tried to explain the significance of the data by relating it to a larger scientific problem, and to clarify the question relating to obesity before introducing the research and its findings. Readers might not want to read about the subject at this time, but the paragraph would not lead them to assume they couldn't. By holding off on the presentation of technical information, you have allowed readers to try reading the paper, and you have given them the option of deciding whether they want to know more.

In another situation, you might want to leave that decision to readers. If you want to win an audience over, you have to present your information in a way that will make them feel interested and comfortable. How can you encourage readers to consider a paper on a technical subject? You have to make your topic appear immediately relevant to your audience. The writer of the following paragraph from a paper entitled, "Genes and Aging: Are We Programmed to Die?" has used this strategy.

```
        Is your life span predetermined? Is it possi-
        ble that you won't live to be over one hundred no
        matter how healthy you are? Recent laboratory ex-
        periments conducted by eminent geneticist Law-
        rence Hayflick strongly suggest this possibility.
        According to Hayflick, both how long we live and
        how we age may be the result of genetic factors
        contained in our cells from the moment we are
        conceived, just as traits such as height and hair
        and eye color are.
```

Although the subject of her article is the research in genetics conducted by Lawrence Hayflick, this writer has placed that research in a context that would interest many readers. Many of us would very much like to know whether exercise or diet really do make a difference in how long or how well we live. In the context the writer has created, reading about Hayflick's research certainly seems worthwhile. We would probably read on also if we had a problem with obesity and the opening sentence of the paper reviewing that research read, "Do you have a problem controlling your weight and sometimes feel as if there's nothing you can do?" The effectiveness of the writing in both of these cases depends on the writer's ability to reach the appropriate and desired audience. Revision, as a result, should focus on changing the tone, language, and overall approach to increase reader interest.

How Does What I Have Done Compare to What Other Writers Have Done?

In some cases it's important that readers recognize your writing as appropriate for its purpose. When you're not sure whether your writing conforms to the conventions of the genre, try comparing your approach to that of other writers (see Chapter 4 for review of the role of conventions in writing). Models are especially helpful when you're writing in a form you're not used to writing in, or when you're writing in a new style, or for an unfamiliar audience. You can compensate for your lack of writing experience by using your experience as a reader to guide you. Although excessive comparison, particularly with well-known writers, can be intimidating, using models to help you see how your choices compare to those made by other writers will make revising less haphazard.

The reading you do to help guide you in composing a paper can also be useful in revising. For example, if you set out to write a book review, you might read some examples of well-written reviews in respected journals, magazines, and newspapers before you begin writing. This type of reading helps you create an image in your head of how a book review looks, and it also helps you conceptualize the book review you intend to write. You notice, for instance, the different formats reviewers follow, the extent to which they summarize the plot or contents of the book, whether or not they compare the books they are reviewing to others written by the same author or different authors, the tone they take, and the extent to which they consider it their responsibility to evaluate the book for readers. Thinking about these issues may seem to be a prerequisite before you begin writing, but reconsidering them after you have drafted your review can prove equally valuable. When you are trying to gain some perspective on your work and to determine whether it achieves the goals you set for it, providing yourself with a basis for comparison can greatly facilitate the process of revising.

Let's assume that you are the student who wrote the following excerpt from a review of *In Search of Excellence*. Read it over, and then read the paragraph that follows it from a review of a different book in the *New York Times Book Review*.

1

In Search of Excellence by Thomas J. Peters
and Robert H. Waterman, Jr., has captured a
large audience due to certain social and economic factors that have a direct bearing on a
great majority of the public. It is relevant
that the book was released during the 1982 reces-
sion, a period of financial difficulty for individuals and companies alike. But the most compelling element of the book is its representation
of how we are reverting back to a people-
oriented way of thinking.

2

This admirably rich book—rich in historical substance, political thought and character portraiture—covers four of the most critical years in American experience. Franklin Roosevelt assumed the Presidency in 1933 at a moment when the country was reeling from a severe social breakdown. Four years later, though recovery was still far away, he had emerged as a popular leader who had initiated, but sometimes merely stumbled along with, a major change in American life: the beginnings of our semi-welfare state.

As the writer of the review of *In Search of Excellence*, what can you learn from Irving Howe's review of *FDR: The New Deal Years 1933–1937* in the

New York Times Book Review? You might note that Howe assumes greater authority than you do and takes a more assertive stance as a reviewer. Part of his authority derives from his knowledge of Roosevelt's presidency, which allows him to claim that the four years covered in the book represent some of the "most critical years in American experience." Part also derives, however, from his obvious comfort with his role. He sounds like an experienced reviewer. Couldn't you sound more authoritative?

   In addition to authority, though, your introduction lacks substance, which makes your paragraph sound less credible. You don't sound as if you really know what you're talking about. You rely on general statements, failing to indicate, for example, which economic and social factors you have in mind, and you never define what you mean by a "people-oriented way of thinking," which is one of your most important points. Perhaps you need to think some more about what you want to say. You might want to look at the book again or read more about the economic or social climate, so that you can include more specifics. In an effort to be more concrete, command greater authority, and bolster your credibility, you rewrite the paragraph:

```
     Released during the economic recession of
1982, In Search of Excellence, which offers some
valuable pointers about achieving economic well-
being, captured a large audience. At a time when
too many American workers felt like mere cogs in
the great economic machine, the book by Thomas J.
Peters and Robert H. Waterman, Jr., reassured
them that the most successful companies in Amer-
ica actually take people into consideration as
they make the giant decisions that affect us all.
```

This version of the paragraph sounds more polished. You present yourself as knowledgeable about economic conditions and confident about your ability to evaluate this particular book. You have decided not to reveal your opinion about the book yet. You want to concentrate, instead, on the question of its popularity, making the reasons for its success more explicit. Your new approach, which is much like the one Howe chooses, contributes to your credibility. You have reserved your description of the content of the book, as you did before and as Howe did, for the next paragraph.

Even though you're not writing for readers of the *New York Times*, you can pick up some useful pointers by reading the *Book Review*. When you're not sure how close you've come to achieving an appropriate style or tone, or following an appropriate format, a model can provide welcome direction.

Revising with Feedback from Readers

When you have satisfied your own concerns in revising, you are still only halfway toward being finished. Frequently, problems with a draft are difficult, if not impossible, for the writer to spot. In addition, solutions to problems you do spot don't always leap to your mind. To help you achieve additional perspective on your writing, you need to enlist the services of at least one and preferably two or more outside readers.

Merely handing a roommate or friend a draft and asking for an opinion, however, will not provide the feedback you need. Both drafts and readers need preparation before they interact, and it is the writer's responsibility to prepare both. Since you've presumably given yourself feedback first, your drafts should be fairly well thought-out, written with readers in mind, and in reasonable condition so that readers can read them easily; readers should be motivated, practiced, if possible, and clear about their function. These conditions do not occur automatically, nor are they easy to achieve; but if you agree to less, you risk receiving feedback that lacks credibility.

Overcoming Defensiveness

As much as you may value good reader feedback, it can, at times, be difficult to accept when you acquire it. For many writers, the first and most stubborn obstacle they have to overcome is their own defensiveness about their writing. It's easy to tell yourself you shouldn't feel defensive, but that doesn't help much when your writing is being harshly criticized by even a well-intentioned reader.

To avoid feeling hurt and overwhelmed by feedback, try first to separate yourself from your writing. Don't interpret an attack on your writing as a personal attack on you. Your readers may hardly know you. Cast yourself in a professional role. You have a job to do, and reader feedback is going to help you do it better. Above all, remember that it's not the draft, but what you do with the draft, that matters.

The more control you take of the process of getting feedback, the happier you're likely to feel about it. When you just turn your writing over to readers without instruction, you're inviting them to do with it what they will. Unless you're willing to hear whatever they might say, don't give them that chance. As much as you can, encourage them to respond to your agenda rather than allowing them to create their own. In addition, the better prepared the reader is, the more useful the feedback is likely to be.

If the prospect of reader feedback on a draft still terrifies you, even after suitable preparation, try doing the following exercise. Take a paper you've written and imagine the responses of various readers. First, think of the worst reader you can envision, one who would hate everything you write and never say anything good. Write an imaginary dialogue with that reader about this paper. Begin by asking your reader, "What do you think?" What might your reader answer? Think of the worst scenario you can imagine. Can you think of statements more offensive than "I hate it," or "It's horrible," or "It's the worst thing I've ever read"? Try.

Once you've gotten that on the table, think of the best reader you can imagine, the person who would most appreciate your writing. What would that reader say? How might your conversation go? Would "It's the best thing I've ever read; it's publishable" be high enough praise to satisfy you? What's the ultimate compliment you long to hear? Go ahead and put those words in your reader's mouth. Let yourself feel good about it.

If you've already heard the worst and the best that you could hear about your writing, the in-between feedback you will probably get should seem less threatening. Besides, it will probably be more useful. It's nice to hear flattering things about what you write, but what you really need is good feedback. If you want to write better and not just feel better, try hard to get the honest feedback you need to help you revise.

Preparing a Draft for Review

To ensure that you get what you want out of the review process, take a little time to prepare for it. As you look over your work, note the attitude you convey to your readers. If you want other people to take your work seriously, first you have to take it seriously yourself. A sloppy, poorly written draft conveys a lack of caring to readers who will take their cues from you. If you want readers to respond to your ideas and the form of your expression, rather than your spelling, grammar, and punctuation, then leave them with nothing to distract them from the larger concerns. Don't spend a lot of time retyping and correcting a draft which in all likelihood will look very different before it's finished, but make sure you review it carefully yourself. A paragraph like the following one cries out for editing:

```
    Interviewing Mark about his pest and expecta-
tions was an intresting and educational experi-
ence, This being the first interview I ever con-
ducted, was made very easy by my host insistance
that I must try to relax as much as possible as
this will help him as much as it will help me
conduct a well rounded interview, We both agreed
how difficult it is to tell some of your life
story to a tatal stranger especially if you are a
firm believer in total privacy.
```

Not even the most well-intentioned reader could refrain from grabbing a red pen and going to work. The following paragraph, however, demands a different type of response:

```
    As a freshman, I saw the college fraterni-
ties as nothing more than elitist social clubs of
which I wanted no part. Gradually, I realized
that fraternities on this campus are more than
just a social organization. They raise money for
charities; they provide housing alternatives;
they are responsible for much of the college's
organized social life, and they provide members
with a personal support system within the larger,
colder university community. They also provide an
established power structure within which frater-
nity brothers may practice student leadership.
But I also realized that a gaping hole stares at
```

```
me when I look for where I fit into the frater-
nity structure. The space for women in the col-
lege's Greek system is grossly inadequate, and I
resent that.
```

Even the most compulsive editor will have to focus on the ideas expressed in this passage, on how successfully the writer communicates those ideas, and on how persuasive they are. If you want this type of feedback from readers, then present them with a text that leaves them with no alternative.

Although spoken interaction with readers can suffice, a written record of your comments and questions will make your readers' job easier. A Writer Review Form, such as the following, or draft cover letter will serve this purpose. It need not be very elaborate or detailed, but it should answer some basic questions about your writing, as well as raising others. Begin by informing readers about the purpose of the paper, its intended audience, why you chose the subject, why you chose this strategy, and what particular strengths and weaknesses you perceive. After these brief comments, you can list specific questions which you would like readers to address. Here is a completed sample Writer Review Form.

Writer Review Form

1. *Who is the audience for this paper?* The audience I have in mind consists of readers of a light, artsy type of campus magazine.
2. *What is this paper's central idea?* I want both to criticize and satirize the relationship between students of the different schools at the university and especially to criticize the attitudes of some non–liberal arts students toward education. The topic could also be universalized to encompass divergent types in society and their philosophies, but that is not my main point.
3. *Why did you choose to write on this topic or in this form?* I wrote on this topic because it is important to me, probably because I need to justify my preference for liberal arts to myself. I wrote in this form because I thought a dialogue would be an effective way of expressing conflicting views.
4. *What is the paper's greatest strength?* I think I captured my opponent's argument well, keeping the paper from becoming one-sided in my direction.
5. *What is its most obvious weakness?* I overemphasize my opponent's argument and don't express mine thoroughly enough, since it is firmly implanted in my mind.

6. *What questions do you have for the reader?* Do I make you laugh enough or at all? Does the paper seem repetitive? Does my topic strike you as unrealistic because everyone can see the importance of liberal arts or do you think it is a relevant point to make? Is the lack of specific examples a problem?

This writer has a clear sense of her goals and she has thought about what she still needs to do in order to accomplish them. Before she proceeds, however, she is asking readers to confirm her view. If she receives the feedback she expects, she will revise as she has planned. If she receives feedback she does not expect, she will have to reconsider her work. This reconsideration, even if time-consuming, will help her write a more effective paper.

By creating a context for your readers to use in evaluating your work, you maximize your chances of receiving constructive feedback. Rather than following their own inclinations as they respond and focusing on details or one particular issue that strikes them, they will follow your direction. By taking charge of the review process, you help to ensure that aspects of the work you consider important receive adequate attention.

Recruiting Readers

Many conscientious readers experience responding to writing as a burden, even if not an unwelcome one. Taking a friendly reader out for lunch can definitely make the burden feel lighter. Readers who are familiar with your subject, as well as interested in it, are more likely to respond effectively. Instructors, teaching assistants, or graduate students in the field in which you are writing make suitable readers for academic writing, although they may not always be available. In work situations, colleagues will often volunteer to act as readers. If they can accurately represent your intended audience, welcome their assistance.

The most accessible pool of readers consists of roommates and friends who are often willing to read over a paper, especially if you will reciprocate. Such readers, however, often lack formal experience (even the English majors) and tend to base their responses on their knowledge of you rather than on their reaction to the text. Supportive comments, such as "I like it. It's great," abound, since friends assume that they should take a supportive stance. Be sure to prepare them by explaining what you're doing and being clear about the type of feedback you want. You want support, but you also need constructive criticism.

Small groups of writers can serve as readers for each other, and such groups often form naturally among students taking the same course or majoring in the same subject, among professionals working together, or among colleagues in the same field. If you're reading this book in a writing course, you can exchange papers with your classmates. Sometimes just an interest in writing will draw people to each other, especially when they realize they will learn about their own writing by reading the work of other writers. You can often find compatible readers through college writing centers or organizations of professional writers.

Even if you can find just one other person who will read your work or with whom you can trade work, the presence of that one reader can make the writing process simpler, more concrete, and more pleasurable. Knowing that someone will respond constructively to your writing and will help you out when you are stuck or overwhelmed can increase your motivation enormously. When you envision personal interaction with a receptive and experienced reader rather than simply the production of pages of text as the outcome of writing, the whole process seems more rewarding.

In addition to offering responses to a text, readers provide you with a mental image of an audience as you work. When your actual readers are not present, you can imagine their responses, even imagine dialogues that you might have with them, to help you decide on strategy or style. In the same way that you need an image of a completed text in your head with which you can compare your achievement as you go along, you need an imagined audience with whom you can confer to shape your decision making. Just as you need to believe that your ideal text is possible to achieve, you also need to believe that your audience exists. Your sample readers help you believe in your audience.

Preparing Readers

In most cases writers receive the feedback they deserve. If you prepare your readers thoroughly, you will almost inevitably find that they respond more ably. Only well-prepared readers can give you the thoughtful responses you seek.

In addition to raising specific questions for readers on the Writer Review Form, provide questions for them to answer, or at least consider, on a separate sheet, or sit down with them and ask them to discuss some specific questions with you. Although this may seem like a lot of work, a carefully structured list of questions will help readers orient their responses around your concerns rather than their own. For example, if you ask readers to reflect on the purpose of the paper and its intended audience, you can check to see whether their impression conforms to your intention. Since clarity tends to emerge as a primary concern for most writers, asking readers which ideas seemed particularly clear or unclear can prove useful. Inquiring about whether readers enjoyed the writing, whether they learned from it, and whether it sustained their interest can also produce valuable information, provided the questions require readers to provide specific examples and pinpoint certain portions of the text in their responses.

You might want to use a form to help your readers structure their responses. A form works especially well in a classroom situation where classmates are reviewing each other's work, but don't be embarrassed to ask a friend, teaching assistant, professor, or employer to answer your questions orally or in writing. The following is a completed sample Reader Response Form.

Reader Response Form

1. *What would you say is the point of this paper, its thesis or central idea?* This paper argues that people who belong to immigrant groups, whose native language is not English, should be free to speak their native language among themselves. You try to persuade us to accept their use of their native languages without bias and point out the value of bilingual education.

2. *Who would you say is its intended audience?* The audience for this paper is native English speakers who think that students who speak other languages don't want to become Americans.

3. *Why do you think I wrote about this topic in this way?* I think you regard people who have this bias against non-native speakers as ignorant, and you want to show up their ignorance and try to get readers to think differently.

4. *Did this paper sustain your interest? If so, why? If not, where did you lose interest and why?* I enjoyed reading this paper because you chose an everyday situation, lunch in a dining hall, to illustrate your point, and you conveyed your message through a dialogue, which was easy to understand and relate to. Towards the end I felt a little frustrated, though. You don't really make any progress with your friend, and the argument doesn't seem to go anywhere.

5. *What parts of it struck you as particularly clear or unclear? (Please be specific!)* I had trouble following who was speaking because you didn't set the quotations apart, starting a new paragraph for each. Otherwise, I had no problem with clarity.

6. *What were this paper's greatest strengths? (Please be specific!)* I thought your obvious sincerity really influenced me more than anything.

Just knowing how you feel about it will make me reexamine my attitudes.

7. *What were its most obvious weaknesses? (Please be specific!)* I didn't find your friend very convincing, but maybe that's what you intended. He just seems ignorant and stupid. Also, you don't really settle anything with him. He just runs away. Is that a solution?

8. *What suggestions do you have for revisions?* I wonder why it is your friend seems to feel so threatened by a group of Spanish-speaking students in the dining hall. That's never clear to me. I know I sometimes feel uncomfortable when a group of students different from me is having a good time, but I don't think I blame them. Why do people not want others to speak their own languages? I would like to see that question addressed in your paper.

9. *Questions (from* Writer Review Form*): Did you understand why I referred to Sociology 6 at the end of the paper?* Yes, I did understand why you mentioned that he was hurrying off to Sociology 6. You wanted to show that even a student of modern sociology doesn't necessarily understand modern social problems. Of course, that reference wouldn't work for anyone who doesn't go to school here.

Because this form is very similar to the Writer Review Form you filled out, you can compare your readers' responses to your own answers to the same questions. Did your readers understand that you were writing for the audience you specified? Did they identify your central idea correctly? They can also use your answers to guide their responses. If they realize that they misunderstood your central idea, they can call your attention to that. If their sense of the strengths and weaknesses of the paper don't match yours, they can point out the differences and possibly consider more carefully why they responded differently from the way you intended.

A Reader Response Form will help you educate your readers and need not prohibit them from initiating questions of their own. The formality of this procedure, however, can frustrate some readers whose responses to your writing don't correspond to the questions included on the form. Consequently, it often works better if you ask readers to cover these questions and any others they want to raise in a way that suits them, rather than insist that they fill out the questionnaire. You don't want whimsical or irrelevant comments, but you also don't want readers to resent you and possibly take their resentment out in their comments. You also never know what you might learn from a reader's open-ended response. Obviously, you want to strike the right balance of structure and openness in your requests for feedback from readers.

Interacting with Readers

Whenever possible, try to speak with your readers and don't rely on written comments alone. Even carefully structured written responses sometimes defy interpretation. When a reader remarks, "I didn't think the introduction worked," you long to ask, "What do you mean by 'work'?" Take advantage of any opportunity to discuss their reactions with your readers and avoid depending on the one-way-at-a-time communication to which writing back and forth restricts you. You usually learn much more from half an hour of conversation than you do from even exhaustive and conscientiously detailed written responses. Besides, personal interaction— especially lively questioning and answering—will stimulate you and help you return to work more eagerly and with renewed enthusiasm.

Interpreting Feedback

No matter how much you trust your readers, the final decision about changes in your text always rests with you. Even if a decision not to make suggested changes might alienate some readers, no one knows your text or your intentions as well as you do. Any reader can turn out to be dead wrong about how a technique will affect a larger audience, for example, and blaming the reader afterwards will not relieve you of responsibility for the decision. In the process of drafting and revising, the readers' responses provide you with additional resources. They all deserve consideration, but only those that make sense to you demand attention.

Interpreting feedback and deciding what to do about it becomes easier with practice. At first, however, don't blindly accept comments that call for major rethinking and rewriting, but don't resist them either. When a reader questions the point of your paper, question it yourself. Is it possible that you have not made your purpose clear? Before you decide what, if anything, to change, consider your options. How might you direct your readers' attention more effectively to your main idea? If small changes would make a big difference, why not make them? If big changes might have to be made, don't decide until you've looked at all your feedback together. If several readers confirm the problem, or if other feedback from the same reader reinforces your concern, then you'd better take the problem seriously. If you only have comments from one reader, seek out another opinion before you decide.

No matter how carefully you prepare for review, sometimes feedback may surprise you. When you receive feedback you did not expect, how do you know whether it's reliable? Trust responses that reflect the reader's experience. In other words, give comments such as "I'm confused" or "I've lost the main point" and questions such as "Why did you use this example?" considerable authority. When a reader expresses confusion, doubt, or distaste—even if you finally determine that the reader's response is idiosyncratic—you have to take it seriously. Responses that reflect the reader's experience carry more weight than advice such as "Make this point first," which assumes that the reader knows more than you the writer. While you shouldn't simply ignore dictatorial advice, you also shouldn't rely solely on the reader's judgment about what needs to be done. Only you can finally determine how best to accomplish your own goals. Again, if you can talk with readers about their advice, you may find their suggestions more useful.

Not infrequently, marginal comments in particular are hard to interpret. For example, determining what "awk" means can prove difficult. Treat ambiguous remarks as if they said, "Take a look at this. I don't like it." If you don't like it either, or if it's hard to read or understand, then change it. Perhaps the comment actually points to a larger problem with syntax or signals that the reader is misunderstanding the sentence or paragraph. Consider all possibilities, but don't spend too much time trying to decipher what the reader meant. If you still don't get it after a second or third look, ignore it.

Setting Priorities for Revising

Once you have accumulated and interpreted your feedback, where do you go from there? Before you make any changes, set some priorities. Put off responding to comments at the section, paragraph, or sentence level until you have reconsidered issues that pertain to the whole piece of writing. Responses that relate to your overall purpose, the effectiveness of your strategy, and your ability to reach your chosen audience demand attention first. Let's use the following paragraph as an example:

Since the 1930's, Western political thought[1] has enjoyed analyzing that extraordinary European phenomenon[2] known as totalitarianism. Stalinist Russia and Nazi Germany provide the standard and perhaps[3] only models of totalitarian states

by which Western political scientists and historians have formulated viable definitions of this
form[4] of government. No one definition is correct. Yet I[5] see most as incorporating the following fundamental characteristics: single party
control of the government and economy, tolerat-
ing no opposition; state control of all mediums
of expression and education; and state control
of every aspect[6] of individual life. Police ter-
ror would[7] enforce such rule under the will of a
single dictator. Stalin's Russia and Hitler's
Germany easily illustrate the applicability[8] of
this definition of totalitarianism.

The reader has noted a number of problems:

1. Can "thought" enjoy analyzing? What do you mean by "enjoy"?
2. I don't follow this. Why is totalitarianism an "extraordinary European phenomenon"? This sounds facetious. Is it?
3. Perhaps? Yes or no?
4. "Formulated" followed by "form" doesn't sound good.
5. Who is "I"? What authority does "I" have?
6. Every aspect? That sounds a little extreme.
7. You seem to switch tenses. I find that confusing.
8. Applicability to what? I think I'm missing the point.

What should the writer respond to first? Comments 2 and 8 merit immediate attention. Comment 2 suggests that the writer's intention is not coming through, and comment 8 at the end confirms that it never did. The
reader does not understand that the writer intends to define totalitarianism
in this paper using Nazi Germany and Stalinist Russia as examples. Clarifying his intention becomes the writer's top priority. How should he proceed? The first sentence apparently creates much of the confusion and
could be replaced by a clearer statement of the writer's central idea: "Western political analysts have offered various definitions of European totalitarianism, but none adequately describes the regimes established by Hitler and
Stalin." The writer's own definition would follow. This new opening sen-

tence takes care of the problem of thought analyzing (comment 1) and also responds to the question of authority (comments 3 and 5). This approach might not be perfect, but it's an appropriate response to the feedback the writer has received. If this reader or another one still doesn't get the point, the writer will have to think again.

After you attend to all the larger issues, you can then turn to paragraphs, sentences, and eventually words, responding both to feedback you have given yourself and to comments from readers. In general, the more limited the ramifications of the choice, the less time you should spend on the decision. Unless you're writing poetry, where every word counts, there is simply no reason to obsess over word choice. Similarly, don't let yourself spend hours debating the merits of sentence-level feedback. Unless it points you toward a bigger problem, take a few minutes to consider the comment and then move on.

Almost every good style book offers writers a checklist for revising. Pick one you find easy to use, or invent one of your own that pays special attention to your quirks as a writer. The list should remind you of everything you need to think about before you finish revising. A sample revision checklist might look something like this:

1. Global concerns
      Is my central idea clear?
      Is it an important idea?
      Have I considered my audience?
      Are my audience's needs met?
      Have I established the right tone?
2. Section or chapter level
      Is each section coherent?
      Does every section contribute to the central idea?
      Do the sections fit together?
3. Paragraph level
      Is each paragraph complete?
      Does every paragraph relate to the paragraph that precedes it
        and the one that follows it?
4. Sentence level
      Are all sentences clearly written and correct?
      Do my words mean what I want them to?
      Have I expressed myself as well as I can?

Global concerns should be a top priority; sentence structure problems should be addressed last. Sort your feedback and assign each comment to a level of priority on your checklist. When appropriate, you can let the specific assignment determine how you define your priorities. For example, in a lab report you might want to review each section independently from top to bottom before reviewing the report as a whole. If you organize your lower levels of feedback into related areas, you can probably respond to several levels at once. There's no need to go all the way through a paper checking only for sentence structure when you can pay attention to transitions and word choice at the same time. Depending on how skillful you are, you can keep multiple concerns in your head as you revise. Just be careful not to overload your system by trying to respond to everything in a single reading.

Making Changes

Any number of problems might lead a reader to express confusion or doubt. Perhaps you've left out information the reader needs in order to follow your argument. Or you might also have pursued too many tangents, which distract the reader from the main point. On the other hand, the problem could result from overly complex sentence structure or even poorly articulated transitions. With all these possibilities, how do you know what to change?

When you revise with feedback from readers, you have to recognize any dissatisfaction a reader might have and then hunt for the problem that gave rise to it. For example, tracking down the source of a bad connection between reader and writer can take some detective work. Why do you imagine the reader of the following paragraph from a paper on Descartes found the writer's assertion that "what we think of as awake is more real than being asleep" unconvincing?

> Furthermore, when I am awake, I can think
> about my dreams as things that aren't real; I can
> contemplate dreaming. But when I am engaged in
> what I now think of as dreaming, I cannot contem-
> plate that I am awake. To the response that some-
> times one dreams that one is awake, I reply that
> even though this fact might be true, one still
> doesn't contemplate being awake in the fullest
> sense of the word. For example, I might be dream-
> ing that I am lying awake on my couch in the

living room, but I don't think about being awake,
about what it means to be awake. I just exist in
my dream as waking. I can, however, be awake and
think about being asleep, about what it means to
be asleep, about all the possible dreams I might
have while I am asleep. In other words, contemplating dreaming while one is awake is more complete than contemplating waking while one is
asleep. And it makes absolute sense to me that
reality must be more complete than dreaming.
Thus, what we think of as awake is more real than
being asleep.

If the writer were revising this paragraph to make the assertion more
convincing, what would you suggest she change? Is it the writer's reliance
on personal experience that fails to convince? Perhaps she simply hasn't
had the right kind of dreams. If she hasn't, how might she make her point
stronger? Or is her failure to define her terms a problem? What does "more
complete" mean? And how does she define "awake" in the "fullest sense of
the word"?

In a situation like this one, you have to try making changes one at a
time until you've done the best you can to satisfy your reader's concern.
The reader has given feedback but no direction, and you have to experiment with different ways of solving the problem. Talking with the reader
would probably be very helpful. If possible, go back to the same reader
once you have revised and see if the response is different. You could also
ask another reader's opinion if someone else is available. You may have to
revise several times before you accomplish your purpose.

As you begin to revise, it helps to make a list, at least a mental list and
preferably a written list, of what you intend to change. Working from your
revision checklist, which helped you pinpoint problems, what are you now
going to do? For example, you might remind yourself to

1. clarify the relationship between the two main points
2. reorganize paragraphs on page 6
3. work on transitions
4. rework the conclusion

Such a list allows you to check off tasks as you accomplish them and reassure yourself that you are making progress. Revision becomes a fairly straightforward and manageable procedure if you can continue to maintain an overview of the task by working, one at a time, toward a set of concrete goals.

This stage of writing emerges for many writers as the most satisfying part of the process. Although you may experience getting ideas down on paper as cathartic, the process of revising usually produces a much greater sense of control. Reinforce your sense of authority by developing a sense of the whole work, identifying priorities, and setting concrete goals based not just on hunches but on convictions. Use skills that you have worked hard to hone. As you realize that what you have accomplished is moving increasingly closer to what you envisioned, you will feel that you command the writing process rather than that the process controls you. When you set out to write for a good reason—to create a specific form, to convey an important message, to influence readers—and you accomplish those goals, you will know the joys and not just the frustrations of being a writer.

Revising with a Word Processor

The technological revolution that brought us word processors has profoundly changed the way we write. Not only has the computer relieved us of the mechanical strain of writing by hand and typing, but it has also opened up possibilities for our writing that we previously never allowed ourselves to consider. Now when an undergraduate sits down to write an honors thesis or a researcher begins to write a grant report, the possibility of producing a finished piece of publishable writing at some point in the not-too-distant future strikes these writers as more realistic. The technology of word processing invites all of us to become professional writers, and for many of us the call is irresistible.

Although the new writing-related software being developed almost daily can help you with every stage of the writing process from thinking to editing, revising has a special relationship to word processing. The computer has virtually eliminated the most onerous aspect of revising—the need for recopying by hand or retyping multiple drafts of a paper—which was also the most common excuse for not revising. If you compose at the keyboard as well, you have a further advantage, since you don't have to bother to type handwritten text into the computer. The ease with which you can change your text at any stage should make the prospect of even major revision seem more a welcome opportunity to improve your writing and less an unpleasant chore.

Computers offer an array of functions to assist you in the revising process. Take full advantage of those capabilities. Don't just insert and delete words, sentences, or even paragraphs; don't just rearrange words within a sentence or sentences within a paragraph; and don't just move paragraphs from one part of the text to another. Don't waste the computer's capacity for helping you with every aspect of revising. In this chapter we will discuss ways of using the computer as a comprehensive aid to revision. This discussion, however, will be far from exhaustive. Use the suggestions that follow to stimulate your thinking about how you can use word processing to help you as a writer. Since the technology changes constantly, you'll have to investigate the capabilities of specific software on your own.

Getting to Know Your Machine

To take full advantage of the new technology, first you need to get to know your machine. Read about it and play with it until you feel completely comfortable and are confident that you can make it do what you want. When your machine occasionally breaks down or literally eats your words, you may regard it as your worst enemy. For the most part, however, try to feel computer-friendly and look forward to interacting with your machine on a regular basis. Many writers experience the computer as company for them as they write. Those who work in a lab setting or who exchange writing with classmates through a network or through electronic mail find writing with a word processor less lonely than writing by themselves.

As you learn about your machine, learn your word processing program as well. Once you learn the basics, keep learning new functions until you have command of your program. Although adding and deleting are useful functions, make sure you learn all the commands that facilitate revising. Don't tempt yourself to forget about making a change because you don't know how to do it. Learn how to mark and move blocks of text, how to copy sections of text, how to remove and save text for later use, how to copy from one file to another, how to search for specific portions of text, how to move around in your file, how to print portions of a file, how to divide the screen so that you can look at two alternative versions of a paragraph, how to use windows to gain access to information stored on another file or somewhere else in your file, how to use all the functions your program can perform to facilitate revising.

In most instances, learning these functions is not at all complicated. With a little practice, you can add any of them to your repertoire. Working in a computer lab where someone can help you if you get stuck will make the learning process less frustrating. If you know someone else who uses the same program, you can get together and pool your experience. Even if you have to rely on the manual, however, it's worth the time it will take to get control of your program before you risk making a mistake in the middle of a paper.

Using the Computer to Achieve Perspective

Perspective is the key to revising, but it can be difficult to achieve. Because computers so rapidly transform your thinking into writing, they help you gain perspective. Seeing your words reflected back at you on the screen or, even more powerful, handsomely printed on the page gives you a sense of perspective that is difficult to achieve by handwriting or typing. It used to require a leap of faith to imagine a scribbled document as a finished, neatly typed paper, but word processors help you to recognize the potential in even your most garbled prose. You perceive what you're doing not just from the inside, as ideas struggling for expression, but from the outside, as writing awaiting reading. You achieve these two perspectives almost simultaneously as you write at the keyboard and read the screen, write and read, write and read, in sequence. It's sometimes hard to believe how suddenly an impression you have floating around in your head appears as words on the screen. One minute it's a vague, unarticulated idea, and the next minute it's there in front of you in prose.

As we have seen, you can acquire the ability to distance yourself from your writing without the computer's assistance, but the computer makes the process easier and faster. You don't have to wait until your paper is typed to see how it reads. You can almost instantly read it off the screen or print it out and look at it as if it were ready for review. You don't have to wait for a reader to help you see your writing from the outside. The computer can't tell you whether it understands what you've written (at least not yet), but it can show you your writing the way a reader will see it. This seemingly minor alteration in your perspective can help you get a jump on the revising process.

Using the Computer As a Tool for Revising

INCREASING YOUR SELF-CONSCIOUSNESS

In a number of word processing programs and programs designed to assist writers, the computer and the writer interact. Usually the interaction consists of the computer prompting the writer with a question, such as "Does this paragraph have a main point?" If the writer answers in the negative, the computer might suggest a strategy for finding a main point. An interaction of this sort simulates interaction between a teacher and student or a writer and reader and can make you feel as if you have interacted with another person, although you have been alone with the computer the whole time. In time you will presumably internalize the questions the computer asks and will no longer need either the computer or an outside reader to raise your level of consciousness about your writing. Sometimes, however, even experienced writers benefit from such prompts.

Even when you aren't using an interactive program, you can use almost any word processing program to create the same illusion. If you like, you can prompt yourself by throwing questions up on the screen at appropriate points, such as "What is the relationship betwen this idea and the one before it?" or "What expectations does my introduction raise in the reader?" You can also program writer review questions into your computer so that it will remind you to ask yourself, "What is my main point?" and "Who is my audience?" as you think about what to change and why.

This dialogue model offers one way of using the computer to your advantage in writing. In the conversations that take place between your writer-self and your reader-self, the computer can play one role and you can play the other. This may seem to some people to be a game of pretend or an effort to make the computer seem more intelligent than it is. The ability to gain perspective on your work, however, remains one of the most elusive skills in writing. If the computer can help you acquire this skill, it deserves a lot of credit.

ASSISTING IN DECISION MAKING

As you make decisions about revising your text, a number of computer programs can provide relevant information or guidelines. For example, before you decide whether to reorganize your essay, you can use a program to review what goes into choosing a successful method of organization. To help you determine whether your paper has coherence, the program might suggest that you outline your draft. Once you go through your essay and mark the main points, the computer can help you produce them in outline form. If you have trouble creating the outline, then the structure of your paper probably needs attention.

Some programs designed to assist writers with revising can help make you more aware of decisions you need to make. A program might identify potential problems in your text, such as vague words, and call them to your attention so that you can decide whether to make changes. Questions such as "Does this paragraph have a clear focus?" and "Have you provided enough detail to convince the reader?" also prompt you to make decisions you might have ignored. If you need more information before you can make a decision—such as a reminder about why the passive voice should be avoided in some cases—the program will offer you an explanation.

ANALYZING YOUR TEXT

There are numerous text analysis programs that can give you quantita-tive information about your writing. They can provide you with such potentially useful information as your readability index; the average sen-tence or paragraph length in your text; the number of times a given word, phrase, or part of speech appears; and the number of sentences that begin with prepositional phrases or other specific constructions. Many programs will call uses of the passive voice or the verb *to be* to your attention, or mark all your gender references. You can even customize some text analy-sis programs to point out quirks in your writing, such as a tendency to overuse a certain word, phrase, or sentence structure.

Computer analyses of text can prove valuable if they are used in an appropriate context and if you use the information they provide with discretion, always relying finally on your own judgment. They can help you to avoid sounding monotonous. They can also point out a predisposi-tion toward sentences that are either very long or very short and that might make your prose ponderous or choppy. Text analysis tends to focus on sentence-level concerns of revising, but many sentence-level problems add up to general stylistic problems when they occur repeatedly. If you're going to use text analysis, use it primarily to heighten your awareness of trends in your writing, and only after you have resolved the broader issues.

ENCOURAGING FEEDBACK

Just as word processing can make writing easier, it can also simplify responding to writing. If you can send your paper to readers through electronic mail and they can compose their comments on the computer instead of having to write them out by hand, the process is less work for all concerned. Even if you don't have access to electronic mail, you could invite your readers to read and respond at the computer by offering your work on a disk. The ease with which they can write comments on the computer might also encourage them to say more.

EDITING YOUR TEXT

When you're ready to attend to the details of your writing, the computer offers you numerous aids. Spelling checkers, on-line dictionaries, on-line thesauruses, and on-line style and grammar manuals can greatly simplify the editing process. All these programs have their limitations, which you should learn and respect. For example, a spelling checker won't tell you to use *effect* instead of *affect.* You can't surrender responsibility for the appropriateness or correctness of your prose to computer programs, but you can get a lot of help if you know how to use such programs.

Avoiding the Pitfalls of Word Processing

As useful a tool as computers have become, they can also be a trap for unsuspecting writers. Just because writing looks good on the screen or on the printed page does not mean that it reads well or that its content is of any significance. Although the printed page inspires more credibility than handwriting, the printing process does nothing to make writing better. In fact, a poorly conceived idea or poorly organized argument stands out even more when the appearance of the writing makes a claim to professional status that the writing itself does not deserve. When you professionalize the appearance of your work, professionalize the writing as well.

In some ways the quantitative stylistic analysis many computer programs offer suits the type of prose becoming increasingly characteristic of writers using word processors. Although not all of it reads as if it were written by a computer, processed prose tends to share specific traits. First of all, there's usually too much of it. Writing on a word processor requires so little exertion that you will probably find yourself going on and on, losing track of how much you've composed and forgetting that brevity as well as clarity are virtues. At the same time, as your writing disappears up inside the screen, you may forget just what you have and have not already said. Unless you print regularly and look over the text, you may lose track of what you've done and end up repeating the same ideas, the same sentence structure, or even the same words. Because so-called surface changes are so easy to make, you may continually add, delete, or substitute words as you draft and then deceive yourself into thinking that those minor alterations in the text constitute a revision. And because you don't have to confront what you've written when you type it, you can avoid scrutinizing your own words and convince yourself, as page after pristine page emerges from the printer, that the prodigious quantity of writing you have produced just has to be good. The advice that follows will help you avoid these pitfalls.

PRINTING OFTEN

In some writing labs you will find notices posted urging you to print often. You should print often as well as save often and back up your files to prevent you from losing text in the event of a power failure, a computer malfunction, or a problem with a disk. But printing frequently also helps to promote good writing. It helps you keep track of what you've done, so that you won't repeat yourself and so that the product of your forward progress bears a direct relationship to what has come before it. Looking backward as well as forward as you write helps you maintain continuity and prevents you from discovering, for example, that you have already filled ten pages and failed to arrive at the main point. When you do look back, instead of scribbles and arrows that can be difficult to follow, you have the luxury of clean, printed pages to review. Printing often also helps writers who don't relate well to their writing on the screen to feel closer to their work and to evaluate it more accurately.

WORKING FROM A PLAN

Because you can so easily change what you've written on a word processor, you may be tempted to skip the thinking and planning stages and go directly to drafting. If you think by writing out your ideas, feel free to do so on a word processor, but don't assume that the computer has eliminated the need to work from a plan. As your prose disappears up the screen, it's easy to lose track of your thinking. If you don't plan, how will you know what comes next?

If you compose at the keyboard and don't work from a plan, revising can become quite difficult. Even if you print a copy of your draft to use for reference, you have no record of what you intended to write. The notes you would have left on handwritten sheets that indicate what you were thinking and the remains of false starts have all been deleted. How can you possibly remember hours or even days later what you had in mind?

Use a planning program if you prefer to do all your work at the keyboard. Don't be lured into thinking you can skip the planning stage.

Unless you have a prodigious memory, you'll need help keeping track of your goals on a word processor as your writing quickly disappears from view. As you write, keep good records on the screen or on paper to help you remember your thinking, and always write and revise from a plan.

COMPLETING A DRAFT BEFORE YOU MAKE CHANGES

Once you begin drafting, resist tinkering with the details of your writing and concentrate on working through the whole piece. Not only does frequent adding, deleting, and substituting distract you from your goal of creating a whole form which you can modify later, it often fails to improve your writing. It may even do it damage, since you have not yet developed any criteria you can use to evaluate the merits of specific changes. By the time you begin revising, you have a much clearer vision of what you want to accomplish and how to go about it. At that point you can make as many changes as you like without risking the continuity of your thinking and writing.

REVISING YOUR COMPLETED DRAFT FREELY

Many writers find it helpful to review hard copy of a draft before revising on the screen. You can mark parts of your draft that need revision on your hard copy and then find them easily on your disk by using the search command of your word processing program. Going back and forth between your hard copy and the screen can also help you make judgments about what needs revising. If you're not sure whether you covered material earlier in your draft, you can quickly refer to your hard copy rather than scroll back to a previous page. That way you can keep the section you're working on in front of you while you look through other parts of your paper.

If you keep in mind the advisability of writing less and revising more on a word processor, you will probably make the best use you can of the new technology. To do so, you should focus on global rather than surface changes: practice moving whole blocks of text from one part of a document to another, cut and store (or cut and delete) sections of your text, cut and paste without hesitation whenever you think a sentence or paragraph belongs elsewhere, split the screen and consider two alternative versions of a paragraph when you can't decide which one works best. You should also allow the machine to take all the pain out of documenting research and providing references. When you do all these things as a function of revising, you will be using the power of word processing to make you both a happier and better writer. Most importantly of all, you will be controlling the technology and making the computer work for you, enhancing rather than restricting your capacity to write well.

Advice about Word Processing

To recapitulate, the following advice will help you take full advantage of word processing and increase your control over the revising process:

1. Print often and read back over what you've written.
2. Plan conscientiously to help keep track of your intention as your writing disappears up the screen.
3. Resist the urge to revise as you draft and enjoy instead the sense of fluency that the ease of word processing promotes.
4. Learn the commands in your program that facilitate revising, such as those that allow you to move blocks of text, delete and store text until you decide where to put it, split the screen and consider alternative versions of the same text, move rapidly around in your document, and locate specific portions of your text when you need them. Use those functions readily.
5. Go back and forth freely between your hard copy and the screen.
6. Mark places that need attention on your hard copy and then make changes at the keyboard.
7. Write less and revise more.

This Chapter in Brief

Revising well takes more than time and energy. It requires both motivation and skill. Much of the skill you need to revise follows from the ability to acquire perspective on your writing, which you can achieve by cultivating your critical reading abilities, by using outside readers, and by taking advantage of the computer. In addition to perspective, however, you have to know yourself and your writing intimately enough to set concrete goals in relation to which you can evaluate your success.

More than anything else, revising effectively both demands and promotes a sense of control. You need control over your writing to direct your revision; at the same time, as you see your writing coming closer to your ideal, you feel increased control over it. Where you start in most cases bears little resemblance to where you can end up. For this reason, view revising as the heart of writing.

Remember:

1. Rewrite for yourself first, but not obsessively.
2. Prepare the text for outside reading.
3. Locate interested, intelligent readers you can trust.
4. Educate your readers.
5. Evaluate the feedback you receive in relation to your purpose, your intended audience, and the image you had in mind.
6. Decide what changes you want to make.
7. Revise.
8. Use a word processor to simplify the process and increase your sense of control.

The Libraries Are Appreciated, by Jacob Lawrence

4

The Conventions of Writing

The individual readers to whom you write almost always belong to a group that has certain characteristics in common. Many groups form because they share common interests, such as sports or fashion. Almost every discipline has its own community of readers and writers (the community of biologists or psychologists, for example) as does almost every profession (lawyers, doctors, accountants). These groups are called discourse communities, and through the influence of their professional organizations and publications members of the groups set the standard for communication in their communities. Generally, anyone who wants to be part of the community has to conform to the common standard.

Standards in writing reveal themselves as conventions. Every form of writing, from an interoffice memo to a novel, has conventions associated with it. These conventions define the form for both writers and readers. The community of writers and readers who use or enjoy a particular form determine the conventions that apply to it. Conventions consist of rules of grammar, punctuation, style, presentation, and documentation, along with other customs that are particular to a specific field or specific type of writing. Writers learn about conventions by reading about them in style books and by observing them in representative writings. Knowledge of conventions is essential for any serious writer.

Since conventions change over time and vary from one setting to another as well as from one discipline or genre to another, they cannot be learned once and for all. You must rethink the conventions associated with a particular form almost every time you write that form, especially if it's one you haven't used or read examples of in a long time. For example, if you sit down to write a poem, how do you know what a poem is? Conventional poetry is rhymed and metered and divided into stanzas of a certain length, depending on what type of poetry you're considering. It also usually addresses traditional subjects, such as love and nature. Consider, as an example, a stanza written by William Wordsworth in 1804:

> I wandered lonely as a cloud
> That floats on high o'er vales and hills,
> When all at once I saw a crowd,
> A host, of golden daffodils;
> Beside the lake, beneath the trees,
> Fluttering and dancing in the breeze.

More modern poetry doesn't always follow these conventions, however. Modern poets don't restrict their subjects, often dispense with rhyme, and use more natural rhythms, rather than strict metrical patterns, to make their phrases sound pleasing to the ear. "The Red Wheelbarrow" by William Carlos Williams illustrates this point:

> so much depends
> upon
>
> a red wheel
> barrow
>
> glazed with rain
> water
>
> beside the white
> chickens

Like Wordsworth, Williams writes in stanzas, and he places his words on the page so that they give the impression of a poem. Yet his subject is not traditional, nor does he use rhyme or regular meter. If we're used to modern poetry, we recognize it immediately as a poem. But why? What conveys the idea of poetry? If you wanted to write a poem in the modern tradition, what would you need to do to ensure that it *is* a poem?

The best way to learn about conventions is to read. If you want to know what makes a poem a poem, read poetry. If you want to know how writers conventionally approach a particular subject, look at what previous writers have done. If you want to know what type of articles a given journal publishes, read a sampling of articles. If you want to determine the best style to use in a proposal to the National Science Foundation, locate proposals that have been successful and read them. Referring to style books and asking for advice from more experienced writers can also help. In the absence of advisors, however, you can learn all you need to know about what a particular community of writers considers appropriate and about the range of alternatives a community will accept by reading.

Conventions and Contracts

You use specific conventions when you write, not to satisfy some rule makers who might be evaluating your performance, but to meet the needs of your readers. For example, you can't write a technical paper about the structure of DNA for an audience of musicians as you would write about DNA for an audience of biologists. The musicians won't understand what you're talking about. Not only will the subject be difficult for them to comprehend, but the way the paper is written will seem alien. You have to choose conventions that signal readers that this paper is addressed to them. A title such as "Cognitive Correlates of Teacher Stress and Depressive Symptoms: Implications for Attributional Models of Depression" speaks directly to its target audience and warns off the casual lay reader for whom the article obviously was not intended.

Many common writing practices, such as beginning an essay or report with an introduction that indicates what the paper is about, represent conventions that function like the title quoted above. To assist readers trying to read efficiently—who need to be able to predict from the first few sentences what will follow in the rest of the paper—you introduce the material you plan to cover or you provide an abstract. Readers of fiction or poetry, however, who are reading for enjoyment rather than information, are likely to tolerate or even welcome unpredictability. For them you can eliminate the introduction and just begin presenting the subject. In an essay, however, such a beginning would strike many readers as unconventional.

The practice of following conventions allows you to create a contract with readers you have never met. Your observance of specific conventions says implicitly to readers: "I agree to write in ways you expect and are used to, in return for which you agree to confer on me the same authority other practitioners of this type of writing claim." By following the same practices previous writers have used to express similar messages to the same audience, you invite readers to treat you as a member of the same community. You identify yourself with a field or school of other writers by the conventions you choose to follow in your writing.

Let's take a simple example to illustrate this contract. Invitations represent a highly conventionalized form of writing. Many people accept the conventions associated with invitations so readily that they purchase cards with the message already written rather than bothering to compose their own. The recipients of such invitations don't fault the senders; they too understand that the information contained in an invitation must be presented in a standard form.

Convention requires that specific information appear in an invitation. You must indicate the type of gathering you are having and the occasion for it—whether it is a birthday or anniversary, for example, or a seasonal celebration, such as a Halloween or Christmas party. This information enables prospective guests to understand the invitation and to think through details such as whether a gift is in order and how to dress for the occasion. Of course, it also helps them decide whether or not they want to attend. Additional information must include the date, time, and place.

Even within the context of these fairly rigid conventions, considerable variation can occur. When you want to convey to your audience that the occasion will be a formal one—a wedding, for example—you have invitations printed which present a ritualized message with the appropriate personal information inserted (see Figure 4-1). The recipients understand from this format, which is exactly like that of many other invitations they have received, and from the language used, just what you intend to convey. When you want your audience to understand that a party will be informal, you write a few words by hand indicating your intention and perhaps letting them know that the time is flexible (7–10 in contrast to the more formally precise eleven o'clock). You also generally sign your name, dispensing with your title, and feel free to add a personal note without having to worry about disturbing the aura a formal invitation is designed to convey.

Should you send, out of ignorance or by mistake, a formal invitation for a casual Saturday night get-together or an informal invitation for a church or synagogue wedding, you would confuse your audience. The

> *Mr. and Mrs. Horace Walpole*
> *Request the Honour of Your Presence*
> *at the Marriage of Their Daughter*
> *Liza Ruth*
> *to Mr. Jeremy James Temptation*
> *on Saturday, May 28, 1988*
> *at eleven o'clock*
> *Our Lady of Consolation Cathedral*
> *777 West Orange Avenue*
> *Pelham, Pennsylvania*

Figure 4-1

usual guidelines, which the conventions associated with invitations pro-vide, would be useless. Unless you provided some explanation of what you were doing, your audience would not know what to expect or how to respond. They would either dismiss your invitation as a joke or assume that you had made a serious mistake. If you want to be taken seriously, you must acknowledge the relevant conventions.

How do these principles apply in other forms of written communica-tion? In most respects, issues about propriety remain the same, although the specific conventions vary. Depending on the type of writing, you follow the guidelines writers before you have established, and members of your audience, acknowledging your adherence to conventions they under-stand, accept your message. When those guidelines appear obsolete or irrelevant, which often happens over time, writers initiate new conven-tions, and forms evolve. When the parents of grooms begin sharing the costs of weddings, for example, their names begin to appear on invitations. However, you need to become familiar with the standard conventions of writing before trying to change them. (For a discussion of alternatives to conventional practice, see Chapter 5.)

Categories of Conventions

When you're writing invitations, the conventions are easy to identify, and your decision-making process is straightforward. In many less ritualized forms of writing, the conventions are not as obvious, and decision making becomes more complicated. Basic stylistic conventions, such as methods of documentation, are usually available in handbooks. Other conventions are always observable if you look at models. But how do you know what to look for?

Whenever you write, you consciously or unconsciously ask yourself questions about the appropriate way to present your ideas and information. Your answers help you ensure that your audience will accept your writing as appropriate. Questions such as "How much background should I provide?" "How much should I assume my reader knows?" "How much documentation must I supply?" and "What kinds of examples will be most convincing?" reflect your desire to conform to common practice. As you well know, the difference between an A paper and a C paper often rests on your understanding of how a paper in a given field should be written.

The answers to these questions about common practice reveal the existence of conventions, although you may not identify them as such. You may realize, for example, that you can't use anecdotal evidence in a formal research paper, but you may not realize that you have identified a convention. Yet your observation that in a formal research paper only objective data is accepted as evidence to support an argument highlights a convention. Numerous similar conventions exist in every form of writing; some are obvious and others are harder to recognize.

If you read widely in a discipline, you intuitively pick up a sense of conventional practice. When you're new to a field, however, or when your status as a writer changes, such as when you switch from writing undergraduate papers to graduate or professional school papers, you need to educate yourself about conventions. When you lack experience in a field, look carefully at what respected writers do and imitate them. Begin by answering the following questions:

1. What authority does this discipline use to regulate basic style?
2. What are the most common forms writers in this discipline use? What distinguishes those forms?
3. What kinds of questions do writers in this discipline ask? How does this discipline present an argument? What constitutes valid evidence?
4. What methods do researchers/writers in this discipline use? How are those methods incorporated in their writing?
5. What type of language do writers in this discipline use?

Questions like these can help you become familiar with common practice quickly. You may not have the breadth of experience that extensive reading offers, but you can acquire enough information to write appropriately for colleagues in the field.

There are also some identifiable categories of conventions that can guide you when you're trying to understand how to approach a writing task. Looking at conventions category by category can give you a more effective grasp of how the whole paper becomes representative of conventional practice in any given instance.

Conventions of Basic Style

At the most basic level, conventions consist of the rules of grammar, punctuation, and style that a community of writers agrees to follow. Most writers in the social sciences adhere to the practice advocated in the American Psychological Association's handbook. In the humanities, the Modern Language Association sets the standard, and many scientists follow the recommendations of the Council of Biology Editors. Writers in many professions also use *The Chicago Manual of Style*. Many instructors and editors insist that writers follow the guidelines provided in one or another of these handbooks. These guidelines include instructions for documentation (footnotes and bibliography) and presentation (size of margins, appearance of title page, number of words per page, typefaces, etc.), as well as advice about style (using *I* vs. *this investigator*, formal vs. informal tone, etc.). So, first of all, determine what authority your readers (including your instructors) will expect you to follow, and then make sure that your text conforms to that standard.

Conventions of Form

Every field requires its practitioners to write in specific forms that present information in ways the discipline expects. Although many disciplines share forms, some forms are characteristic of certain fields. For example, science and engineering students write lab reports; students of business write case analyses; literature students write critical essays; and students in the social sciences write research reports. Each form has rules that govern its presentation, and you must follow those rules if you want readers to recognize the form. Some of these rules are provided in field-specific style books. Exactly how you apply those rules, however, depends on your audience and your purpose and requires your best judgment as a writer to determine.

Usually the form you use and the audience for which you are writing go together. For example, you would probably write a report rather than an essay for a board of directors, because a report is what they would expect and understand. The same is true of your purpose; certain forms suggest distinct purposes. For example, you wouldn't write a lab report, the purpose of which is to report results, when you're requesting funding. You'd write a proposal. Sometimes, however, the question of what form to use is not so clear. How should you present statistical data to parents in a school district? Should you follow the conventions of a social science paper, a technical report, or an informal essay? If you don't answer this question correctly, you might choose a form that is inappropriate for your audience and purpose. Consequently, when you have such a choice to make, look at the conventions that define a form and consider whether those conventions suit your purpose and whether your audience will understand them. Then make your decisions accordingly.

Conventions of Argument and Evidence

In order for readers to accept your writing as representative of the field, it must reflect how people in the field think. If part of your goal involves influencing your readers to accept your point of view, then you'll need to know what questions or problems the field considers significant and what type of argument the field respects. Should you begin with observations and argue toward conclusions, or should you start with a thesis and provide evidence to support it? What constitutes valid evidence in any given discipline? Precedent plays a major role in legal argument. Evidence produced from interviews could prove highly persuasive in a folklore or sociology class. In a history class, however, you would need evidence from historical documents, and in an English class you would need to support your claims with evidence from the text you are discussing. Your style of argument and type of evidence should always be appropriate for your field.

Conventions of Method

You must also employ methods that reflect the process of inquiry that characterizes the discipline. Historians, for example, construct arguments about what happened in the past and why, based on their readings of primary and secondary sources. Sociologists frame questions about people in society and then gather data in order to supply answers. Physical scientists generate research questions and then design experiments that allow them to draw conclusions. Writing effectively in any given field requires you to use appropriate methodology or approach your subject in an acceptable way. If you mistakenly approach a problem in psychology as if it were a literary question and try to interpret a study in a way that proves your thesis instead of presenting data, you will lose your credibility with social scientists. Always make sure that your methodology conforms to the standards in the field.

Conventions of Language

As you learn about a field, you learn a specialized vocabulary and a particular way of using vocabulary, which incorporates your knowledge about your subject. Although most style books advise you to avoid jargon (which is good advice in principle), you should always use language appropriate to the form and discipline in which you are writing, especially if it will facilitate communication with your audience. Technical terms are out of place in a report to the public about new methods of treating cancer but not in a report to the medical profession. Most types of writing are defined by specific language. Any writer in the field should be familiar with the appropriate standard of expression.

Convention and Choice

The reward for knowing the conventions of a field well and understanding why those particular conventions are observed is often increased flexibility. The more experience you have reading and writing, the more freedom of choice you can permit yourself in regard to conventions. At the same time, more conventions become available to you. This, of course, complicates your decision making.

Let's look at a typical choice writers in engineering have to make. How do you organize information about a design problem for presentation to an architect? Technical report formats, with which you would be familiar, can serve as useful models, but no single format fits your information perfectly or perfectly suits this particular audience. Since the problem has two parts, you're not sure whether to cover both recommendations simultaneously or to write, in effect, two reports. Since your reader is a professional who has hired you to design supports for a building, should you include a conventional abstract, or should you just write a cover letter summarizing what you've done and giving your recommendations? How do you know what is correct in this situation?

Given the number of choices like these that any conscientious writer must make, you do well to read often in your field and to practice writing. Although some rules must be followed, many can be bent or circumvented if you're familiar with both common practice and the exceptions to common practice. When your subject does not lend itself to conventional treatment, or when you want to make an unconventional point, rely on your experience to suggest ways of rethinking the rules. Conventions exist to set a standard for common practice, not to dictate what writers can and cannot do. If you can meet that standard differently, your readers will not hold it against you. In many instances, you may have no other choice.

Writing in Conventional Forms

Although exceptions always exist, many forms besides invitations require you to follow a strict set of rules. In some cases, you must follow the rules to be credible. In other cases, you have more freedom of choice. You can't make intelligent choices, however, unless you understand why the rules exist. Although some conventions—such as the practice of placing footnotes at the bottom of the page—seem simply like hurdles, many have histories which explain their functions. Once you understand the purpose of a convention, you can more easily adapt to it or change it by substituting a practice which performs the same function.

In the following pages, we will review three student papers, representing three conventional forms: the lab report, the social science research paper, and the critical essay in literature. We will begin with a form governed by strict conventions and progress to forms that are less regulated. By examining what conventions define each form and how each student interpreted the conventions, we can acquire a sense of both the limitations conventions impose and the opportunities they create.

We will look at these papers, not as unique pieces of writing, but as representatives of types. We will read them critically, using the categories of conventions set out above to help identify standard practice in each case. Whether or not you write lab reports or literary criticism does not matter. The goal of this exercise is not to instruct you in how to write these forms, but to help you identify their distinctive characteristics. This type of reading should become a staple for any writer when confronted with an unfamiliar form or a new field. You have to depend on your reading to inform your writing at points where the style books leave off. Whatever textbooks (including this one) tell you, the experience, judgment, and taste you acquire from reading and from writing and receiving feedback teach you most about writing well.

The Conventions of the Lab Report

The most common writing assignment for students in the sciences and engineering is the lab report, a form with strict conventions. If you were a student in one of these fields, learning to write a good lab report would be essential. An overview of the rules that govern the form will give you a context for interpreting what writers have done when you look at some model lab reports. Any handbook for writing in science or engineering would include information like that in the following paragraphs.

In beginning classes, lab reports are based on classic experiments which students must replicate, and the reports serve as a means of testing the students' understanding of and ability to follow scientific method. Each section of a lab report serves a precise function and makes a distinct contribution to accomplishing the goals of the report. As a result, students need to become familiar with the content appropriate for each section. In addition, they need to communicate that content clearly. Mastery of the form of the lab report demonstrates knowledge of scientific method, which is obviously essential for anyone who purports to be a scientist.

Students and many professionals use the same form for the lab report—abstract, introduction, methods, results, and discussion—or a variation of that form. Lab reports, especially in entry-level classes, contain no surprises. The task of the writer consists primarily of organizing information effectively and presenting it clearly.

Because scientists and engineers strive for objectivity, they almost never use *I* in lab reports. They want to ensure that the experiment has integrity apart from the experimenter. In addition, any researcher should be able to duplicate an experiment and achieve the same or similar results. To achieve these ends, science writers avoid imprecise words (such as *maybe* or *probably*), or words that convey opinion (such as *believe* or *think*) or reveal bias (such as *obviously* or *of course*), unless they are pointing out problems, or they intend to cast doubt on the reliability of their observations or conclusions.

Using this type of information as a guide to conventions of form, method, and language, you can go on to look at models to see how writers use these conventions and others in practice. Let's look together at selections from a lab report and see how they conform to or vary from the norm

just described. From these observations, we can draw some conclusions
about the conventions of lab reports.

THE SECTIONS OF THE LAB REPORT

1. ABSTRACT: SUMMARIZING THE MAIN POINTS

An abstract of a lab report is a short summary of the report designed to
inform readers about the experiment and the conclusions reached. Along
with the title, the abstract helps readers decide whether or not to read the
report. Because readers from a variety of backgrounds read abstracts, abstracts generally should not include a lot of technical language. Other
parts of the report are written for a specific group of technical readers, but
the abstract should appeal to a broader technical audience.

Of course, in any particular case, the wording chosen will depend on
the intended audience. Since many scientific papers are intended for science readers, even abstracts often sound highly technical to the lay person. The following abstract written by a student in a biology course on
plant development illustrates the point:

> In this experiment, the silique plastocron
> index (S.P.I) was used to characterize em-
> bryogenesis in Arabidopsis thaliana, a plant com-
> monly used for study in genetics. The growth rate
> and stage of differentiation of embryos was ob-
> served in plants with more than 25 siliques on a
> ramet. The rate of embryo expansion was exponen-
> tial and biphasic between S.P.I. 21 and 9. From
> S.P.I. 21 to 14 the embryo grew rapidly. After
> S.P.I. 13 the embryo grew more slowly and dis-
> played no further morphological change. These re-
> sults indicate that the S.P.I. is useful in deter-
> mining the age of the embryo and evaluating its
> developmental state.

The amount of technical language used here is conventional for lab reports
and other technical forms like project reports and proposals. The student

casts the technical terms, however, in relatively short and uncomplicated sentences and paragraphs which make their meaning easier to understand. Readers unfamiliar with *Arabidopsis thaliana* or embryogenesis probably won't be interested in reading the report. The writer recognizes that when she decides what vocabulary to use. For a nontechnical audience, she would need to define her terms or use different ones.

This student also relies heavily on the passive voice, as do most writers of lab reports. Use of the passive voice is also conventional in this type of writing. The student writer could have started by saying, "In this experiment, *we* examined," but she chose instead to stick to conventional practice. Readers of lab reports expect writers to avoid intruding themselves on their experiments as much as possible. They don't really want to know who is performing the experiment, because anyone should be able to follow the same procedure and produce the same or similar results. The writer's use of the passive voice demonstrates her awareness of that expectation and her desire to make her research objectively valid. If you're writing for a similar audience, you would do well to follow her example.

2. INTRODUCTION: CREATING A CONTEXT

The introduction creates a context for understanding the experiment. Writers generally include any background information, including references to previous experiments, that might help readers understand the significance of the experiment. In addition to a clear statement of the problem, a description of what is being tested, and the hypothesis, the introduction should also present any limitations readers should be aware of and any assumptions on which the work is based. Like the abstract, the introduction does not need to sound highly technical, but it should include technical vocabulary for technical audiences when less technical language will not convey the same meaning.

The student lab report on "Embryogeny in *Arabidopsis Thaliana*" continues with the following introduction:

Arabidopsis thaliana is a small angiosperm
of the mustard family. The species has been shown
to have great potential for experiments in molecular biology. Consequently, the need for accurate
development indices has become apparent
(Meyerowitz and Pruitt 1985). In this experiment,

embryogenesis in <u>Arabidopsis</u> was characterized
with respect to the silique plastocron index
(S.P.I.), a time-independent developmental parameter. Embryo dimensions were plotted against the
S.P.I. to yield absolute and relative one-
dimensional expansion rates for the embryo proper
and cotyledons between distinct plastocrons. Once
the rate of silique initiation had been determined, expansion rates could be expressed in
units of time. This result allows approximation
of the age of embryos in successive siliques.

To the uninitiated, this paragraph may read like a foreign language. Yet such language is conventional in lab reports, and readers expect it. The language the writer uses seems appropriate to the context. In her introduction the writer explains not only what she has done, but why she has done it. We learn that because of the importance of this plant to research in molecular biology, the writer proposes to use an index to measure the plant's development.

As in the abstract, the writer uses the passive voice frequently in the introduction to avoid personalizing the experiment. She also talks about the experiment in the past tense, since she has completed her work by the time she writes her report, and writing in the past tense is customary in lab reports. In these ways and as a result of the context she creates for under-standing her experiment, this writer identifies herself as a member of the community of scientific researchers. Through her observance of the appro-priate conventions of writing, she earns the respect of readers in the same community.

3. METHODS: ESTABLISHING CREDIBILITY

The Methods section is designed for other professionals who might wish to replicate the experiment. Consequently, the information pre-sented here must be clear, complete, and easy to follow. Depending on the audience, this section should provide as much detail as readers will require to accept the results. The researcher should avoid any impulse to analyze and instead stick closely to the facts. Readers will not believe the results of an experiment unless they are convinced that the methods used to achieve them were sound.

The Materials and Methods section of the report on plant development follows:

> *Arabidopsis thaliana* was grown under standard greenhouse conditions. In determining the rate of silique initiation, both siliques and open flowers (with petals showing) were counted at 24-hour intervals. For embryo characterization, plants with more than 25 siliques along a single ramet were selected. Siliques were numbered in the order of appearance, removed from the plant, and dissected under a dissecting scope. A 5% NaOH solution was applied to facilitate clearing of the embryo from the excised seeds. A cover glass was applied, and the slide was placed under a light microscope. Dimensions were recorded using an ocular micrometer. At least two embryos from each silique were measured.

The procedures used in this experiment are clear even to nontechnical readers. They may not understand the terminology employed or how to perform the experiment, but the uncomplicated sentence structure and clear statement of procedures make it possible for anyone to understand in general terms what methods the experimenter used. Prose that maximizes clarity for all readers is a desirable feature in any type of writing. Although only a technical reader can evaluate the report, this section sounds complete and thorough and convincing. The experimenter speaks clearly, provides sufficient detail to convince readers of the validity of her experiment, and presents her information efficiently, all of which increases her credibility as a researcher.

4. RESULTS: PROVIDING THE EVIDENCE

The results of an experiment supply the evidence to support the claims made in the Discussion section which follows. Presenting the results of an experiment challenges a writer's organizational skills. The section may begin with the most significant results and proceed to the least significant, or begin with the broadest ones and proceed to the most specific, whatever seems appropriate for the audience and the experiment. Results may be compared to those produced by previous or concurrent experiments, but the writer should not comment on the similarities or differences. Graphs and tables which summarize findings belong in the Results section.

In the plant experiment, the results consist primarily of numbers, which the writer presents in paragraph form, followed by graphs and charts:

> The rate of silique initiation was deter-
> mined from a plot of the number of open flowers
> and siliques against time (in days) for two
> plants (Fig. 1). With the exception of the first
> 48 hours after the first flower opened, the
> points for both plants fit straight lines, both
> giving a rate of 2.7 + 0.1 siliques per day, or
> a plastocron of 0.37 + 0.1 days. Siliques are
> initiated (flowers open) therefore every 8.9 +
> 0.2 hours. During the first 48 hours, the rate
> appears to be in a "lag phase." It was noted that
> only open flowers could be seen on the axis dur-
> ing this period.

After a middle paragraph, this section concludes:

> A plot of the log of the length of the em-
> bryo proper against the S.P.I between S.P.I. 9
> and 21 yielded a straight line with a slope of
> 0.24 + 0.04 per plastocron, or 0.65 + 0.01 per
> day. Hence over 11 plastocrons showing biphasic
> absolute expansion rates, the length of the em-
> bryo proper is increasing by between 22 and 26%
> per plastocron, or by between 55 and 65% per day
> (Fig. 3).

Maintaining a strictly neutral stance toward the data, the writer refrains from making any interpretations at this point. She simply reports what she observed, in keeping with the sense of objectivity that the writer of a lab report strives to create. She also notes any patterns that emerge in her data—for example, that the plot yields a straight line—but withholds comment on the significance of that pattern until the next section. She also refrains from allowing her personality to appear in her presentation. Every effort is made to present the data so that it can be easily understood. She also records the data in graphs and tables. Some readers will want to review such visual aids along with the paragraphs which highlight the most important information conveyed visually. Some data, such as the graph of expansion rates, which yields a straight line, also lends itself better to visual representation.

5. DISCUSSION: EXPLAINING THE RESULTS
AND DRAWING CONCLUSIONS

This section explains the implications of the results and draws conclusions. It reviews whether or not the results were conclusive and why, and mentions the limitations of the research. It is important to indicate here how this work fits into the context of other research and to suggest what further work needs to be done to produce more significant or more conclusive results. In this section, the writer interprets the evidence in a way that will lead readers to accept and approve the work the report represents.

In effectively written scientific research, the conclusions appear to present themselves. Although the writer analyzes the results according to frameworks developed for the experiment, readers will expect the conclusions to appear objective and inevitable, not the result of personal opinion or speculation. Speculation may be part of the discussion, but conclusions should sound definite.

In the lab report we have been following, the writer divides the last section into two parts. Under Discussion, she interprets the results of the experiment. She uses statements such as:

```
In this study, an observed developmental change
in the embryo seems to correlate with the
biphasic expansion rates of the embryo proper.
```

and

```
If growth is considered both as a function of
morphological differences, a function of nutrient
```

transport via the suspensor through most of the
heart—shape stage, and a function of photosynthe-
sis in the mature stage, then it is logical to
expect two different absolute expansion rates
from the embryo proper, as reflected in Figure 2.

These statements help readers understand her results and encourage them
to see what she sees. Once she has explained how she achieved her results,
she draws her conclusions in a separate section:

The silique plastocron index was shown to be
useful for the characterization of embryogenesis
in Arabidopsis, because it is time—independent
yet can relate developmental events indirectly to
time. It is easier to keep track of the S.P.I.
than to do a time—dependent study. Any significant developmental parameter may be defined and
characterized in terms of the S.P.I., such as
fresh or dry weight, or any parameter that is
relevant to a particular experiment. For species
like Arabidopsis that form seed pods along a single ramet, the S.P.I. should be used. For species
that do not show this kind of seed pod pattern,
another plastocron index should be used, because
developmental events will be more easily, and
probably more accurately, defined in terms of the
plastocron index than as a direct function of
time.

In writing a lab report, be careful that you do not claim more in your
conclusions than you have proven with your results or qualified in your
discussion. If you follow this guideline, you should have an easy time
influencing readers to accept your assertions. Especially because conclusions come at the end, when you have had an opportunity to support them

with evidence and with analysis, they should seem to write themselves. This effect represents exactly what the method is designed to promote. Your mastery of scientific method should reveal itself in the clarity and invisibility of your prose. If you have performed your duties as a competent scientist, the presentation of your work will justify itself.

PERSONAL STYLE IN THE LAB REPORT

In actuality, however, the facts cannot present themselves; writers have to present them. As a result, even lab reports have different styles, which reflect the character of individual writers. Although some scientists might argue that personal style is out of place in a lab report, a certain amount of personal style is inevitable and desirable. As long as you follow correct procedures and the presentation reflects correct use of scientific method, personal style can make the report more interesting.

This is not to recommend excessive use of colorful language or inappropriately casual prose; such stylistic flavor might understandably cause readers to doubt the authenticity of your research. However, many factors that create interest in writing—factors such as variation in sentence and paragraph length and structure or the use of strong verbs and of interesting, descriptive nouns—can enliven lab reports without offending the reader's sense of correctness. Let's look at a few examples. Compare these sentences from the introduction to a lab report on cell aggregation with the alternative version which follows them.

1

The importance of each factor in the aggregation factor complex was examined. A proteolytic enzyme and a saccharide specific enzyme were used. Their effects on the aggregation rate were determined. The question of whether protein or sugar is the active component in cell adhesion was addressed. An example of a calcium cofactor for protein action was recorded. The number of variables to be taken into consideration when planning research and examining species specificity was noted.

2

This lab tried to discover the role played by
each of the major constituents of the aggregation
factor complex. Because the aggregation factor is
a glycopolypeptide, a protein destroying enzyme
and a sugar specific enzyme were used to study the
effects on the aggregation rate. The results were
expected to show whether protein or sugar is the
active component in cell adhesion, and in so doing, to demonstrate the major structural constitu-
ent of cell binding for all multicellular orga-
nisms. It provided an example of a calcium
cofactor or controlling switch for protein action
and emphasized the number of variables which must
be taken into consideration when examining species specificity and planning research.

Although either of these versions is acceptable according to the conventions of lab reports, the second is livelier and makes the same information
sound more interesting. Some readers might object to the longer, more
complicated sentences, but they help to break up the monotony induced by
repeating the same sentence structure and sentence length in the first paragraph. Most importantly, communication is not obscured by the more fluid
writing in the second paragraph. In fact, the relationship between the
sentences and between the ideas contained in them (expressed, for example, in the phrase "in so doing") is more clearly stated in the second version.

In the same lab report, the writer used categories slightly different from
the conventional ones to organize her presentation. She used the following headings in this order: Introduction, Results, Observations (consisting
of graphs and tables), Discussion of Variables, Discussion, and Conclusion. The most obvious omission in this list is the Materials and Methods
section. Since the lab was assigned and performed in a classroom, and
since students worked together in groups, a description of materials and
methods was unnecessary. The most obvious addition to the lab report is
the section headed Discussion of Variables. The writer added this category
as a result of the unique character of the lab:

This lab allowed for a large number of seemingly uncontrollable variables. The involvement of many people throughout the process increased the possibility of human error.

Possible variables included:

1. Error through judgment: debris counted as cells, chosen field not representational, or fudge-factor--deliberate alteration of the count because it seemed disproportionate.

2. Malfunction or denaturation of enzymes due to improper storage or wrong amount of enzyme in flask.

3. Temperature: increase in aggregation or overheating from too much exposure to microscope light. If optimum temperature exists, activity could speed up geometrically when this is reached. An imbalance in the count could result.

4. Movement of liquid on slide; flow of cells through viewing field.

5. Lack of uniformity: in taking aliquots, varying size of same, inadequate mixing of liquid in flask, microscope magnification, size of field between different brands of microscopes.

6. Time: the time it takes to count cells, flasks to reach tables, slides to reach microscopes or time it takes to get slides ready.

The group eventually reduced some of the possibilities for error by making the production of slides uniform, but discrepancies still appeared. At the eight-minute interval, the count for one group member seemed too large, and it was disallowed. Table 4 shows variance in the count for the total number of units from one interval to the next. If the account is accurate, and if a representative field is chosen, the total number of cells should remain the same. This does not happen. It varies from 48 to 231, a more than fourfold increase. Sometimes the count remains steady; sometimes it decreases or increases by half. The individual and group graphs show the same fluctuation.

The variables and obvious mistakes mentioned above are evidence of all that must be taken into account when an experiment is conducted. If these are not controlled, the results are not accurate and cannot be duplicated.

Because of the context for this lab, the changes in conventional format appear completely justified. These changes make this particular experiment simpler and clearer. The reader of this report already knows what methods were used. On the other hand, the large number of students involved in this experiment created a situation that deserved comment. The writer's decision to explain that situation in a separate section contributes to the reader's ability to comprehend the results. Although scientists place a high value on conventional presentation for reasons already stated, the existence of conventions does not exempt an individual writer from exercising judgment. Even in a form rigidly governed by conventional practice, you must choose those options that best contribute to accurate and successful communication of the subject matter. Reading examples of lab reports that readers respect will help you determine your options.

The Conventions of the Social Science Research Paper

Different fields of social sciences use different research methods and present their work somewhat differently. In sociology, you might begin by identifying a problem and formulating a research question, and then read articles or books or collect data from other sources, analyze the information, and draw conclusions. In psychology, you might first formulate a hypothesis before investigating sources or collecting data. The exact form of the paper depends on the field, the methodology you have used, and the nature of the assignment, but research papers have certain characteristics in common.

Although the conventions of the research paper are not as formalized as those for the lab report, most research papers have a distinctive form. They begin with an introductory section, which poses the question or states the thesis of the paper; they have a body, in which the writer reports findings or provides evidence to support the thesis; and they have a concluding section, which summarizes the research and its implications. Although it is customary to write a research paper in three such parts, you have more leeway in determining just how you want to organize and present your subject in each part. However, you must show in a research paper, just as you must show in a lab report, that you have used methods appropriate for the field and the task. Your method of presentation should reflect your research methods.

THE METHOD OF SOCIAL SCIENCE RESEARCH

Just as some professors assign lab reports to teach students scientific method, other professors require research papers to ensure that students learn how to perform research in social science. Practitioners in any field need to know how to raise questions, develop hypotheses, acquire information, and use that information to prove a hypothesis or make inferences. Following this method helps ensure objectivity and may create new knowledge, the goal of most research.

Although social scientists strive for objectivity, they acknowledge, more than natural scientists do, the inevitable subjectivity that research entails. To offset that subjectivity, social scientists demand that writers present evidence to prove that they gathered information as objectively as possible and that their interpretations are at least appropriate, if not shown to be true by some objective standard.

As you move away from the more ritualized methodology represented in a lab report, convention demands that you not only use appropriate methods for gathering information and support your claims with evidence, but that you indicate through appropriate documentation in what ways your sources influenced you. In any type of research paper, some ideas will be original and others will be taken from your sources. Often original work synthesizes or extends previous research. In order to prove yourself as a social scientist, you have to show through quotations, citations, and other references how your thinking relates to accepted thinking in the community of social scientists.

The form of the research paper requires writers to follow standard methods for doing research. Beyond that, however, you decide how to organize your presentation so that you demonstrate that your methods conform to this standard. You have to *summarize* your investigation in the introduction, *select* the sources that are most useful and most convincing in the body of the paper, and *influence* readers to accept the validity of your methods and your findings in the conclusion. You don't have to include everything you did, as you would if you were writing a lab report, nor do you have to maintain strict neutrality toward your subject. If the paper demonstrates good reasoning, proceeds logically, and establishes its authority, and if you express your ideas clearly, the reader's expectations for a conventional research paper will be met. Let's look at a model and see how one student interpreted the conventions of a research paper.

THE FORM OF A RESEARCH PAPER

1. THE INTRODUCTION: BEGINNING AND ASSERTING

The following excerpt, which is the third chapter of a long research paper for a history course, reveals some of the conventions of a social science research paper. Although it is only a portion of the paper, the form of the chapter corresponds to the form used in the presentation of the whole paper. The paper is entitled "The Role of Student Media in Student Political Participation." This chapter is called "The Conservative Movement and the Campus Press." The chapter begins:

> Although most students may be "turned off"
> from all forms of political participation because
> of preprofessionalism, a sense of inefficacy, or
> the ideology of specialization, student political
> activity goes on through lobbying groups, minor-
> ity associations, political research, and cam-
> paign work. Perhaps because these activities tend
> to be low key, part of the status quo, and noncon-
> frontational, they are largely ignored by the na-

tional and even campus media. But since 1980, a
new brand of true activism has arrived on the
campus. It uses the student communications media
as its weapon, tends towards ideological and personal confrontation, and is funded mostly from
outside the campus. It is represented by Young
Americans for Freedom, a large number of College
Republicans, and "underground" conservative papers like the Dartmouth Review. It can be inflam-
matory, unrestrained, confrontational radicalism
coming into conflict with university administra-
tions and liberal campus groups. And it is part
of a new trend in the campus media which has the
potential to bring about a return of political
debate among students through the college press.

This introductory paragraph previews the presentation which follows
and provides a context for the reader, a necessity in any form of writing,
but especially important in a research paper. In order to capture the
attention of the audience, the writer has to establish the significance of his
question or thesis. Before readers can evaluate evidence, they need to view
the question in a larger framework. This paragraph asserts that the conservative student movement represents a new form of student activism,
which has found expression in the campus press and may create renewed
political debate among students. This assertion seems acceptable as a
thesis and significant enough to warrant investigation. It is also likely to
create interest, especially for a campus audience. Unless they have reason
to think differently, readers will probably await the evidence before making up their minds. They look for direction and authority in an introduction, and convention demands that the writer provide it.

Convention does not require that a paper begin with an introduction
of this form, however. In your own papers you could begin with a quotation, with a definition, with background information, or with a summary
of your presentation. You must, however, provide a context readers can
use to make sense out of your work. The context must establish the
importance of what you have to say and influence readers to accept the
point you are trying to make.

Although you might assume that research papers should simply report information, readers usually expect writers of such papers to assert a point of view. Your individual perspective on the information and the use you make of it are at least as important as the information itself. Unlike the results of science experiments, social science data must be interpreted. As long as you follow correct methodology, you can interpret the data in your own voice without worrying about contaminating your results. Consequently, the writer of the social science research paper does not rely on the passive voice as heavily as the science writer does. This student writer does not refer to himself as *I*, which some readers might construe as too informal, but neither does he refer to himself in the third person (as *this researcher*). He chooses a matter-of-fact, reportorial style, even though much of what he reports is clearly open to interpretation. The confidence his style conveys interacts with the evidence he uses to support his assertions and to convince readers that his point of view is valid. Although it is acceptable on occasion to assert more than one point of view or to express ambivalence about a subject, social science writers conventionally take a position and support it in the body of their papers.

2. THE BODY: SUPPORTING AND PROVIDING EVIDENCE

The middle section of a research paper supports the assertion made in the introduction by offering appropriate evidence. The nature of evidence varies from field to field, but evidence often involves bringing in outside experts and offering concrete examples and data which help prove your point. In the paper we are discussing, the writer does both:

```
    Much of the sharp decrease in student politi-
cal activity in the 1970s may have been due to
the national media's lack of interest in the new
forms of political participation that replaced
the mass protest movements (Altbach 46). In 1976,
for example, as many as 18.6 percent of under-
graduates reported that they had engaged in some
form of activism (Altbach 23). And in 1979, PIRGs
(Public Interest Research Groups) staffed by stu-
dents on campuses around the country had more
than 700,000 undergraduates paying dues through
```

their schools (Altbach 46). In fact, PIRGs have
become so powerful that the conservative student
movement has singled them out for destruction (Interview with Dave Donabedian, Summer 1983). Ob-
servers agree, however, that at least in the late
seventies,

> The campus reverted to a political
> level not unlike the 1950s. . . . Even the
> traditionally most active campuses, such as
> the University of California at Berkeley,
> Harvard, and the University of Chicago, have
> only a few small, relatively inactive, and
> usually weak, political organizations func-
> tioning (Altbach 23).

But while the lack of viable organizations
may persist, politics on the campus, especially
concerning student governments such as Penn's Undergraduate Assembly (UA), has risen to a renewed
significance. Philip Altbach, in a book on student activism, observes that "while student governments have not become primarily political
entities in the seventies, the political consciousness and power of student governments has
been enhanced" (25). Student governments have become the arena of campus politics perhaps by de-
fault, as isolated issues fail to produce durable
political organizations. Also, student activity
fund committees, as well as university con-
sultative committees, have become a focus of political activity because they deal with large
sums of money, some of which may be used to fund
political organizations. Largely, the record

shows that students have tended to limit their
activities to political issues that are somehow
related to the campus through university policy
of some sort (Altbach 23-4)--external/internal
politics (Seminar discussions, June 1983). Examples of external/internal politics are the recent
controversy at Penn over army discrimination
against homosexuals, the South African divestment
movement, and the demonstrations against defense
research projects in the late sixties.

In the documentation for these paragraphs, the author acknowledges, in
addition to Altbach's book, conversations with the Executive Director of
College Republicans of the state of Pennsylvania and seminar discussions.
Later in the chapter he cites a dissertation on undergraduate newspapers,
as well as articles in the *New York Times* and the *Christian Science Monitor.*
His references to events on the campus of the University of Pennsylvania
(Penn), where he is a student, might not convince outside readers, but
they work effectively for his immediate audience, his professor and peers at
Penn. The evidence he offers is appropriate for his purpose and for his
readers. If he were to rewrite this paper for national distribution, however,
he would need to refer to Penn—at least initially—as the University of
Pennsylvania and possibly to provide more information about these events
to ensure that outside readers understand his meaning.

The writer begins the next paragraph with a reference to a quote two
paragraphs back. Such tight connections between paragraphs add unity and
coherence to writing, characteristics that increase the writer's credibility.

The parallel between the fifties and seventies goes beyond the widespread apathy and
careerism among students. In the 1980s we are seeing a resurgence in student political participation coming from the same direction from which
the nascent campus political awareness of the fifties was born--from the right. One of the largest
student organizations of the fifties was the con-

servative Students for America (SFA), founded in
1952. The SFA was funded by nonstudent conservatives and published a national journal called the
American Student, which railed against campus
radicalism and subversion. In fact, the organization had a National Security Director who was assigned the task of watching radical movements and
reporting suspected communists to the proper "au-
thorities" (Altbach 165–6). And in 1960, the
Young Americans for Freedom (YAF) was formed on
the Connecticut estate of the prominent right-
wing intellectual, William F. Buckley.

In the remaining paragraphs that make up the body of the chapter, the
writer proceeds as follows, paragraph by paragraph, to say that

1. The conservative movement was overshadowed by the New Left.
   When the underground leftist press disappeared from campuses, a
   vacuum was created.
2. That created an opportunity which the conservative movement
   seized. The nonstudent American right has taken the initiative and
   is funding and advising the conservative student movement and its
   press.
3. Prominent people including William Simon, Secretary of the Trea-
   sury under Ford and Nixon, and Irving Kristol have supported the
   conservative movement. Simon and Kristol founded the Institute
   for Educational Affairs (IEA), which has given over $1 million to
   undergraduate student publications.
4. Other sources, including individuals and corporations, have provided funding as well.
5. There seems to be an increase in conservative views on campus,
   and more reflective and intellectual conservatism has appeared in
   many campus publications.

In the body of the paper, the author relies primarily on raw data to make
his case. Methodically he shows readers how the expression of conservative views on college campuses has continued to grow in recent years,
supported by leading conservatives around the country. By the fifth para-

graph in this sequence, which summarizes the previous paragraphs, we note a transition into a concluding section. The author has supported his assertion with appropriate and convincing evidence; all that remains is for him to conclude.

3. THE CONCLUSION: MAKING YOUR MARK

The conclusion of a research paper can serve a number of functions—for example, it can summarize, reinforce the central idea, or point out the need for further research—but it must leave readers feeling satisfied that the paper has ended, not leave them hunting around for a possible lost last page. In our example, the writer uses the last two paragraphs to emphasize the point made in his introduction about the role the conservative press can play in reintroducing political debate on college campuses:

> Of course there is the question of whether using the student press as a political weapon is appropriate in the context of American educational and political values. But the new conservative student press, regardless of the source of its funding, represents an opportunity, not a danger, to broad political education in the United States. While the initial flow of dollars may have weighted the marketplace of ideas in favor of the right, the left certainly has the resources for an adequate response which could only benefit the intellectual and political climate on college campuses. Even without such a response, however, the new voices promise to stir the mainstream student media, often liberal or left-leaning, into a new political awareness. Certainly the appearance of the Red and Blue at the University of Pennsylvania prompted a response by the Daily Pennsylvanian. Unfortunately, that response seemed to be an attempt to discredit the paper even before it appeared.

> If leftist student journals do not appear,
> the debates that could stimulate students to
> think about politics--the values and policies
> that will shape America's future--can easily take
> place on a college daily's "op-ed" page. All that
> is required is for student media managers to be
> aware of this potential, seize upon opportuni-
> ties, and actively aid the development of intel-
> lectual communication of political opinions about
> significant national issues.

Readers recognize an ending here because what the writer proposed to do in the first paragraph reaches its conclusion. The evidence which has filled the body of the chapter leads logically to the conclusions the writer draws. The writer had proposed to prove to readers that campus conservatism has flourished during the 1980s, finding expression in numerous publications, and that this movement could lead to a resurgence of political debate on college campuses. He has fulfilled the contract he made with his readers in the introduction and in the process made his mark on the reader's understanding of the subject.

The conventions of the research paper are designed to show whether you have actually performed the tasks that are required of you, and to make it simpler for readers to understand, evaluate, and learn from the paper. Because readers read research papers primarily to acquire new information or to discover a new perspective on old information, they have little patience with unconventional presentation. Breaking the rules can make a subject more interesting and might even make a paper more informative, but it makes it difficult for you to establish credibility and for the reader to evaluate your reliability. If you don't demonstrate that you used conventional methods by writing a conventional paper, how can readers be certain that they can trust your conclusions? This uncertainty leads many readers of social science research to prefer conventional presentation.

ALTERNATIVE FORMS FOR RESEARCH PAPERS

On the other hand, if you think your audience would appreciate something out of the ordinary, you might like to try something unconventional, at least once in a while. Omitting an introduction or failing to support your points with evidence, however, does not fall into the category of acceptable unconventional writing. No matter what form your presentation takes, you have to convince your readers that you have met the standards of your field. A weak argument is not convincing. A new type of argument might be.

As an alternative to a conventional research paper in a political science course on American constitutional law, one student chose to write a paper as if it were a decision of the United States Supreme Court:

> In this case we are asked to decide whether the ruling of the New Jersey Supreme Court, which permits a nonstudent to distribute literature on the campus of a private university, violates the university's property rights under the Fifth and Fourteenth Amendments and the university's free speech rights under the First Amendment.

The writer of this paper worked with a law student, who helped her capture the voice of a Supreme Court justice, and met regularly with her instructor to ensure his approval of the project. This paper not only meets, but exceeds, the requirements for most conventional research papers. The writer demonstrates the scope of the information she has acquired and puts that information to use.

A student in a history of education course came up with an equally acceptable alternative to the conventional research paper. She wanted to write about the educational philosopher John Dewey and his relationship to mainstream thinking about education in his day. She received permission from her instructor to write a transcript of an interview John Dewey might have had for a position as school superintendent in a midwestern town. She had different members of the school board represent different attitudes toward education at the time and showed, through the questioning and answering in the interview, how Dewey's ideas conflicted with those of many of his contemporaries. She also managed to elucidate the other schools of thought by presenting their responses to Dewey.

In a nursing course on maternal and child welfare, a student decided to present her argument for women using midwives instead of obstetricians in the form of questions and answers, rather than write a conventional research paper. Addressing a hypothetical woman trying to decide which type of care she would prefer, the writer generates and then answers typical questions women have about nurse-midwifery:

```
Question: If I wanted a clinical nurse-midwife to
supervise my pregnancy and assist with the birth
of my baby, what would my options be in terms of
birth setting?
Answer: Clinical nurse-midwives manage births pri-
marily in hospitals, but some offer home births
if certain safety criteria are met, and some CNMs
manage deliveries in birthing settings. In gen-
eral, a particular CNM will offer only one to two
of these options. If you are interested in an
"alternative" birth setting, it would be impor-
tant to find a CNM who typically attends births
in that setting.
```

By framing her discussion in this way, the writer made her paper more interesting for a lay audience. At the same time, the writer was able to demonstrate her command of the subject for a more informed reader, such as her instructor. An audience of experts might find the paper too simplistic to satisfy their interests, but for less informed readers, the paper provides a great deal of information.

The personal essay offers a riskier and more difficult alternative approach to presenting research but one which can prove highly workable. This form lends itself particularly to research projects in which the writer has participated, and it can convey the nuances of experience much more effectively than the conventional research paper. A student who worked in a soup kitchen recorded his experiences in an informal personal essay:

```
I was working behind the counter washing
dishes during the midday coffee and doughnut
drop-in hours at a soup kitchen in what's some-
times called a hardscrabble part of the city. I
remember that bright noontime--it crystallized
```

and will always be there, one of those pictures
we carry around with us. The girl on my right has
since become a good friend. The guy on my left
was killed in an abandoned-house fire a couple of
weeks afterward. We worked, three young people of
widely divergent backgrounds and outlooks. None
of us was bound to the work and so it was light
for us; as a result we talked freely and lightly.
Well, when you can accept ugliness and go beyond
it and find some time of happiness or beauty—
that's a rare thing, a good thing.

This essay has literary qualities which are not mandatory when your
purpose is not to entertain but to convey information. Such qualities,
however, add to the reader's enjoyment of the essay and increase the
likelihood that readers will receive the message about urban decay the
writer is trying to communicate. Later in the essay, he presents some of his
findings about the sociology of the city to a group interested in the problems of runaways, abused children, and children who hustle on the streets:

We told stories, pointed out prominent land-
marks. Sometimes we told jokes. Finally the three
of us Philadelphians explained what we thought
should be done. Philly, we explained, isn't like
Manhattan. Philly is neighborhoods. It's not a
lot of downtown. You don't get a whole lot of
outside kids—maybe they're hidden and you don't
see them—anyway not like New York. If you're going to do something in Philly, it's not going to
work to build a big hotel way downtown because
they already have stuff like that and it doesn't
seem to be in danger of being overrun. Quite the
contrary. If you're going to fight problems
you're going to fight them at the neighborhood

```
level. And maybe a lot of people don't want to be
helped. That's where your real struggle's going
to be. Neighborhood centers, not one big place--
that's what you want.
```

Do conclusions such as these hold up under the scrutiny of sociologists? Certainly not when they expect more conventional methods and more conventional presentation. This essay does not have the credibility more objectively obtained data would have for the professional. Yet when done well, such subjective presentations can often influence nonprofessional audiences more effectively than the objectivity of a more conventional research paper.

Each of these examples suggests a somewhat different way of thinking about presenting research, a way that is rooted in the subject under study. You couldn't, for example, present what you learned working in a soup kitchen in the form of a Supreme Court decision without altering the experience or adding to it considerably. The form of presentation, in order to accomplish its purpose, must suit the subject.

At the same time, audience remains a primary concern. When making a decision to try something unconventional, you have to consider whether you can elicit a positive response from your readers, whether your readers are your professors, your peers, or fellow social science researchers. After all, they are probably expecting something standard, and they're going to need some help from you in order to be able to appreciate the merits of your work. Because of these obstacles to effective communication, it's best to attempt an unconventional presentation only if you follow a few basic guidelines:

1. Don't risk more than you can afford to lose. If a grade or publication depends on the approval of specific readers, clear your ideas with them first. Don't surprise them with a creative, new approach.
2. Make sure you can do what you want to do well. If you want to be the exception, make your work exceptional.
3. Know your audience's needs. Don't offer a short story to your employer in lieu of a monthly financial statement.
4. Keep your goal in mind. Unconventional presentation should not be an end in itself, but a means to an end.
5. Remember the reasons conventions exist. Establish some common ground with your readers to hold their attention and convince them that your point of view is well founded. Help them understand what you're doing and why.

The Conventions of Literary Criticism

Although the process of analyzing a literary text follows a set of rules, there are few formal conventions that govern its presentation, and the conventions that exist are more flexible than those that characterize lab reports or social science research papers. Humanists, unlike scientists, have no need to duplicate another investigator's analysis. If the interpretation provides insight into a text, they value the interpretation. In literary criticism, method matters less than the interpretation. Critics of literature, especially, concentrate primarily on presenting a text in a way that elucidates the text for readers. There is no single correct method which all writers must follow and, consequently, no single correct form for literary criticism. Good writers invent both the interpretation and the form.

Writers take various approaches to literary criticism, some incompatible with others. For example, some critics refuse to consider anything except the text itself, while others insist that literature can't be understood without understanding the author, the intellectual climate, and the historical period. Some writers approach a text as a representative of a genre—as a novel, for example—and compare it to other examples of that genre. Other critics might look at the same text in relation to other works of literature written during the same period.

The approach writers take in literary criticism determines the type of questions they can legitimately ask and influences the form of their writing. For example, if you were to approach Ralph Waldo Emerson from a historical perspective, you might ask how his writings incorporate transcendentalism, which was popular during his lifetime. To write an essay on this subject, you might begin by explaining transcendentalism and then show how it influenced Emerson by using examples from his work. You could construct your essay differently, but this form seems appropriate and makes sense.

Literary criticism does not have the ready-made forms that are available for lab reports or even social science research papers, but there are conventions that must be followed. When formally interpreting a literary work, for example, you must root all interpretations in the text you are discussing. An effective example of literary criticism will make frequent reference to the text, including direct quotations wherever appropriate. Fidelity to the text is a prerequisite for credibility. Only by showing that your interpretation has a solid base in the text can you convince readers of the validity of your interpretation. Your thoughts and feelings about what a text means have little relevance unless you can demonstrate how you derived those thoughts and feelings from the words on the page.

When you analyze nonliterary texts—for example, in sociology or political science—you try to understand correctly what they mean and why they're important. When you analyze a literary text, however, there is rarely one correct interpretation. In the way you analyze the text, you try to help your readers achieve insight they did not have on their own. Your interpretation succeeds not if you follow the correct procedures, but if readers accept it. You must present your interpretation in a way that allows readers to follow the development of your thinking, supported by evidence from the text and, sometimes, from other sources. The evidence readers rely on most is the evidence of experience. You have to help them experience the text the way you have so that they will draw the same conclusions.

AN EXAMPLE OF LITERARY CRITICISM

In an essay entitled "Henry James and Lambert Strether: Two Lives in the World of Imagination," a student writer uses two texts to develop a thesis about author Henry James's attitude toward imagination and its opposition to the world of action. The student uses James himself as a character in his autobiography and compares him to the character Lambert Strether in James's novel *The Ambassadors*. By examining in detail a carefully selected set of events and observations from the texts, he shows readers already familiar with James how this evidence leads him to draw specific conclusions.

Because the paper is a long one (twenty pages), the writer divides his work into the following six parts:

    Introduction
I.   Fate, Failure, and Passivity
II. Envy and Isolation
III. The World of Imagination
IV. A Pair of Confrontations
    Conclusion

This structure conforms, at least on the surface, to the tripartite structure typical of research papers and academic papers in general. However, the four sections which represent the body of the text reflect how the writer has chosen to present his interpretation rather than a conventional

method of organization. He may have chosen a structure that reveals the
methods he used to gather information to support his thesis, or he may
have simply designed the structure to make the most persuasive argument
he could. In order for the interpretation to prove convincing, however,
the reader must, by the end of the paper, perceive and accept the writer's
rationale for the way he has structured his essay.

In its way, this essay is as highly technical as a report in engineering or
science, although not because the writer has to follow a rigid format.
Readers unfamiliar with literary criticism and with Henry James lack the
context necessary for understanding the writer's idea. A critic obviously
cannot interpret a text for readers who have not read the text or who have
no interest in this type of technical analysis. For the right audience,
however, the paper has significance. The writer knows this and doesn't
waste any time. He doesn't explain the texts or summarize them, nor does
he explain his method. He starts by presenting the view of James he will
attempt to prove in the body of his paper:

> In many of Henry James's tales and novels,
> characters confront the advantages and the conse-
> quences of two wholly distinct modes of living,
> two alternatives which James discusses in <u>A Small</u>
> <u>Boy and Others</u>:
>
>> There was the difference and the opposi-
>> tion, as I really believe I was already
>> aware——that one way of taking life was to go
>> in for everything and everyone, which kept
>> you abundantly occupied, and the other way
>> was to be occupied, quite as occupied, just
>> with the sense and image of it all, and on
>> only a fifth of the actual immersion: a cir-
>> cumstance extremely strange.
>
> Strange, indeed, for the two options——pursuing
> life either in the world of action or in the
> world of imagination——remain entirely incompati-
> ble. The dualism is absolute; the choices are mu-

tually exclusive. In the realm of fiction, James
creates Lambert Strether as an agent of the world
of imagination. In the realm of real life, James
presents himself as a young boy, who also tra-
verses the country of the imagination. What factors have led these two characters to make such a
choice? Is choice actually involved? How do their
imaginative minds operate? What similarities do
the characters share? Such questions will be addressed below, followed by a comparison of a pair
of confrontations, each involving a moment of
revelation for the characters.

By including in the first paragraph the quotation from James, the
writer validates his claim that this topic stems from James's concern and
not the writer's own, and, consequently, deserves the reader's attention.
Experienced readers of literary criticism will dismiss topics that seem trivial
or questions that seem mere products of the writer's imagination. In order
to ensure the reader's cooperation, the writer must prove that the discussion addresses issues readers recognize as important according to the accepted standard in literary criticism. At the same time, the writer invites
the reader to consider relevant questions, which help focus the reader on
the method of inquiry the writer plans to pursue.

Like the writer of the social science paper, this writer begins by assert-
ing a position—that James represents the worlds of imagination and action
as totally distinct—which he then prepares to explore. He has already
validated his assertion by quoting James on the subject. What remains,
then, is for him to prove that this point has significance in relation to
James's art. If he can demonstrate that his point sheds light on James's
work and helps readers gain insight into the meaning of his texts, the
paper will succeed. He must, consequently, organize his paper in a way
that convinces his readers that viewing the novelist from this perspective
adds something to their reading of James.

Each section of this essay helps to accomplish this purpose, although
the purpose only becomes clear as we read. In "Fate, Failure, and Passivity," the writer shows how living in the imagination creates passivity and
feelings of failure in both Strether and James:

For Strether, the cultivation of imagination
results not from a conscious choice, but rather
from the unintelligible twists and turns of fate.
Strether's statements carry a certain amount of
self-pity as he attempts to relate his unfortu-
nate position to others. In his world, where action and accomplishment exist as polar opposites
to imagination, Strether believes his life to be
completely bereft of success; his admissions of
failure echo throughout The Ambassadors.

When Strether meets Maria Gostrey in Ches-
ter, after only two days he cannot help but inform her of his situation, his life's shortcom-
ings. Speaking about his traveling companion
Waymarsh, Strether remarks, "He's a success of a
kind that I haven't approached . . . he makes
[money]--to my belief. And I . . . though with a
back as bent, have never made anything. I'm a
perfectly equipped failure" (40). Later, Maria
Gostrey learns of Mrs. Newsome and then of the
Woolett Review, which Strether edits. Belittling
his position, Strether tells her: "It's exactly
the thing that I'm reduced to doing for myself.
It seems to rescue a little, you see, from the
wreck of hopes and ambitions, the refuse-heap of
disappointments and failures, my one presentable
little scrap of identity" (52).

Despite his elaborate imaginative escapes,
Strether can never completely subjugate "the fact
that he had failed, as he considered, in everything, in each relation and in half a dozen
trades. . . ." (62). As the lemon-colored vol-

umes, symbolic of the unfulfilled dreams of
youth, play in his memory, Strether experiences
the depth of his life's meagerness, "a meagerness
that sprawled, in this retrospect, vague and comprehensive, stretching back like some unmapped
Hinterland from a rough-coast settlement" (64).

In the next paragraph, the writer turns to James:

The life of the young Henry James is not
without its episodes of failure either, and the
role of fate looms even larger than for Strether
in The Ambassadors. The predilection toward a
life of imagination extends to include more than
just James, enveloping two entire generations of
the family; his fatalistic language returns as he
comments:

. . . we appear to have held our agreement
as loyally and to have accepted our doom as
serenely as if our faith had been pledged.
The rupture with my grandfather's tradition
and attitude was complete; we were never in
a single case, I think, for two generations,
guilty of a stroke of business (109).

In a series of assertions, immediately substantiated with evidence from the
text, the writer convinces readers that both Strether and James feel like
failures, and that they feel cut off from the world of action by circumstances beyond their control. With this much established, the writer
moves on to his next point in the next section.

In "Envy and Isolation," the writer shows how the characters similarly
feel isolated from the world around them:

What one lacks—and lacks the spirit to
pursue—becomes an object of attention if present

in others. Disqualified from activity in the outside world, with success unattainable, Strether
and James fixate on qualities of accomplishment
and success in the people they encounter. The
first of these figures for Strether is Gloriani.
At a lavish garden party, the talented sculptor
is introduced to Strether, who reflects upon the
"genius in his eyes, his manners on his lips, his
long career behind him and his honours and rewards all round" (125). Envious of Gloriani's success as both an artist and man capable of function-
ing in society, Strether again feels victimized
by fate and adds: "The deep human expertness in
Gloriani's charming smile--oh the terrible life
behind it!--was flashed upon him as a test of his
stuff" (126). . . .

After presenting in a similar fashion a number of figures James envied, the writer points out that both characters lived in solitude, aware of their difference from other people and isolated in the world of the mind.

The train of thought continues in "The World of Imagination":

Thus foiled by fate and unable to operate in
the world of action, hounded by memories of failure and inadequacy, the characters revel in the
world left to them, the world of imagination.

Over several pages, the writer gives examples of the delights of imagina-
tion the two characters enjoy. Yet the imagination continues to exist in opposition to a more concrete physical world, and in spite of the richness of imaginative experience, the characters continue to feel isolated and estranged from the life around them. "Indeed," the writer concludes in this section, "where life is small, imagination grows large."

In the final section, "A Pair of Confrontations," the writer presents each character in a moment of crisis when the imagination and reality confront each other. Although James fares better than Strether, neither character succeeds in harmonizing the worlds of imagination and action. This leads the writer to conclude:

From the examples presented, the similarities between the characters of Henry James and Lambert Strether extend over a wide range. Their dependency on the powers of the imagination lies at the center of all these similarities, serving as the impetus for the feelings of isolation, failure, and fated existence that ultimately result. The ability to create the artistic and the sublime from the mundane and marginal displays its dark side in both works. Differences exist mainly in the presentation of these qualities. The sense of the free play of imagination comes through stronger in A Small Boy and Others, whereas The Ambassadors juxtaposes such play with its consequences, many of which are severe. The consequences might have weighed heavily in the mind of James as he wrote his autobiography, but only a diluted amount of that anxiety reaches the text. What A Small Boy and Others seems more concerned with than the costs of living in the world of imagination are the historical, almost genetic, factors that have placed James in his isolated position. The question that then arises is "Does the dualism between the two worlds exist at all?"--a question that most would confidently answer in the negative. But to better understand the intricate mental operations of characters like Strether and James himself, a positive response is required.

In this last paragraph there are no surprises. The writer reiterates the points he has emphasized throughout his paper: James and Strether are alike in relying on the imagination to create meaning in their lives, and the imaginative life leaves both of them isolated, feeling helpless and like failures. Because readers of *A Small Boy and Others* might draw different conclusions, the writer qualifies his claims. He still asserts, however, that for the purposes of understanding the characters, it is imperative to treat the worlds of imagination and action as totally separate.

Although these conclusions reaffirm the assertions made in the introduction, they have more concrete significance in the conclusion. When initially offered, the writer's claims are more suggestive than informative. Readers may have some idea what the writer means by living in the world of action or the world of imagination, but that idea gathers substance in the body of the paper as examples are given and interpretations made. By the end, readers understand the terms at a level they could not initially. As a result, the writer's claim has greater significance. The writer's effect on the reader is cumulative. Only after he has approached his subject from the various perspectives presented in the middle sections does the whole design emerge.

WRITING LITERARY CRITICISM

If you were writing a lab report, you would follow the guidelines for lab reports, possibly making a few modifications in the format if your experiment did not fit the usual standard. You would concentrate on providing appropriate information in each section of the report, presenting your information clearly, and maintaining your objectivity. If you were writing a research paper in social science, you would follow the method required in your field, making sure that your presentation of your research showed that you used correct methodology. After raising your research question or stating your thesis and establishing its significance, you would present appropriate evidence, ordered logically, in the sequence you thought would most effectively make your case.

If you were writing literary criticism, you could use the tripartite form of the research paper as a base. Demonstrating the method of interpretation you have used, however, would make your paper quite different from one in social science. The points you might set out to prove in a work of literary criticism are not as concrete as research questions in social science. Proving that campus media can play a major role in encouraging student political activity seems objectively more verifiable than proving that

Henry James represents the worlds of imagination and action as completely separate. Yet both the writers on both of these topics offered convincing evidence to support their claims.

Although both papers followed a similar form and tried to accomplish similar tasks, the nature of the evidence in each case differed markedly, as did the reasons readers might find the evidence convincing. Sociologists would hardly look on quotations from a novel as a reason for altering their beliefs, nor would literature professors accept statistics as a reason for changing their interpretation of a poem. What do these differences signify?

Scientists rely on empirical evidence to influence their audiences. Such evidence appeals to their readers' sense of truth, which must be satisfied in order for readers to accept a researcher's findings. Social scientists use data to support their claims, data that consists of information gathered from readings, textual analysis, or field research. Like scientists, they appeal to truth as a standard against which they measure their findings, but their truth admits a human element, which scientists take pains to exclude. Readers of social science are more susceptible to logic, reason, and common sense than are readers of science, who expect strict objectivity.

Writers of literary criticism have no comparably objective truth on which they can rely to substantiate their claims. They must create their own truth. Because interpretations of literature depend less on reason and logic and more on emotions, perceptions, feelings, and values, they must rely less on a predetermined and predictable structure and more on creating an experience for readers that will lead them to draw the desired conclusions. If you can make readers think, feel, or believe the way you do, you succeed as a writer, whatever methods you employ and whatever form you use.

Logic and reason should be used as effectively in literary criticism as they are in science and social science writing, but often logic does not prevail until the end of the essay. Although literary criticism should be as carefully reasoned as any other type of argument, readers will accept a variety of styles of reasoning as legitimate. Literary criticism often does not proceed from assertion to evidence to conclusion. The writer may choose to give several assertions equal weight in an essay and, rather than state them at the outset, reveal them only as they become relevant. Not infrequently, whatever assertions the writer is making become clear only at the end of an essay, when all the evidence has been presented. Works of literary criticism commonly have an introduction, body, and conclusion, but the introduction may provide background, place the subject in a larger context, or set the scene for the discussion that will follow without ever stating a thesis. At the other end, the conclusion, rather than summarizing the argument, may finally reveal the thesis. Many writers present the text and then apply critical frameworks which allow them to make interpretations. This method often results in writing that leads readers through the same process. As a result, readers don't understand the writer's point until they have read the essay through to the end.

This process also occurs at the level of language. Scientists use discipline-specific words (such as *metabolic rate, embryo,* and *species*) confidently because they assume that those words have essentially the same meaning for all scientists (at least scientists in the same field). Literary critics, however, do not share a common definition of imagination. Part of the purpose of an essay like the one we just read is to define imagination and action in terms that support the writer's position. These definitions are not simply stated, however. They emerge in the essay as the writer demonstrates what he means by using quotations from the text and by analyzing the text in a way that proves his point. Not until the end of the essay do the definitions become clear. If the writer does not succeed, the definitions may never become clear.

As a writer of literary criticism, you obviously have considerable leeway, but you still have to conform to the standard in your discipline. How do you know when you are meeting that standard? This determination is not easy to make. Although reading models can help, in this case the variety that characterizes accepted models can be confusing. The format used by another writer to discuss images of death in the modern novel could prove totally inappropriate for your paper on metaphor in Renaissance poetry. Even two writers writing about the same subject might approach it completely differently and produce two papers that have different forms, cite different evidence, and represent different methods.

To ensure that you meet the common standard for literary criticism, you would do well to follow the example of our student writer and use the form of the research paper as a model. In this case, you begin by raising a question (What is Henry James's attitude toward imagination and how does imagination relate to action?). You then propose an answer (Henry James sees the worlds of imagination and action as totally separate) and provide evidence to convince your readers that your answer is acceptable because it contributes to understanding the work of the author. The body of the paper can have as many parts as you like in whatever order makes sense as long as your readers can follow what you're doing. The way you present your evidence should help your readers understand and accept your point of view as valid.

Another appropriate way to proceed is to try to re-create for your readers the experience that led you to the insight you achieved. This method is harder to do well but is often followed by literary critics. Using this approach, your essay will take shape around the stages your thinking went through on the way to making your interpretation. Obviously the form of this type of essay is idiosyncratic, depending on the thought processes of the individual writer. Yet this method can prove highly effective at inducing readers to see what you see and believe what you believe when your responses to literature have little to do with logic or sound reasoning. Always keep in mind, however, the difficulty of persuading readers to see through your eyes. Particularly when those readers are professors or professional critics with views of their own, influencing them can pose quite a challenge. Relying on your personal way of making meaning to substantiate your claims makes that challenge even more difficult. If you want to make an original contribution, however, this method is worth the risk.

Good literary criticism can follow any number of approaches and take a variety of forms. As a result, it's difficult to cite examples of standard and unconventional practice. Papers written in an informal style, like reviews of books for the popular press, can be considered literary criticism as long as the writer interprets the book and doesn't merely describe it. For example, the style of the following sentences from a student review sounds unconventionally easygoing for standard literary criticism, but the writer's point is still well-taken:

> Some critics will wish longingly for a biographer's steadying presence to provide some moral context. "To feel this need is to miss the point with Edie," and to prefer the easy indulgence of normalcy or coherence. Others will claim thematic cowardice, but there is meaning in Stein's refusal to draw conclusions.

An imitation or parody of a writer's style can be fun to write and could serve as an alternative for more formal stylistic analysis. In an assignment asking students to choose one of Grimm's fairy tales and rewrite it in the style of Edgar Allan Poe, one professor pointed out that a successful paper would depend not only on capturing Poe's narrative voice and getting the incidents of the story to sound like a Poe plot, but on imitating his word choice, sentence rhythms, paragraph structures, and punctuation. Trying to parody a writer's style can teach you a lot about style. To parody another's style well, you have to understand the style you're imitating better than you probably understand your own style.

Even in a field which accepts a broad range of forms as within the standard of conventional practice, you still can't do just anything. Be sure when you write literary criticism especially that you have reasons for writing the way you do. If your reasons aren't obvious to your readers, make them obvious. Don't assume that an informed reader will figure them out or stick with you until the end if there's no payoff before then. Explain how you're going to look at a text at the beginning, even if the whole view doesn't crystallize until the end. You can try all kinds of approaches in many different forms as long as you use appropriate methods, but you must convince your readers that both what you have to say and how you say it will enhance their understanding. Unless you're sure you can live up to the expectations you create when you try something unconventional, choose a more conservative mode of presentation.

Defying the Conventions of Writing

All of the generalizations just made about writing in different disciplines require qualification. Even science writing can sometimes be highly speculative and appeal to the reader's imagination just as poetry does. By the same token, careful linguistic analysis of prose fiction can resemble science writing more than it resembles any genre in the humanities. Consequently, you must look at each writing task in its own context before deciding which conventions apply. You can rely on experience, custom, or tradition to guide you.

In an influential essay entitled "Tradition and the Individual Talent," T. S. Eliot discusses the relationship between literary tradition and the significance of contemporary literature. He argues that no writer has meaning alone, that readers can only value writers by comparing and contrasting their work to the work of those who preceded them. The "historical sense," a prerequisite for writers according to Eliot,

> involves a perception, not only of the pastness of the past, but of its presence; the historical sense compels a man to write not merely with his own generation in his bones, but with a feeling that the whole of

the literature of Europe from Homer and within it the whole of the literature of his own country has a simultaneous existence and composes a simultaneous order. This historical sense, which is a sense of the timeless as well as of the temporal and of the timeless and of the temporal together, is what makes a writer traditional. And it is at the same time what makes a writer most acutely conscious of his place in time, of his own contemporaneity.

Although Eliot refers exclusively to literature, his remarks are equally applicable to nonfiction. Readers of any type of writing can only determine its merits by assessing it in relation to other work that is part of the same tradition.

Conventions stand for tradition in nonfiction. Your adherence to convention allies you with the tradition of the genre in which you are writing. As Eliot points out, however, a sense of tradition should not simply breed repetition. All forms benefit from occasional modification. In some cases, changes in the external world or in the discipline necessitate changes in convention. A new field, like computer science, enters the arena and demands a new definition of and format for lab reports. A community of readers and writers decides to alter its practice, as the American Psychological Association did when it decided that researchers should refer to themselves as I, rather than in the third person. Women readers and writers point out the prevalence of language that excludes them, and the standard of common practice changes so that all references to people include both men and women. In individual cases, writers ignore or change conventions when they feel such conventions do not suit their own purposes.

We have looked at a few ways of altering conventions without unduly offending readers. Some changes, however, are bound to cause offense. Some readers will undoubtedly experience variation from convention—from the acceptance of split infinitives to the increased informality of previously formal prose—as an attack on tradition, which they like, feel part of, and want to preserve. Consequently, writers who choose defiance should be aware of the potential consequences. If you have previously proven that you appreciate the traditions of your discipline or field, you have more freedom. Newcomers to a particular type of writing, however, should exercise due caution.

On the other hand, no change would ever occur if courageous individuals weren't willing to take risks. Overzealous adherence to tradition can greatly restrict your thinking and make it more difficult to generate original ideas. Like any professional, you want to be familiar with the established customs in your field. As a serious writer, however, you also want to leave yourself free to create new conventions. The radical changes of today quickly become tomorrow's tradition.

This Chapter in Brief

In order to write well, you need to become familiar with the range of conventions that define forms in writing and that are commonly used in different disciplines. You can learn about conventions

1. by referring to appropriate style books,
2. by reading models,
3. by asking other writers.

Each time you write in a new form or in an unfamiliar field

1. study the conventions other writers use,
2. assess the role these conventions play in the discipline,
3. understand the function of conventions,
4. note how frequently writers use alternatives to conventional practice,
5. consider the consequences of varying from the norm,
6. choose which conventions you will follow.

On a larger scale, read what other writers have written to gain a sense of the tradition in your field. Then, establish yourself in relation to your tradition.

The Thinker, by Auguste Rodin

5

Writers
and
Their Ideas

Writing and Thinking

Many people underestimate the significance of the role thinking plays in writing. They reduce writing to its most mechanical elements and separate thinking, which comes first, from the process of recording thought, which defines writing. In practice, however, the relationship between thinking and writing is highly complex.

At one time people who studied the writing process believed that thinking inspired writing and that, consequently, writers needed dynamic thoughts to get their writing going. They believed that, once in motion, writing created its own momentum, so that a good idea could sustain a writer for some time. The energy of the idea freed the writer to concentrate on its articulation. Whatever mental activity the writer performed in the writing stage related to mundane issues surrounding sentence structure, word choice, and usage. The idea existed in its entirety before the writer expressed it in writing, and the goal of the writing process was simply to capture that idea in permanent form.

In actuality, the need for thinking and rethinking continues throughout the writing process. Attempting to avoid the intrusion of conscious thought can prove counterproductive. You can expend so much effort trying to avoid thinking that you lose touch with your message and the context for writing. Welcome the stimulation thinking provides, and use the energy to enhance rather than inhibit your concentration. Of course, not all thinking will assist concentration. Wondering about what to have for lunch or when to do laundry won't help, nor will protracted debates about minor details, like whether to use the word *hard* or the word *difficult*. Thoughts about strategy, direction, or style, however, or a brief discussion with yourself about when to begin a new paragraph or provide an example, will help keep you engaged and focused.

To control the writing process, you need to take an active, intellectually alert stance toward your writing from beginning to end. Never assume that you have your whole paper thought out. As you write, let what you have written influence your thinking so that the process of learning and rethinking continues until you're finished. Much of your thinking, particularly in the early stages of writing, will focus on your subject itself. Later, as you revise, your thoughts may focus more on writing about your subject or on writing itself. Whatever you're thinking about, you want to keep your mind open and active.

In the following pages we will explore the relationship between thinking and writing, particularly the way creative or original thinking can enliven the writing process and lead to a more exciting outcome. We will read examples from some writers renowned for their creative nonfiction and then review some strategies any writer can use to promote creative thinking in writing. Use the techniques suggested to assist you at any stage of the writing process when thinking or rethinking is in order. If you can't decide what to write next, visualize several possibilities. If you can't think of more examples, brainstorm. As you become familiar with the variety of techniques you can use to enhance your thinking, you will find that uses for those techniques present themselves regularly when you write.

Thinking Creatively

Readers expect creativity from fiction and poetry, but they generally have no such expectations for nonfiction. Academic writing, reports, proposals, essays, magazine and newspaper articles, and much of the writing we do every day falls into the category of "uncreative" writing. Why uncreative? Because writers tend to put the need to communicate information clearly above any interest they or their readers might have in prose that is entertaining or aesthetically pleasing. While novelists and poets invent people, places, events, and even words and forms, writers of nonfiction have to stick to the facts and the required conventions. Like an appropriately dark, well-tailored business suit, good nonfiction communicates its message and fades into the background.

All writing, however, demands that you create; not even the facts write themselves. No matter how mundane or prescribed the task, you must interpret the conventions and make choices that result in writing that conveys your unique style and voice. Even a reminder to committee members about a meeting offers you a number of decisions to make: Should you write it as a memo or a letter? Should you mention that attendance in the past has been poor, or will that just put your readers off? Should you remind them of their obligations to the program, or will that just annoy them? If you give them the agenda ahead of time, will some of them decide that nothing interests them? What tone should you take? You are the committee chairperson, but these members are your peers, not your subordinates. Do you have any right to do more than encourage them to attend?

The perception that options exist transforms a mundane communication like a memo into an opportunity for creative expression. You don't have to write what everyone else writes. You can write something that is unique to you. You can't invent the facts, but you can express them in your own unique way. For example, the following communication could have been written as a straightforward reminder of a meeting; instead, the writer thought about what he wanted to accomplish and personalized his communication:

Dear Members of the Theater Arts Program:

Those of you who were at the last meeting know that our final meeting of the year will be on Tuesday, May 2, at 8:00 P.M. in the Theater Arts office. We are extremely anxious to have everyone there so that we can make plans for next year. Even if you haven't been attending regularly, please try to come. We want everyone's help to ensure that next year's program will be a success.

I would also like to get a chance to thank you all personally for your support this year. Before I graduate, I have a few words of wisdom to impart, and like good theatergoers, I hope you will provide an audience for my brief (I promise) remarks. See you on May 2.

The obvious thinking that went into this communication not only gets the reader's attention, but it also gives voice to the unique character of the writer. Like this writer, you can express yourself along with your ideas instead of sounding like everyone else when you write.

THE RISKS INVOLVED

As suggested in Chapter 4, writers can often satisfy standards and still permit themselves considerable flexibility in relation to form, tone, and other aspects of writing. In addition, some audiences—like readers of journals of opinion—have few preconceived notions about what conventions must be observed. More often than you may suspect, you can meet your readers' expectations and be creative at the same time. You should, however, recognize the risks involved.

If you write exactly the way other people would write in the same situation, exactly the way you were taught to write, you know you're safe. You might not inspire admiration, but you're confident you'll get the information across without embarrassing yourself or offending your readers— legitimate concerns for any writer. Following the established format for a lab report or a social science research paper ensures that your readers will understand your intention, accept your efforts at face value, and evaluate them according to established standards. In college or graduate school, you know you can do well with papers that conform to those standards. Why take risks by trying to be creative?

Originality involves risk; yet the original, the unusual, and the unexpected interest readers, and writing with these qualities often influences readers more than ordinary prose. As a creative writer, you need to assess the risks each time you think about writing and determine how much creativity the subject merits and how much your audience will bear. Sometimes quite ordinary subjects take on unforeseen significance in the mind of a creative writer.

THE GOALS ACHIEVED

Creative uncreative writing abounds in all fields. Almost any writer who has chosen to relate technical subjects for nontechnical readers, for example, has had to invent new strategies. In order for readers to develop an interest in subjects about which they know nothing, they need to see how those subjects might relate to them personally. Writers trying to communicate with such readers, or with interested readers who just do not share the writer's expertise or vocabulary, need to think creatively about their writing and how they might reach readers with whom they don't have a great deal in common.

One of the most popular contemporary writers about science for nonscientists is Stephen Jay Gould, whose writings about natural history have earned him a National Book Award. The following excerpt consists of the first three paragraphs of his essay "Were Dinosaurs Dumb?"

> When Muhammad Ali flunked his army intelligence test, he quipped (with a wit that belied his performance on the exam): "I only said I was the greatest; I never said I was the smartest." In our metaphors and fairy tales, size and power are almost always balanced by a want of intelligence. Cunning is the refuge of the little guy. Think of Br'er Rabbit and Br'er Bear; David smiting Goliath with a slingshot; Jack chopping down the beanstalk. Slow wit is the tragic flaw of a giant.
>
> The discovery of dinosaurs in the nineteenth century provided, or so it appeared, a quintessential case for the negative correlation of size and smarts. With their pea brains and giant bodies, dinosaurs became a symbol of lumbering stupidity. Their extinction seemed only to confirm their flawed design.
>
> Dinosaurs were not even granted the usual solace of a giant—great physical prowess. God maintained a discreet silence about the brains of behemoth, but he certainly marveled at its strength: "Lo, now, his strength is in his loins, and his force is in the navel of his belly. He moveth his tail like a cedar. . . . His bones are as strong pieces of brass; his bones are like bars of iron" [Job 40:16–18]. Dinosaurs, on the other hand, have usually been reconstructed as slow and clumsy. In the standard illustration, *Brontosaurus* wades in a murky pond because he cannot hold up his own weight on land.

Gould's style and his ability to engage readers in thinking about subjects they might not ordinarily find interesting have distinguished him from many other scientists. Both in spite of and because of his lack of orthodoxy, many readers find him both informative and entertaining, a winning combination for a writer. By using concrete and everyday examples to illustrate his thinking, he invites any reader to explore with him a world which previously appeared mysterious and inaccessible. He does not simply explain his subject clearly for his audience, however. He explains it cleverly as well.

In an essay about fourteenth-century Europe entitled "History As Mirror," Barbara Tuchman uses an approach similar to Gould's: she seeks to make history come alive for her readers. We read not simply about corruption in the Church or the spread of the Black Death during the years 1347–1349, but about the progression of events over time and how that progression relates to our own world and our own image of ourselves in history:

> The afflictions of the fourteenth century were the classic riders of the Apocalypse—famine, plague, war, and death, this time on a black horse. These combined to produce an epidemic of violence, depopulation, bad government, oppressive taxes, an accelerated breakdown of feudal bonds, working class insurrection, monetary crisis, decline of morals and rise in crime, decay of chivalry, the governing idea of the governing class, and above all, corruption of society's central institution, the Church, whose loss of authority and prestige deprived man of his accustomed guide in a darkening world.
>
> Yet amidst the disintegration were sprouting, invisible to contemporaries, the green shoots of the Renaissance to come. In human affairs as in nature, decay is compost for new growth.
>
> Some medievalists reject the title of decline for the fourteenth century, asserting instead that it was the dawn of a new age. Since the processes obviously overlap, I am not sure the question is worth arguing, but it becomes poignantly interesting when applied to ourselves. Do *we* walk amidst trends of a new world without knowing it? How far ahead is the dividing line? Or are we on it? What designation will our age earn from historians six hundred years hence? One wishes one could make a pact with the devil like Enoch Soames, the neglected poet in Max Beerbohm's story, allowing us to return and look ourselves up in the library catalogue. In that future history book, shall we find the chapter title for the twentieth century reading Decline and Fall, or Eve of Revival?

I cite these two examples as creative uncreative writing because they defy our stereotypes for nonfiction. We think of writing about academic subjects—such as history and science—as irrelevant to everyday experience. However, the essays from which these examples are taken involve us in questions that touch our lives now. These two authors help us recognize the relevance of history to contemporary living, and any time a subject presents itself as immediately relevant, we are more likely to sit up and pay attention.

Taking a past event or a period in history and helping the reader perceive its relevance represents only one strategy for enlivening nonfiction. Maintaining a distinctly personal style represents another. In both these examples the writer clearly communicates a particular point of view. The voices of both authors sound real, and both of them seem enthusiastic about the material they are discussing and committed to their views of their material. It is difficult as a reader to avoid responding with anything less than respect and curiosity. If this subject interests the author to such an extent, might it not interest us if we tried to understand it? Sincere voices, which we don't always find in this type of nonfiction, evoke sincere interest in readers.

Creative thinking does more than arouse interest, however. It also provides insight. By putting dinosaurs and Muhammad Ali on the same platform and using the Bible to substantiate his claim that people expect big animals to be dumb, Gould makes readers perceive dinosaurs differently and may permanently alter their ideas about dinosaurs. This ability to affect the thoughts and perceptions of readers characterizes creative writing. Such unusual thinking surprises readers who would not have had such thoughts unaided.

From the reader's perspective, creative uncreative writing distinguishes itself from other writings about the same subject or in the same genre. It strikes the reader as different and often better or more interesting. From the writer's point of view, writing creatively involves rejecting the obvious and searching for new approaches, unusual contexts, distinctive styles, or analogies no one else has thought of using. The creative writer of nonfiction often has more in common with the novelist or poet than with fellow professionals in science or history, although not always. Frequently, the creative writer and the inventor, discoverer, or originator of new ideas turn out to be the same person.

Thinking Creatively about Writing

Knowing how to write creatively greatly expands your horizons as a writer. Instead of perceiving writing as a chore, you are able to view it as an opportunity and a challenge, a chance to assert your individuality, even in the most ordinary circumstances. No matter how uninteresting an assignment or writing task may appear, the possibility of responding creatively can usually redeem it.

Learning to be creative is something every writer can do. Simply allow your individuality to emerge. The conventions of writing enable you to perform in a social context and to communicate effectively with others, and on a larger scale, learning to conform to conventions plays a critical role in helping you integrate into society. Yet at certain points, you need to examine certain requirements carefully and begin to make distinctions about when you should or should not conform.

As long as you know the basic conventions of written English and can use the language correctly, there is no need to be a slave to common practice. In many instances, uncommon practice will actually influence readers more and bring about better results than meticulously imitating the norm. As a result, it is to your advantage to nurture your creativity, to cultivate the differences that define you as an individual, and to translate those differences into techniques and stylistic traits that characterize your writing and other forms of self-expression. How can you discover your creativity and learn to use it effectively? The following advice may help.

THINKING THROUGHOUT THE WRITING PROCESS

From the initial brainstorming that leads you to the selection of a topic to the final proofreading you do before a paper is released to its audience, you should think while you write. Not all thinking produces the same results, of course, but constant thinking can check any innate tendencies toward passivity, which undermines creativity. In many instances, it is easy enough to sit back and allow the familiar words and phrases to flow: "I am writing to inquire about the position of Account Executive you advertised in the *Wall Street Journal.*" Anyone could have written such a sentence, however. Writing that strikes readers as something special requires an active, inventive thinker who can produce a surprising turn of phrase: "Your advertisement for an Account Executive in the *Wall Street Journal* caught my attention."

If you don't already, you certainly should try talking to yourself while you write. Although too frequent dialogues between your reader-self and your writer-self can slow the pace of writing, regular and informative exchanges between the different perspectives you maintain mentally can help you resist the obvious and the ordinary. For example, if you find yourself at a turning point in an argument about the value of sports in college life, you might think the next step through in dialogue between your writer-self and reader-self:

> *Writer (writes):* Anyone who has ever attended a college with a winning football team can testify to the effect the team's victory has on the morale of the whole student body.

Reader (*thinks*): But that doesn't really prove the point. Lots of schools don't have football teams and still manage to maintain morale. It's losing that hurts, and if you don't have a team, you can't lose. Maybe I should restrict my argument to schools that already have strong athletic programs.

Writer (*writes*): Anyone who has ever attended a college with a strong sports program and has experienced the joys of winning and the heartbreak of losing will recall those moments as among the most exquisite of any college career.

Reader (*thinks*): That makes sports sound pretty attractive, I think. This is beginning to read like a defense of athletics in schools that emphasize athletics. Is that what I really want? Do I want to suggest that all colleges should emphasize athletics? No, not really. I guess I'll focus on why we should maintain sports programs where they exist and fight people who think college should be just for studying.

Writer (*writes*): The rewards of passing tests and even of acquiring knowledge simply cannot compete with the immediate gratification of a 24–7 rout of a detested rival on the field, and why should they? Why should Shakespeare or Freud have to compete with the intense emotional highs and lows and the joy of competition sports inject into undergraduate life? Isn't it possible that the demands of sports enrich rather than impoverish college life? Students who have played out their tensions in the stadium or the gym over the weekend are surely more likely to return to their studies on Sunday with renewed energy.

Reader (*thinks*): There, now I've reached my stride. I like the way this is shaping up, and this is definitely the argument I want to make. Now I need to get more concrete. I have to prove that people do get back to studying and that the games don't interfere. How can I do that? Should I quote students or cite experts who advocate the importance of breaks from academic routine? I think the experts are likely to be more persuasive, but I don't want this to turn into a research paper. How can I handle it so that it stays informal but sounds authoritative? Let's see. . . .

This type of lively interchange going on in the writer's mind is much more likely to lead to writing that is the unique expression of the particular writer/thinker. An argument inevitably ends up stronger and probably more original as a result of a writer's persistent self-consciousness. You don't need to torture yourself by constantly questioning your own judgment. Talking through questions with yourself, however, is much more

likely to lead to creative thinking and creative writing than blandly following the familiar cadences of someone else's, or everyone else's, style.

Although good writing demands that the writer think throughout the
writing process, certain stages notoriously require more thinking than
others. The choice of subject, when the subject is not predetermined, can
demand a great deal of mental energy, as can the choice of an angle on the
subject once it is chosen. Later on, the writer's revision strategy often
requires some thinking, especially if the writer hasn't considered the angle
in enough detail. Decisions about style, tone, and voice demand thought
as well.

CHOOSING A SUBJECT

When you are required to write about subjects that don't interest you,
you are much more likely to write uncreatively. In such circumstances, you
may be tempted to put your brain on hold and rely on what other people
have told you to do or on common models. Unconscious imitation of
models and slavish fidelity to prescriptions, however, will almost certainly
deter originality.

Even when an instructor requires you to compare Freud's view of man
with Plato's, for example, you can still choose your subject. How you define
"view of man" can greatly influence your response to this assignment. If you
choose to focus on the role of reason vs. emotion, which may be the most
obvious response to the assignment, you are certainly on firm ground. You
could also, however, decide to discuss Freud and Plato as revolutionary
thinkers or compare Plato's attitude toward form with Freud's emphasis on
experience. You could also comment on their definitions of *man* and the
relationship of *man* to woman. Nothing forces you to select the most obvious response, and certainly nothing ensures that the most obvious response
will interest you or result in the best writing. From a writer's point of view,
you will produce a better paper if you choose your subject thoughtfully rather
than allow your automatic reactions to choose for you.

DEVELOPING AN ANGLE ON YOUR SUBJECT

After you choose your subject, you need to develop an angle on it. For
example, if you choose to approach Freud and Plato as revolutionary
thinkers, you might compare their ideas and the amount of influence each
has had on others. Or, to develop another angle on this subject, you might

compare the intellectual climates that gave birth to each man as a revolutionary thinker.

As another example, suppose you have chosen to write on the influence of Keynesian economics on the British economy since World War II. First you should determine what you have to say about the subject. Simply describing the influence, as you understand it from your reading, proves that you read the books but will probably not advance the reader's understanding. Most readers prefer that writers form an opinion and assert a point of view on the subject, and the process of establishing an opinion establishes the paper as an original piece of work. Do you believe that Britain's economic ills in recent years stem from adherence to Keynesian principles? Or, in your opinion, have the British failed to institutionalize Keynes in a beneficial way? Whatever your attitude toward your subject, your ability to present the material convincingly to readers and to influence their thinking will distinguish your writing from other papers on the same subject.

When your vision is partially blocked by people sitting in front of you at the theater and, consequently, you can only clearly see a portion of the stage and the profiles of the actors, who are facing to your left, you perceive the action from a specific and limited angle. If you compare notes with someone who sat on the other side or in the balcony, you may discover marked differences in that person's experience of the drama, particularly in relation to the fine points determined by facial expressions, movement on stage, and gestures. Since no one can take in all of the activity on the stage from all perspectives, no single angle reflects a more truthful interpretation of the play than any other. Each angle conveys its own truth, and by becoming familiar with angles other than your own, you enrich your understanding of the original experience.

The unique angle on an experience or an idea that only an individual thinker can offer creates writing that sustains the interest of readers and frequently teaches them something new about the subject or themselves. In his essay "On Warts," for example, Lewis Thomas offers his unique biologically-based perspective:

> Warts are wonderful structures. They can appear overnight on any part of the skin, like mushrooms on a damp lawn, full grown and splendid in the complexity of their architecture. Viewed in stained sections under a microscope, they are the most specialized of cellular arrangements, constructed as though for a purpose. They sit there like

turreted mounds of dense, impenetrable horn, impregnable, designed
for defense against the world outside.

In a certain sense, warts are both useful and essential, but not for
us. As it turns out, the exuberant cells of a wart are the elaborate
reproductive apparatus of a virus.

Few readers would be likely to imagine warts as architectural structures
without Lewis's assistance. His approach to warts through a discussion of
their structure unifies the essay, helps him to get his message across, and
promotes the reader's understanding. By taking the time to develop an
angle on his subject, rather than just describing warts in technical terms or
in the terms that come most readily to mind, Lewis produces an effective
and creative piece of writing.

Coming up with angles can take more time and creative energy than
any other activity associated with the writing process. Especially when
deadlines loom, angles sometimes seem like gravy. That is, they make the
subject taste better, but they don't alter its essential composition. Consequently, in a pinch, if a good angle doesn't offer itself, the writing may be
presentable without it.

This attitude toward angles, however, ignores the profound changes a
good angle can work on a subject and on a text. Besides, inventing angles
challenges writers to think in new ways and converts each writing task into
a new and unpredictable opportunity. Much of the work involved in
determining an angle can be done in your head—while driving in a car,
riding the bus, walking to class, eating, or jogging, for example. You don't
need to isolate yourself to discover an angle, nor do you need your computer or even a pencil and paper. All you require is an open, uncluttered
mind and some space which it can freely explore.

Free association can often lead you to an angle on your subject if you
let your mind roam. The subject of food, for example, might lead you quite
effortlessly to think about diets, exercise, anorexia and bulimia, health,
nutrition, mothering, body makeup (we are what we eat), farming, poverty, Third World countries, and many other related ideas. A paper on the
average American diet, for example, could focus not just on the foods we
eat but on how we take care of ourselves or how our body and cell structures compare with those of malnourished people in Third World nations.
You could also write an essay about food production by restricting yourself
to one food—the apple, for example—and reviewing how apples are produced in the United States or in other countries. Following the life of one
particular apple could also prove instructive and might lead to an interest-

ing paper or article. Once you put aside the ordinary way of handling a subject, the possibilities for angles abound.

Certain subjects and certain types of writing lend themselves more readily to presentation through angles than others. Even lab reports or project write-ups, however, benefit from presentation that highlights some features, discoveries, methods of inquiry, or results over others. Although the accepted formats for lab reports sometimes deprive the writer of opportunities for innovation, an abstract can offer the writer some choice about what merits emphasizing and how the reader might view the experiment constructively. Within even rigid formats, writers have some leeway in organizing sentences and designing paragraphs. In order to make such a routine writing task more challenging for yourself, as well as more interesting for the reader, think aggressively about an angle on your experiment that will effectively communicate its significance.

Relying, for example, on chronological order to organize a report makes it easy enough to write but fails to emphasize ideas or outcomes that are more important than others. Presenting data by beginning with the most important findings and progressing to the least important or vice versa, or by showing how those findings relate to other important issues, can make a paper much more interesting to read as well as ensure that readers interpret the results the way the writer intends.

DEVELOPING A STRATEGY FOR REVISION

The processes of choosing a subject and developing an angle are the first major thinking activities associated with a writing project; developing a strategy for revision is another. Revision demands that you rethink your overall goals, including the decisions you made about subject and angle, and offers another opportunity to affect the creativity of the whole. In order to make revision a realistic opportunity for creativity, however, you have to take risks. If you limit your rethinking to changes that will require the least rewriting, you are unlikely to allow yourself to think any new thoughts. On the other hand, if you open your thinking to new possibilities, your strategy for revision can improve the creativity of a piece of writing dramatically.

The object of developing a strategy for revision is to encourage rethinking. At a time when you might otherwise go on to other things, serious thinking can help you stay engaged in the task. The prospect of making even major changes doesn't seem onerous when you have a clear picture of what you want to accomplish, especially when the picture excites and energizes you. As long as you have concrete and achievable goals to motivate you and a positive image of where your efforts will lead, the work of rewriting should seem manageable.

To come up with a strategy, compare your goals with your achievement so far and list the changes you need to make to ensure that your objectives and your achievement match. Such a strategy might require you, for example, to redefine a problem in a way that better lends itself to the problem-solving methodology you employ in the paper. Let's say that you started out writing about how gender influences success in the workplace. In the end, though, you transcribed interviews with working women into a discussion of their attitudes toward how their gender influences their success. As a result, you will need to redefine your goals before you rewrite. Then you'll need to reorganize the interviews to show how the majority of the women you interviewed feel that their gender inhibits their success. You'll also have to rethink the introduction and conclusion. If you also found something you hadn't planned on, such as a relationship between a woman's profession and the extent to which she feels gender is a factor in her success, you would probably want to restructure the paper to include that finding. All this requires active and creative thinking.

What if you find yourself with a workable draft of a paper but feel devoid of creativity? The ideas are all there, but they bore you and will probably bore your readers also. The linear thinking you followed doesn't lead anywhere, and you can't seem to loosen up the preconceptions that led you to write this way in the first place. What can you do when you feel you've reached a dead end?

You can't always depend on professors, classmates, or friends to provide the support you feel you need to take risks and to open up your thinking and your writing to new ideas. You must be prepared to trust and support yourself. If you believe that good ideas will occur to you when you need them, you are much more likely to come up with good ideas. On the other hand, if you perceive your conceptual resources as limited or unreliable, you probably won't bother to push yourself. In his book *Conceptual Blockbusting,* James Adams suggests that "an atmosphere of honesty, trust, and support is absolutely necessary if most people are to make the best of their conceptual abilities." Unfortunately, many would-be writers refuse to provide such an atmosphere for themselves. You may well worry that if you do push yourself to open up your thinking, you will find the recesses of your mind empty. This fear, although common, rarely turns out to be justified. You can think and write creatively if you're willing to work at it.

Using Creative Thinking to Enhance Your Writing

With few exceptions, great ideas do not appear full-blown in people's minds. In most cases a great deal of preparatory thinking goes into the formulation of an idea, whether the thinker realizes it or not. Many times the thinking occurs below the level of consciousness, which leads some writers to doubt their ability to control creative thinking. However, you can learn to think creatively with practice.

Overcoming Resistance to New Ideas

Not only your personal limitations, but your culture, upbringing, values, experience, environment, and education can inhibit your creativity. No matter how exhaustive your education, you are trapped, for better or worse, in ways of seeing, thinking, and imagining that you have been perfecting all your life. Unless you choose to break out, to increase your susceptibility to new ideas, and to permit new influences, you will never think or write as creatively as you might.

Resistance to new ideas, particularly ideas that contradict your experience, often takes subtle forms. You don't necessarily think of yourself as resisting when you reject the idea of writing an argument in the form of a dialogue when a friend suggests it, but it is resistance nonetheless. When you can't identify with any point of view except your own and, consequently, can't answer the concerns of readers who disagree with you, you are also resisting. No matter how much you deplore the tactics of terrorists, the more you can think like a terrorist, the more effective you can be as a writer against terrorism.

To stave off resistance, put yourself in another person's shoes. Imagine how you would feel about abortion, for example, if you grew up in a staunch Catholic family or if you found yourself pregnant with an unwanted child. Write out a few paragraphs in the other person's voice, advocating his/her position, or ask a friend to represent your side and try arguing against your own point of view. If you're successful at identifying with another position, you may well find your views softening, even on issues that have been clear in your mind all your life. You may begin to realize the merits of capital punishment, although you have always been against it, or to acknowledge the importance of public assistance for impoverished single mothers, even though you have always believed people should work for the money they receive.

When you approach a subject, try thinking like one of your favorite

authors whose strategy or style you admire. Ask yourself, for example, how
H. L. Mencken would write about the federal deficit, if that is your
assignment, or how E. B. White would describe a computer program.
Imagine Carl Sagan or C. P. Snow writing your chemistry paper. If you're
not familiar with any creative uncreative writers in a particular field, read
through a book of essays designed for college students or ask an instructor
to recommend some readings. Do not imitate textbook writing on a subject unless you want to sound like a textbook. Make yourself think about a
subject like a writer, not a teacher or student. Ask yourself how you can
turn an ordinary academic subject into the material of art.

Whenever you think about a subject, generate more rather than fewer
ideas. In addition, strive for diversity in your thinking. Once you identify a
position you want to take, try taking the opposite position. Where does
that go? What other positions might you take? How many of those are
viable? How viable is your original position from this revised perspective?
How might you change your original idea to incorporate more perspectives? None of these activities need take very long. If you allow plenty of
time for thinking, you should have no trouble resisting the temptation to
cling to the first idea that occurs to you.

Don't take anything for granted when it comes to ideas. When you
brainstorm or list, never reject an idea until you are satisfied that you have
considered the idea fully. Show all your ideas the respect they deserve,
even if they strike you as ridiculous at first. You probably had good reasons
for thinking them, and you never know when one of your ridiculous ideas
is going to lead to a new way of conveying thought in writing. Any new
idea, like the idea that the world is round or that people can fly to the
moon, seems odd or silly in the beginning, but people get used to good new
ideas very quickly.

Always examine your assumptions carefully, especially when you're
writing about controversial subjects or for audiences who don't know you
or have reason to disagree with you. When you approach a subject, think
about how you feel about it first, in detail, and then look at the sources of
your ideas. Where, for example, did you learn that stealing was bad? Did
you learn it from your parents; from your minister, priest, or rabbi; from
your teachers; from other children? Does the biblical injunction against
stealing still have force for you, or do you believe that it's acceptable to
steal in certain circumstances—to buy food for your starving family, for
example, or from large corporations like the phone company? Before you
write to enjoin students from stealing each other's problem solutions off
the computer, explore your own thinking and try to identify with the

students who obviously think that stealing work off the computer doesn't count as stealing. Your writing will almost certainly emerge richer and more effective, as well as more creative, if you open up your thinking before you unconsciously close out your options.

Promoting Creative Thinking

For those of you who are just beginning to develop your creativity, there are some tested methods for promoting creative thinking. Not all of them may appeal to you or work for you, but they do help many people to think differently, especially when they feel stuck in a particular mode of thinking. Frequently, even in the rush of inspiration, your ideas benefit from a strategy that promotes creative thinking.

BRAINSTORMING

Many people in professional life—including engineers, business people, artists, and writers—use brainstorming as a way of opening up their thinking. The object of brainstorming is to come up with as many ideas as possible in a limited amount of time. Best performed in a group, brainstorming involves taking a problem and generating as many solutions as the group can think of in five or ten minutes. Since the most outrageous ideas can often lead to the most original and effective solutions, the more impractical and unlikely the solutions proposed, the more successful the brainstorming. Participants are encouraged to build on each other's ideas and prohibited from making negative comments, which might lead to self-censorship. A playful, supportive, and enthusiastic group will inevitably produce the best results.

Since writing involves a great deal of creative problem solving, brainstorming often works well as a technique for generating alternative approaches to problems. Even if you're working alone, brainstorming can help you expand your thinking, especially if you try to imagine how other people might respond to your problem. Although probably most useful when you're choosing subjects and identifying angles, brainstorming can also help you decide how to organize (or reorganize) a piece of writing, what voice to use, how to write a convincing argument. For example, if you are writing a paper condemning the present system of medical training, whose point of view should you use? A brainstorming session might produce the following alternatives:

the doctor
the nurse
the patient
the intern
the intern's husband/wife/child
the intern's dog
the hospital
the intern's mother
the doctor's mother
a respirator
the emergency room
the emergency room receptionist
a corpse (someone murdered by an overtired medical student in the
    emergency room)
a hospital administrator
an officer in the American Medical Association
an old-fashioned general practitioner
a current medical student
someone who dropped out of medicine

The list could go on and on. Not all of these ideas might strike your fancy
or seem possible or in line with your goals, but the list certainly makes you
aware of alternatives. Although generating quantity is not an end in itself,
you are much more likely to find unusual options on a long list than on a
short one. If you don't censor your thinking prematurely, you will discover
at least one or two approaches that seem impossible at first, or even
ridiculous, but look more promising after some consideration. These seemingly unlikely alternatives often lead to writing that is more creative than
you thought yourself capable of producing.

IMPROVISING

Whenever you're not sure how to handle a subject in writing or what
to write next, it helps to improvise. There are no rules for improvisation;
you simply pretend that whatever comes to mind is what you were supposed to be thinking or writing about before you got stuck. Just take the
first idea that occurs to you and pursue it until another idea takes hold or
leads you in a new direction. Especially when you can't remember what
you had in mind, improvisation will often bring your original thoughts or
better ones to the surface. Whether you've forgotten something or never

had a clear idea to begin with, you can often improve on the quality of your thinking by improvising.

In order to improvise successfully, you need a specific context. Otherwise, your imagination may carry you away. For example, you might be halfway through a draft of a paper on how World War II affected world trade when you lose track of your argument. A look at your plan convinces you that you wanted to discuss American-Japanese relations next, but you can't remember how you were going to get there. Instead of struggling to reconstruct your thinking, you could just as well improvise. So you keep writing about what comes to mind, and what comes to mind in this case is how our conception of "made in Japan" has changed over the last twenty or thirty years. You start describing the Japanese trinkets you had as a child (they always broke the minute you breathed on them) and compare those items to the Toyota and the Sony television you now own. After a while you may or may not remember where you originally intended this argument to go. Focusing on Japan's exports, as perceived through your own experience with Japanese products, seems just as valuable an idea as the one you had originally, if not a better one.

VISUALIZING

Some people are natural visual thinkers and prefer to represent their ideas graphically rather than in words. Even if you don't ordinarily think visually, you can learn to do so with practice. Especially when you're having trouble verbalizing your thinking, try visualizing it instead. Drawing an image of a piece of writing can give you a sense of the form of your work that's very difficult to acquire with words. Ask yourself what image best represents what you are trying to accomplish in writing. Does your argument proceed in a circular fashion, ending where it began, or does the image of a spring seem more appropriate? Do you begin with a single idea and then branch out in several different directions, all of which lead eventually to a single conclusion (see Figure 5-1)? Or do you start with several assertions and then show how they all exist parallel to each other without ever intersecting or influencing one another (see Figure 5-2)?

Securing a visual image of your strategy for writing can greatly help clarify your thinking as well as your sense of direction. You may well find that discovering an image of what you're writing opens up new possibilities that wouldn't occur to you except visually. For example, imagine yourself writing a paper comparing a novel by Zora Neale Hurston (a contemporary

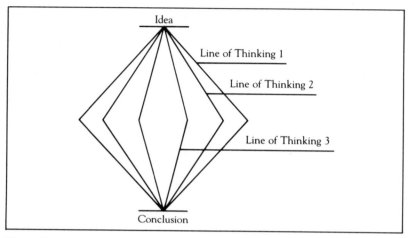

Figure 5-1

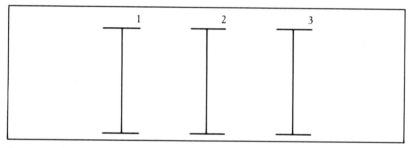

Figure 5-2

black writer) and one by Bobbie Ann Mason (a contemporary southern white writer). Your central idea is that the unique experiences of these two novelists have led them to interpret the conventions of the novel in distinctive ways. Yet both could serve as exemplars of the modern American novelist. How are you going to structure your thinking?

You could begin by looking independently at each writer and then bringing the two together at the end by showing how each novel is typically American. Such an approach might look like the diagram shown in Figure 5-3. The visual representation of your thinking highlights some problems. How are you going to begin the paper? You need some common

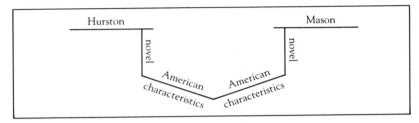

Figure 5-3

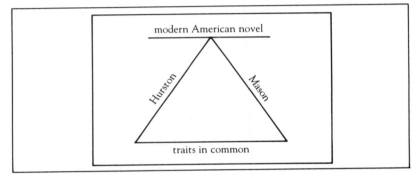

Figure 5-4

ground to create a smooth opening. You're also not sure how to bring the two writers together. Perhaps it would be better if you began with a discussion of the modern American novel, branched off to show how each writer represents that tradition, and then ended with what they have in common (see Figure 5-4).

However, is the modern American novel really one form? Can you adequately represent it as a dot? Perhaps it would be more appropriate to approach the novel as a continuum and show where Hurston and Mason fit (see Figure 5-5). From this perspective both writers originate from and contribute to the same tradition, but they come from and go to different locations. You also have a more distinct form that may be easier to represent in writing than your original idea. By visualizing, you may discover just how your thinking can take shape in writing. You may also find alternative ways of structuring your ideas so that the whole paper fits together better and creates the sense of a definite form.

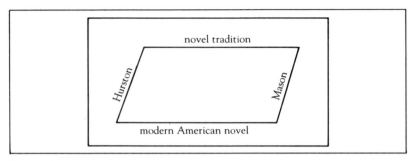

Figure 5-5

INQUIRING AND EXPLORING

Visualization represents one mode of exploring writing, but there are verbal modes that can also help you achieve new perspective. These methods work because they are systematic and force you to think about your subject in ways you would not normally do. In most cases you begin by describing your subject from several angles. For example, you might try looking at your subject as if it were (1) a physical object, (2) part of a system of relationships, and (3) an abstract idea. If you were writing about the Constitution, you might look at it as a piece of paper with writing on it, as the foundation of our government, and as a symbol of democracy.

In the same way, you can describe an object, like a computer, as a plastic box with a television screen, as a device that accepts information and solves problems, and as a means of interacting with people at great distances. You can explore a concept like technology by dividing it into parts (such as computers, calculators, and VCRs), by looking at how the growth of technology has affected people, or by considering the relationship between technology and the acquisition of knowledge in the last decade. It doesn't matter what ideas occur to you. There are no right or wrong answers in exploration. Use the process as a means of evoking images that would not have occurred to you if you had not systematically explored your initial idea.

In each instance just described, we end up with an image or idea that is larger and more complex than the one with which we began. In the case of computers, we start with a clearly defined image of a physical object and progress to an idea that incorporates the computer's vast capabilities and uses. The same type of progression occurs in relation to our perspective on technology. You may not feel that you need such a formal procedure in order to enlarge your thinking, especially when the subject lends itself to expansive thought. In many instances, however, especially if your imagination fails you, a formal structure can prove very useful.

These examples represent only one method out of many for generating perspectives. Depending on your training, your experience, your inclinations, and the type of writing you do, you could come up with other, equally valid ways of helping yourself think more expansively about anything. You could imagine people from different backgrounds or with very different relationships to your subject and look at the subject from their points of view. In the case of the Constitution, you might use the views of a political refugee, a convicted murderer, and a Supreme Court justice to help you think about the subject. To improve your reader awareness, you could explore a subject by explaining its chief characteristics to yourself, to an expert in the field, and to a disinterested bystander before settling on an approach to use for prospective readers.

Let's assume, for example, that you're writing a psychology paper on individual learning styles. Because you have read a great deal about the subject and studied it intensively, you can satisfy yourself by writing, "Although learning styles can be grouped in categories, each child learns a little bit differently from any other." Looking at it from the point of view of an expert, however, you realize how inadequate that statement appears. How do you define learning styles? Can you prove that every child learns differently? A teacher unfamiliar with the field might accept the validity of your assertion based on experience, but would a psychologist? What kind of learning do you have in mind? From the point of view of a bystander, so what? Aren't you just restating the obvious? What's the significance of the fact that learning styles can be grouped into categories? Are you suggesting that every child has to be taught differently in order to learn? By the time you've finished exploring your subject, you should be aware of more perspectives on it than you imagined existed. As a result, the method you choose should be the best one you can imagine to accomplish your purpose for your audience in an interesting way.

COLLABORATING

Although some writers prefer thinking by themselves, you can often accomplish a lot more thinking in a short time by using others to help you shape your thinking. An exchange of ideas with someone whose views you respect often helps you think more effectively than you could without the challenge of another point of view prompting you. A good collaborator will press you to refine your ideas, and the energy generated by discussion will often help you rise to new heights in your thinking. Whether you're just beginning to think through a topic or trying to determine a strategy for revision, collaboration works well as an aid for creative thinking.

Choose a collaborator who will challenge you. If you're arguing for greater government regulation of imports, find someone who disagrees with that position. See how your adversary responds to your argument and try to strengthen it based on that response. In another circumstance, you might want to choose a collaborator who knows a great deal about your subject and will sympathize with your point of view. Often a graduate student or professor can fill this role. A supportive collaborator can help you think through issues you might not have understood or take into consideration ideas you might have ignored.

In many fields, some people collaborate routinely and jointly author any writing they produce. Almost all writers, however, thrive on give-and-take with friends, colleagues, interested bystanders, and potential readers and would have difficulty continuing to write without the support of such collaborators. Even more informal interaction with people will help you maintain momentum and will also stimulate you to think more broadly and to take greater risks with your thinking and writing.

Using All the Resources of a Writer

In addition to your intellect, you have many resources to employ when you write. You may not think that some of these, such as imagination for example, are suitable to use in writing nonfiction. In any kind of writing, however, the more resources you enlist, the richer your writing. Your dreams, your imagination, your feelings, and even your unconscious expand your repertoire of resources. Don't assume that such influences interfere with writing nonfiction. Good writing of any kind results from full use of all your faculties.

Anytime you get stuck or find yourself up against a difficult problem, step back and think through your resources. Let's assume, for example, that you have written a draft of a paper reviewing the outcomes of different types of psychotherapy. You've covered all the data, but you don't feel you really communicate the differences between the therapies and how those differences influence the outcomes. After thinking about it repeatedly, you draw a blank. No matter how you think about it, you can't come up with an alternative way of presenting your ideas.

When straight thinking doesn't work, or for a change, turn to your imagination, your unconscious, or your emotions. For a start, let's approach the problem imaginatively. Try free associating to the word *psychotherapy*. What comes to mind? Imagine a therapy session. How does it go? Pretend you go in to talk with someone about a problem. How might that person respond? Calling on your unconscious, can you bring to mind any associations or experiences with psychotherapy that might help you? How do you respond emotionally to different types of psychotherapy?

Activities like these might lead to several possible solutions. You might think about presenting the types of psychotherapies by giving an example of an interaction between a sample client and several different therapists, highlighting the differences in the way they respond to the same situation. You might also describe the positions different therapists might take on a given issue. Your feelings about different psychotherapies might lead you to look more closely at how you present the outcomes. You review each type of therapy with its outcome in your draft. Would it be more effective to look at all the outcomes together and compare them?

If you have been unable to solve a problem using only logic as a resource, you have not yet begun to fight. To keep your writing lively and interesting and to increase its effectiveness, use all of your resources when you write.

Using Imagination

All of us have the capacity to imagine, to develop images in our minds, and to use those images to create new ideas. Few of us, however, rely on imagination or use it in a constructive way to assist our thinking and writing. Instead of rejecting the apparently fanciful thoughts that cross your mind, pay attention to them. Welcome the images that appear in your mind without warning and at first seem irrelevant to the thought that provoked them. Embedded in those thoughts and images are a rich store of information and ideas that can enliven your writing and help lead your thinking in new directions

───────── EXERCISE: INVOKING IMAGINATION ─────────

Although imagination does not always put itself at your disposal, you can invoke it by creating the right conditions. Looming deadlines and pressure to meet someone else's expectations do not foster the right conditions, nor does an unending expanse of leisure time in which to create. The right combination of structure ("I think I'll begin here") and freedom ("This paper isn't due for a few days") invites the influence of imagination, which, if you pay attention to it, can play a determining part in what and how you decide to write. Try invoking your imagination the next time you're considering how to approach a writing assignment. Sit down under a tree or relax in a comfortable chair and follow the images that occur to you as you concentrate on the task. Before you allow another image to appear, make sure you see how each idea contributes to your thinking about the task, how even though it may seem silly, it does apply in its way. Make a chart or draw a picture of the flow of ideas, indicating how they connect to each other. For example, a chart of your thinking (just before Thanksgiving) about the subject of food production in the Americas might look like that shown in Figure 5-6. How would you translate this chart into prose? Make your own chart and try writing out one of your silliest or most problematic ideas while you're still relaxing. Try connecting an improbable thought (like the lima beans) to your main idea. Later, see if you can't incorporate that bit of imagining and writing when you're working on your assignment.

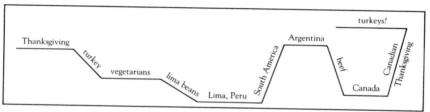

Figure 5-6

Using the Unconscious

The unconscious works much the same way imagination does, although it intrudes more and is more difficult to invoke. Using it consists primarily of recognizing a message from the unconscious when one crosses the boundary into consciousness and recording it before it fades out or you unknowingly chase it away. When you're working hard on a piece of writing, particularly over an extended period of time, you may not notice that your unconscious is working on it too. If you pay attention to your dreams and daydreams, however, you will probably discover that more of yourself than just your conscious mind is working on the problem.

The best part about contributions from the unconscious is that we tend to perceive them as effortless. Solutions to problems that occur in dreams seem as if they required no work at all. It's comforting to think that if you just take a nap, you might have more success at generating a topic than you are having by forcing yourself to think about it. Not even the unconscious, however, can create something out of nothing. You have to prepare your dreams with the raw material they need to provide you with new discoveries. You could probably accomplish the same ends consciously if your inhibitions did not prevent you. Fortunately, unconscious thoughts and images do not bow to the same masters that control your conscious mind. As a result, they offer access to thinking that your consciousness blocks off. Because such thinking has to overcome obstacles to get your attention, it is often even more precious.

Use the unconscious to overcome resistance to new ideas and to get around the restrictions your sense of propriety imposes on you. If you want to sample the resources of your unconscious, try the following exercise.

——— EXERCISE: EVOKING THE UNCONSCIOUS ———

The unconscious emerges most readily in dreams and along the borders between sleeping and waking, and it often expresses itself in visual images, which you have to interpret before they can prove useful to your writing. If you are good at daydreaming, you can use that mode, or you can try thinking about your writing just before you fall asleep. Make sure you have a pencil and paper handy to record your images before they slip your mind. First, clear your mind of everything else by relaxing for a few minutes and allowing intrusive concerns to surface and dissipate. Then focus your attention expectantly on the subject about which you are writing. Don't try to control your thoughts; give in to them. You want to raise to consciousness ideas that exist in your head but have not made themselves known to you. Don't evaluate or analyze what crosses your mind; just try to realize it so that you can recall it later when your mind is less receptive. If you fall asleep, don't worry. As soon as you wake up, write down whatever you can remember about what you were thinking or dreaming. Sometimes unusual and unexpected ideas surface from the unconscious, and it can be difficult to apply them to the immediate problem. Look carefully at and follow through all your ideas, however, and you may find interesting connections that lead to new insights on the material and the writing process.

Using Emotions

Emotions also present a rich resource for writers. We often respond to experiences emotionally but rarely pause to examine our responses or use them as data while we're thinking or writing. When you react to a piece of writing emotionally—by crying or laughing, for example—your reaction becomes part of your experience of the writing and influences how you perceive that piece of writing after that. You respond emotionally to the process of writing and to writing you create as well. If you pay attention to your emotions, they will influence your perception of your writing and provide more information you can use to aid you in decision making.

——— EXERCISE: THINKING ABOUT EMOTIONS ———

While you're writing or thinking about writing, you experience a variety of feelings, most of which you probably ignore or suppress under the assumption that, if you let them, your feelings will interfere with getting the job done. You may feel hungry, lonely, excited, discouraged, anxious, or hundreds of other ways while you're writing or thinking. Next time you're working, try to make yourself aware of how you're feeling. Let your emotions register in your conscious mind and ask yourself why you're experiencing that feeling at this time. If a paragraph you've just written makes you feel uncomfortable, it's probably better to realize that now than to try to override your feelings and forge ahead.

In addition, allowing your emotional self to converse with your conscious mind gives you access to important information. If you're feeling discouraged or bored, then you're probably going to bore your reader as well. If you're feeling excited, that excitement will probably communicate itself through your writing. Whatever your feelings, trust them, examine them critically, and allow them to influence your perceptions. While you're working on a specific writing project, try recording your feelings throughout the process. Can you identify stages that coincide with demands the process of writing makes on you? Do you, for example, need reinforcements (food or human contact) at a certain point or feel like giving up just before you're ready to conclude? Try charting your emotions through several writing projects. Are there many similarities?

If you know that you need emotional support at a certain stage while writing, or that your feelings become too intense if you work too long, you can help yourself by accommodating your emotions. You can also make yourself aware of how your ideas and your expression of them affect you, which can help you imagine how they might affect an audience. For example, if you recognize that your research for a paper on Holocaust survivors is depressing you, you can take steps to alleviate your depression. If you don't realize you're depressed, your feelings can easily overwhelm your thinking. On the other hand, if you use your feelings as a resource, you can consider the fact that many people won't want to read about the Holocaust because they won't want to be depressed. A realization like this one can help you decide to make an effort to get over your depression, thereby lifting a burden from your thinking. With renewed energy, you can address the decisions you have to make.

Heightening Your Consciousness

Many people believe that creativity flows from lack of consciousness and that trying to control creativity destroys it. However, much research shows that creative thinking requires not less consciousness, but more. The most receptive state of mind for creative writing is easy enough to achieve through concentration and self-control. For maximum efficiency, you want to loosen up your conceptual inhibitions and tighten up your instincts and intuitions.

More than anything else, you need to trust your creative potential and have confidence in your ability to develop thinking skills that do justice to your ambitions as a creative writer. Don't surrender your goals for the sake of feasibility, and certainly don't give up just because you're lazy or because inspiration fails to strike on demand. Creativity responds well to nurturing, and if you create a receptive environment for it, the results may surprise you.

For a start, practice extended thinking. Don't come to any conclusions until you have thought through a problem or subject from all the angles you can generate, considered it again from at least two alternative perspectives, sought a response from at least one collaborator, and daydreamed about it. When you're sure you have exhausted the subject, think about it again, this time from a writer's point of view. Try to capture the form of your thinking, possibly in a drawing or diagram. What does this idea remind you of or make you think about? Left to your own devices, with no need to satisfy anyone except yourself, how would you write about this subject? What prevents you from doing it that way?

Keep a notebook or some notecards handy and keep jotting down your thinking. Carry this writing around with you and add to it whenever you have a free moment—riding on a bus or train, eating lunch, or taking a break between classes. Make your writing a high priority among the subjects that are vying for your attention and allow it to distract you from other concerns. Some of the most successful and compelling connections between ideas occur to writers in unlikely contexts because they give themselves permission to think them.

Creative writers experience the act of writing as a release of energies and influences that have filled their minds and preoccupied them for a length of time. Sometimes the length of time spans hours, sometimes months or weeks, sometimes years. However long it takes to reach the point when thinking explodes into writing, the release is just as welcome and the feeling of accomplishment just as gratifying. When you begin writing in earnest, or maybe when you finish, the intensity of your thinking will diminish, and the heightened consciousness that has governed your behavior will recede, its purpose accomplished. If what you write satisfies your ambition, you may never call to mind again the thinking that made it inevitable. However, if you choose to reexamine your thinking, you can always heighten your consciousness and reestablish the concentration required to inspire creative thought.

This Chapter in Brief

No matter how much or how little you write, and no matter how seemingly mundane the writing tasks you do, you can become a creative writer. With practice, you can learn to enlarge and diversify your thinking; you can overcome the limitations imposed by your education and experience; and you can cultivate cognitive, emotional, and psychological resources you never suspected you had. Special genius, unique talent, or a particular facility are not required. If you have courage and commitment and aren't afraid to fail, then you might well succeed.

The preceding pages contain lots of advice about how to cultivate creativity, some of which may have struck you as obvious or preposterous. Perhaps you find yourself grumbling, "Sit down under a tree and daydream, indeed! Bah, humbug!" Consider for a moment, however, that these suggestions might work. Such procedures have helped many writers, and they could help you as well. Nothing, however, will make a difference if you don't believe in your ability to create. Trust yourself first and then

1. Think throughout the writing process. (The need for creativity does not evaporate when you choose your topic.)
2. Take risks.
3. Always write creatively.
4. Practice creative thinking.
5. Use all your resources to enrich your writing.

Self Portrait, by James Ensor

6

The Writer's Personality

Personality and Voice

Do you recognize this voice? "Hello, students. My name is Cad. I am glad to know you. If you ask me questions, I will try to answer them for you. You can ask me anything you want to know about a college in the United States and I will try to find the answer. For example, if you want to know how many students attend the University of Pennsylvania, I can tell you that Penn has approximately eight thousand undergraduates. If you want to know where Evergreen State College is located, I can tell you that it is in Olympia, Washington. I cannot compare colleges or give opinions, but I can give you the facts. Do you understand me? Good, I am sure we can work together. Please ask your first question now and then press Enter. Okay. I'm waiting. Don't forget to press Enter after you type in your question."

If you have used computers to gain information or solve problems, this voice will sound familiar. Although different programs approach users differently, computer voices have a lot in common. What makes this type of prose sound as if it were written by a computer? The sentences tend to be short, simply constructed, and easy to follow. The voice sounds solicitous because its purpose is to serve. Besides introducing itself, the computer wants to convey information as clearly as possible. As a result, it almost always combines pleasantries with instructions. In addition, it tries to give users the impression that they are interacting with an intelligent being rather than a machine, so it pretends to engage in conversation. Its inability to vary from a set script, however, makes it clear to users that, unlike a person, the computer lacks personality.

Vocabulary, sentence structure, style, organization—all these elements combine to create a voice that speaks through any piece of writing. Although we do not hear that voice the way we hear speaking voices, we imagine how it sounds and, more particularly, we imagine who speaks it. We may not be able to picture a person in graphic detail, but we come away with an impression of a personality or a lack of personality, as in the case of the computer. In many, though not all, cases, the more interesting or authoritative we find the personality, the more receptive we are to the writing. We respond not so much to the argument itself, but to the influence of the person who presents the argument, just as we respond face-to-face to a person's appearance, gestures, and tone as well as to the words spoken.

Let's listen to some famous voices in nonfiction. H. L. Mencken's newspaper columns, which appeared largely during the 1920s, made him a well-known voice and commentator on the American scene of his day. Many contemporary readers continue to enjoy his work, not just because of his sometimes seething attacks on middle-class life, but because of his outrageous and commanding voice, which, although full of indignation and authority, speaks in tones the average person can easily comprehend. In "The Penalty of Death," Mencken asserts:

> Of the arguments against capital punishment that issue from uplifters, two are commonly heard most often, to wit:
>
> 1. That hanging a man (or frying him or gassing him) is a dreadful business, degrading to those who have to do it and revolting to those who have to witness it.
> 2. That it is useless, for it does not deter others from the same crime.
>
> The first of these arguments, it seems to me, is plainly too weak to need serious refutation. All it says, in brief, is that the work of the hangman is unpleasant. Granted. But suppose it is? It may be

quite necessary to society for all that. There are, indeed, many other jobs that are unpleasant, and yet no one thinks of abolishing them—that of the plumber, that of the soldier, that of the garbage-man, that of the priest hearing confessions, that of the sand-hog, and so on. Moreover, what evidence is there that any actual hang-man complains of his work? I have heard none. On the contrary, I have known many who delighted in their ancient art, and prac-ticed it proudly.

Whether or not you agree with Mencken's views on capital punishment or find his cynicism merited, his voice provokes a response. He hesitates at nothing, blithely comparing the work of the hangman to that done by plumbers, garbagemen, and even priests. We might ask whether the fact that Mencken has heard no complaint from the hangman really consti-tutes evidence. By the time we've finished arguing that point with him, however, we realize that we've been suckered anyway, since the whole issue has no relevance to the main point, which he hasn't even begun to cover yet. Repeatedly and with gusto, Mencken sets his readers chasing their tails not because he argues persuasively, but because he asserts his views so emphatically. Who is this *I* who presumes he knows it all?

Another famous twentieth-century voice induces quite different feel-ings in readers. Martin Luther King, Jr., a trained and accomplished public speaker, brought the familiar cadences of the sermon to his writings. Even in his "Letter from Birmingham Jail," written in response to a group of clergymen who had published a statement objecting to his policies, King carries readers forward on a tide of rhetoric that leaves his imagined voice ringing in our ears:

> We have waited for more than 340 years for our constitutional and God-given rights. The nations of Asia and Africa are moving with jetlike speed toward gaining political independence, but we still creep at horse-and-buggy pace toward gaining a cup of coffee at a lunch counter. Perhaps it is easy for those who have never felt the stinging darts of segregation to say, "Wait." But when you have seen vicious mobs lynch your mothers and fathers at will and drown your sisters and brothers at whim; when you have seen hate-filled policemen curse, kick and even kill your black brothers and sisters; when you see the vast majority of your twenty million Negro brothers smothering in an airtight cage of poverty in the midst of an affluent society; when you suddenly find your tongue twisted and your speech stammering as you seek to explain to your six-year-old daughter why she can't go to the

public amusement park that has just been advertised on television, and
see tears welling up in her eyes when she is told that Funtown is closed
to colored children, and see ominous clouds of inferiority beginning to
form in her little mental sky, and see her beginning to distort her
personality by developing an unconscious bitterness toward white people; when you have to concoct an answer for a five-year-old son who is
asking: "Daddy, why do white people treat colored people so mean?";
when you take a cross-country drive and find it necessary to sleep night
after night in the uncomfortable corners of your automobile because no
motel will accept you; when you are humiliated day in and day out by
nagging signs reading "white" and "colored"; when your first name
becomes "nigger," your middle name becomes "John," and your wife
and mother are never given the respected title "Mrs."; when you are
harried by day and haunted by night by the fact that you are a Negro,
living constantly at tiptoe stance, never quite knowing what to expect
next, and are plagued with inner fears and outer resentments; when
you are forever fighting a degenerating sense of "nobodiness"—then
you will understand why we find it difficult to wait. There comes a
time when the cup of endurance runs over, and men are no longer
willing to be plunged into the abyss of despair. I hope, sirs, you can
understand our legitimate and unavoidable impatience.

King offers evidence to support his claims, but his powerful voice is
what most commands our attention. Like Mencken, King relies on assertion for his authority, using active verbs and permitting no room in his
argument for alternative points of view. Unlike Mencken, however, King
structures his writing to overpower his readers. Like a preacher, he speaks
at length without hesitation and without showing any obvious concern for
whether his readers are following him. One sentence goes on so long and
contains so many clauses, so many instances of the discrimination he is
trying to document, that the meaning of the individual words is subsumed
in the flow of his prose. We lose track of the specific words and examples
as we get swept up in the emotion King creates. As a result, what we
remember afterwards is not predominantly the language but the cadences
of his speech.

Both Mencken and King have unique voices that communicate distinctive personalities. We have no way of knowing whether the personalities
we experience in their writings represent them accurately, but we relate to
these writers in ways we do not when the writer's voice is less distinct.
When the computer speaks, the message counts most, and the voice exists
only to carry it to the reader. The voices of writers like Mencken and

King, however, are an important part of their messages. We relate to the personalities of these writers, as expressed in their voices, not to their arguments alone. Their voices influence our understanding—probably more effectively than the logic of their prose influences our intelligence.

The Uses of Voice

Traditionally, writers in disciplines that value objectivity have downplayed voice and worked to rid their prose of such characteristics that convey personality. Audiences in these disciplines perceive the subjectivity of personal style as a weakness in the writing. Perhaps you do, too. Certainly, when convention requires you to write impersonally, you take a risk if you permit too much personality to emerge in your writing.

Like other decisions writers have to make, the decision about how much personality to reveal involves trade-offs. For conveying information, even a computer-simulated voice can be effective, and too much personality can inhibit communication of the facts. In other contexts, however, readers read more diligently when they sense a writer through the text. They prefer relating to a person, not just to pages of printed matter.

Although you inherit a voice over which you have no control, anyone can learn to eliminate or cultivate an accent or to speak more softly, boldly, or with greater emphasis or enthusiasm. As a writer, too, you can learn to modulate your voice, disguise it, or cultivate it, if you choose.

How do you know when to personalize your writing, when to speak in your own natural voice? Use your own voice whenever you can. Although flaunting your individuality may offend some readers, most people respect writers who, no matter what role they're playing—that of student, expert, or employee—can be themselves. Sometimes you may feel uncomfortable with a role you are required to play in writing and your writing will reflect your discomfort. Rather than struggling to speak like someone else, try to find a voice that sounds appropriate but also suits your personality. Let's look at some of the options.

Speakers' Voices and Writers' Voices

The writer's voice is always a device, and writers choose their voices as self-consciously as they choose their subjects or forms. Some writers use voice as a means of identifying themselves to their readers. For example, devoted readers would recognize the voice of a favorite columnist, like

Russell Baker or Erma Bombeck, anywhere. Bombeck's harried housewife persona speaks in tones that distinguish her from all imitators. In an article titled "Who Are Harder to Raise—Boys or Girls?" from her collection *Motherhood: The Second Oldest Profession*, Bombeck argues:

> If you want to stir up a hornet's nest, just ask mothers, "Who are harder to raise—boys or girls?"
> The answer will depend on whether they're raising boys or girls. I've had both, so I'll settle the argument once and for all. It's girls.
> With boys you always know where you stand. Right in the path of a hurricane. It's all there. The fruit flies hovering over their waste can, the hamster trying to escape to cleaner air, the bedrooms decorated in Early Bus Station Restroom.
> With girls, everything looks great on the surface. But beware of drawers that won't open. They contain a three-month supply of dirty underwear, unwashed hose, and rubber bands with blobs of hair in them.

Her concentration on the humor in the annoyances of everyday life, her consistent representation of herself as a frustrated housewife and mother, and her closeness to her readers, whom she assumes share her frustrations, make Bombeck easy to identify. In addition, her informal, conversational tone along with her short, punchy sentences and paragraphs and familiar vocabulary create an unmistakable journalistic voice.

Whether Bombeck speaks from the heart, or whether she just pretends, she uses her voice to accomplish purposes she could never accomplish if she represented herself differently. Many writers have written about family life with a great deal of humor, but Bombeck's portrayal of herself as an ordinary housewife and mother has earned her the loyalty and trust of countless readers who identify with her situation. She never uses words her readers wouldn't recognize or talks about subjects that demand any specialized knowledge or experience. Bombeck invites anyone to join her in enjoying the fruits of her unique perspective on American family life.

Erma Bombeck sounds as if she is talking when she writes, making her appear friendly and informal and breaking down any barriers that the printed word might create between her and her readers. Many other writers, however, project voices that take advantage of the distance writing permits. Like Bombeck, Eudora Welty writes about homely subjects in a sincere and friendly voice, but her prose strikes the ear as more "literary." It seems more carefully planned and less as if it just rolled off the tongue in an effusive moment. In her descriptions of life growing up in Mississippi, Welty presents herself more as a chronicler of events, using time as well as a more considered style to create distance between her readers and her narrative. The following passage is from an essay called "The Little Store" in Welty's *The Eye of the Story:*

> My mother considered herself pretty well prepared in her kitchen and pantry for any emergency that, in her words, might choose to present itself. But if she should, all of a sudden, need another lemon or find she was out of bread, all she had to do was call out, "Quick! Who'd like to run down to the Little Store for me?"
>
> I would.
>
> She'd count out the change into my hand, and I was away. I'll bet the nickel that would be left over that all over the country, for those of my day, the neighborhood grocer played a similar part in our growing up.
>
> Our store had its name—it was that of the grocer who owned it, whom I'll call Mr. Sessions—but "the Little Store" is what we called it at home. It was a block down our street toward the capitol and a half a block further, around the corner, toward the cemetery. I knew even the sidewalk to it as well as I knew my own skin. I'd skipped my jumping-rope up and down it, hopped its length through mazes of hopscotch, played jacks in its islands of shade, serpentined along it on my Princess bicycle, skated it backward and forward. In the twilight I had dragged my steamboat by its string (this was homemade out of every new shoebox, with candle in the bottom lighted and shining through colored tissue paper pasted over windows scissored out in the shapes of the sun, moon and stars) across every crack of the walk without letting it bump or catch fire. I'd "played out" on that street after supper with my brothers and friends as long as "first-dark" lasted; I'd caught its lightning bugs. On the first Armistice Day (and this will set the time I'm speaking of) we made our own parade down that walk on a single velocipede—my brother pedaling, our little brother riding the handlebars, and myself standing on the back, all with arms wide, flying flags in each hand. (My father snapped that picture as we raced by. It came out blurred.)

We don't feel as close to Welty as we do to Bombeck, because we have more sense of a writer and less of just an ordinary person. Would a person just telling a story about her childhood to her children or grandchildren or friends think to use expressions like "through mazes of hopscotch" or "played jacks in its islands of shade"? Would she sustain in casual speech such a long and richly detailed image of the activity that took place along the route between home and "the Little Store"? Perhaps. We are more likely to believe, however, that while Bombeck might be cracking jokes to a friend on the telephone or to a neighbor across a back fence, Welty sits somewhere quietly and reflects and writes. We like Welty nonetheless, even though she cultivates this posture. Some of you may even like her more for it.

The Voice of Authority

When trying to sound like an authority, it's not at all difficult to sound like a bore. Writers who become so involved in their subjects that they forget their readers suffer from this tendency. You can deaden even the most stimulating subjects by sounding so uninterested yourself that you put your readers to sleep. You can also enliven the most deadly subjects by sounding like someone readers would enjoy knowing.

Defining terms helps readers share the language that initially separates them from a more knowledgeable writer. An academic writer's willingness to avoid jargon and explain discipline-specific vocabulary reveals a person sensitive to the concerns of readers and interested in involving them in the subject. In his article "Contextual Understanding by Computers," Joseph Weizenbaum demonstrates this kind of concern for his reader's understanding. He begins by explaining:

> I compose my sentences and paragraphs in the belief that I shall be understood—perhaps even that what I write here will prove persuasive. For this faith to be at all meaningful, I must hypothesize at least one reader other than myself. I speak of *understanding*. What I must suppose is clearly that my reader will recognize patterns in these sentences and, on the basis of this recognition, be able to recreate my present thought for himself. Notice the very structure of the word "recognize," that is, know again! I also use the word "recreate." This suggests that the reader is an active participant in the two-person communication. He brings something of himself to it. His understanding is a function of that something as well as of what is written here. I will return to this point later.
>
> Much of the motivation for the word discussed here derives from attempts to program a computer to understand what a human might say to it. Lest it be misunderstood, let me state right away that the input to the computer is in the form of typewritten messages— certainly not human speech. This restriction has the effect of establish-

ing a narrower channel of communication than that available to humans in face-to-face conversations. In the latter, many ideas that potentially aid understanding are communicated by gestures, intonations, pauses, and so on. All of these are unavailable to readers of telegrams—be they computers or humans.

How do you feel about this writer? Since writing about computers tends these days toward a genre unto itself, requiring command of a highly specialized vocabulary in order to follow the logic of a basic argument, Weizenbaum's avoidance of jargon is especially striking. In the process of explaining his terms and his subject, this author reveals himself as a person, offering us not just information to absorb but someone with whom to interact. The interest in himself that Weizenbaum arouses may strike other writers who value objectivity as unnecessary or even inappropriate, but if readers respond positively to a writer's personality, they are more likely to respond with equal enthusiasm to what that writer has to say.

Third-Person Personal Voices

Many writers, like Bombeck and Welty, use the first person because it brings them closer to their readers and because they feel more at home in the first person. Third-person voices do not refer to themselves as *I*. If writers in the third person refer to themselves at all, they usually present themselves as *this writer* or *this researcher*. The effect of this more impersonal style is to create distance between the writer and the reader, leaving the reader free to concentrate on the writing. In many instances, that distance serves the writer's purpose. However, it is also possible to compromise, to write in the third person and still maintain an informal relationship with your readers.

Even when writing about subjects that lend themselves to formal presentation, in some situations writers prefer to use a conversational voice. Rather than putting yourself at a distance, you can speak as if your readers were people you might know, who share your interests and who are familiar with the world as you see it. Lewis Thomas, a doctor and medical administrator, frequently uses such a voice when he writes for general readers. In an essay titled "On Natural Death," he begins:

> There are so many new books about dying that there are now
> special shelves set aside for them in bookshops, along with the health-
> diet and home-repair paperbacks and the sex manuals. Some of them

are so packed with detailed information and step-by-step instructions for performing the function that you'd think this was a new sort of skill which all of us are now required to learn. The stronger impression the casual reader gets, leafing through, is that proper dying has become an extraordinary, even an exotic experience, something only the specially trained get to do.

His everyday language, his effort to engage the reader ("you'd think"), his reference to a common experience (browsing in a bookstore), all combine to make Thomas seem highly approachable and a real person, not just "the writer." His prose sounds more formal than casual conversation, but not contrived. We never lose a sense of the individual writer.

In a more formal voice, Rachel Carson, a scientist, urges her readers to protect the environment. In "The Obligation to Endure," she explains:

> It took hundreds of years to produce the life that now inhabits the earth—eons of time in which that developing and evolving and diversifying life reached a state of adjustment and balance with its surroundings. The environment, rigorously shaping and directing the life it supported, contained elements that were hostile as well as supporting. Certain rocks gave out dangerous radiation; even within the light of the sun, from which all life draws its energy, there were short-wave radiations with power to injure. Given time—time not in years but in millennia—life adjusts, and a balance has been reached. For time is the essential ingredient; but in the modern world there is no time.

In spite of the relative formality of Carson's presentation, she speaks in a clear and identifiable voice. Although she uses more formal syntax and language than Thomas, she communicates her individuality in her willingness to take a stand, to speak what she perceives as the truth, to argue honestly for what she believes. Whether or not we agree with her point of view, we sense a person writing who is willing to reveal not just her reason, but her values and emotions. She sounds in no way like a fanatic or a preacher. On the contrary, her controlled and eloquent prose adds power to the obvious depth of her conviction and helps us see a serious and concerned individual through the words.

Distinctive Voices

The voices that we read that make an impression on us are produced by distinctive writing styles. Such voices do not suit all occasions in writing.

Just as you wouldn't wear a tuxedo to a baseball game, you wouldn't want to assert your personality too much in a scientific paper, where the subject should take precedence. In some instances, however, distinctive voices enrich the subject and give it a level of meaning that a less distinctive voice could never convey.

Much of what we experience as unique about a person we attribute to style—a special way of dressing, an expressive use of body language. In writing, too, we admire style: distinctive uses of language, unusual metaphors and analogies, turns of phrase that please the senses. We don't always require it, but we respond to good style much the way we respond to a great actor. We might have enjoyed a lesser performance, but exposure to a real master raises us to another level entirely.

The achievement of recognizable style in writing depends primarily on the writer's command over the language and its forms. Although not every noteworthy stylist controls a mammoth vocabulary, most serious writers know a lot of words and a lot of ways of putting them together into sentences and paragraphs. In addition, those words need to be familiar enough for the writer to think of using them in unusual and even bizarre contexts. Such fluency is achieved only through practice and after considerable experience.

Of course, quantities of words by themselves add nothing to writing and may even ruin it, particularly if the words are jargon or overused. Familiarity with colloquial usage and with the trendiest new words does not create good style, although it will make a statement about your personality. Respect for some of the more traditional representatives of the language along with a good ear for new sounds, however, can be a great advantage to a writer.

In a traditional vein, E. B. White is considered by most readers to be a master stylist. Not only does he use a great variety of words, but he uses them in ways that create images, arouse feelings in his readers, and create a distinctive voice. In "Once More to the Lake," an essay describing his return to a lake his family had visited for many years while he was growing up, White draws us in and invites us to share his experience with words and images that seem fresh and alive:

> I took along my son, who had never had any fresh water up his nose and who had seen lily pads only from train windows. On the journey over to the lake I began to wonder what it would be like. I wondered how time would have marred this unique, this holy spot—the coves and streams, the hills that the sun set behind, the camps and the paths

behind the camps. I was sure that the tar road would have found it out, and I wondered in what other ways it would be desolated. . . .

From the fresh water up his son's nose to the tar road seeking out his hideaway, we sense a self-conscious writer-personality presenting himself, in his own style, to his audience. He uses words deliberately the way an artist arranges paint on a canvas, but his control extends beyond individual words. Later in the same essay, he stretches the sentence almost to its limit to convey a single idea:

> Summertime, oh, summertime, pattern of life indelible with fade-proof lake, the wood unshatterable, the pasture with the sweetfern and the juniper forever and ever, summer without end; this was the background, and the life along the shore was the design, the cottages with their innocent and tranquil design, their tiny docks with the flagpole and the American flag floating against the white clouds in the blue sky, the little paths over the roots of the trees leading from camp to camp and the paths leading back to the outhouses and the can of lime for sprinkling, and at the souvenir counters at the store the miniature birch-bark canoes and the postcards that showed things looking a little better than they looked.

In this lyrical outburst, White carries the reader from phrase to phrase, just barely pausing at a comma or semicolon until he completes his image and the sentence ends. Such a sentence does not appear by chance. Clearly, White considers what he wants to say and how he wants to sound. This sentence works to convey his distinctive voice.

A distinctively different personality is conveyed through the highly stylized prose of Maxine Hong Kingston. In her effort to represent her Chinese-American heritage in her book *Woman Warrior*, Kingston cultivates a unique style:

> Whenever she had to warn us about life, my mother told stories that ran like this one, a story to grow up on. She tested our strength to establish realities. Those in the emigrant generations who could not reassert brute survival died young and far from home. Those of us in the first American generations have had to figure out how the invisible world the emigrants built around our childhoods fit in solid America.
> The emigrants confused the gods by diverting their curses, misleading them with crooked streets and false names. They must try to confuse their offspring as well, who, I suppose, threaten them in simi-

lar ways—always trying to get things straight, always trying to name the unspeakable. The Chinese I know hide their names; sojourners take new names when their lives change and guard their real names with silence.

Chinese-Americans, when you try to understand what things in you are Chinese, how do you separate what is peculiar to childhood, to poverty, insanities, one family, your mother who marked your growing up with stories, from what is Chinese? What is Chinese tradition and what is the movies?

As she elucidates customary Chinese ideas and images by describing them in the contemporary American idiom, Kingston communicates in a unique voice. Even the title of her essay, "No Name Woman," speaks of a culture removed from the American mainstream, yet one which, by finding expression in standard English, asserts its place in the American tradition. Phrases like "the emigrants confused the gods by diverting their curses" or "the Chinese . . . guard their real names with silence" may strike some readers as exotic, and they do represent ideas associated with traditional Chinese culture rather than contemporary America. Kingston's effort to express these ideas in language modern American readers can absorb, however, creates a completely original writer-personality, a blend of the two cultures with which she identifies.

Although writing teachers frequently counsel students to resist cultivating style in their writing until they have a firm grasp of basic modes of expression, style is hard for writers to avoid. You may not have a good singing voice, but you still have a voice; and, by the same token, you may not write beautifully, but you certainly have a personal style. At some point, if you take yourself seriously as a writer, you will need to work on your style and develop your own voice as a writer. The style you possess by virtue of being an individual will express itself inevitably in your writing, but not necessarily to your advantage. In the same way that you can work at achieving style in the way you dress, you can develop, alter, or enhance your writing style.

Establishing Your Own Voice

You don't want to sound like a nonentity in your writing, but you also don't want to overwhelm your audience with your personality or embarrass them. Readers do not want to feel as if they're eavesdropping, reading someone's private diary: "I cried and cried when I found out Grandpa had cancer. I really freaked out." You also want to come across as the right kind of person, not just some person: "When the nurse mentioned the oncology unit, my stomach dropped. I thought that *oncology* meant cancer, but I wasn't sure. When we walked down the hall, I knew. Each person we passed was bald."

If you're writing about space exploration, you may want to sound curious, excited, perhaps even a little in awe or fearful, but you don't want to sound like an amateur stargazer. Whether or not you are a professional astronomer or astronaut, you should behave like a professional writer. Inform yourself about your subject, organize your information, and present your ideas clearly and coherently. Within that framework, you have plenty of room to express your personality without embarrassing your readers or yourself.

Expressing Your True Self

Before you seek out any other methods for cultivating personality in your writing, try relaxing and allowing your personality to emerge in your natural voice. Before you begin to write, think about your subject for a while, about what you have learned while researching it or exploring it in your mind, about how you feel about it. What kinds of emotions does this subject arouse in you? Which, if any, of those emotions do you want to convey, or even reveal, to your readers? How do you feel about your readers? How much do you want to share with them? Do you want them to understand that you enjoyed this project more than anything you've undertaken in the field or, on the other hand, do you want them to know that sociology bores you to death? How frank do you want to be or should you be?

Through answers to questions like these, you can begin to construct an image of your personality, as you perceive it and as it might become, at this moment and in relation to this specific context. For example, you might feel eager to communicate in writing your newly developed appreciation for modern art or genetics. You might need to tone down such sentiments for the sake of professionalism, but trying to suppress your enthusiasm or banish your feelings would harm your paper. Instead, as a strategy, you can use your process of discovery as a model for teaching your readers and try to infuse in them the same exhilaration you experienced when you came to understand the intricacies of the subject.

Frequently, the concern student writers have with evaluation colors their relationship to their subject, leading them to adopt the personality of the dutiful student, whether or not they identify with that personality, and whether or not it has any relationship to the topic they are pursuing. Self-examination, experience, and assurance from the instructor that the writer's independent stance has value can encourage student writers to stop substituting a stereotype for the genuine article. Instead of sounding like everyone else, be yourself, assuming you have information, ideas, observations, and intuitions that merit communicating to readers. When your overriding interest requires you to put expressing your subject ahead of your interest in self-expression, you can freely choose to do that, adopting a professional stance toward your topic and avoiding personal idiosyncrasies that would seem inconsistent with that stance. In many instances, however, expressing some aspect of yourself is one of the most satisfying and pleasurable outcomes of writing, so relax and enjoy it.

Developing a Repertoire of Voices

Close your eyes and concentrate on hearing a familiar voice. What characteristics make that voice unique? What kind of vocabulary does the voice use? Does it use a lot of nouns or verbs? Does it favor a particular sentence structure or tend to speak in phrases rather than sentences? Does it express a specific attitude toward itself, toward the listener, or toward its subject? Can you capture that voice in writing?

Although some people think of voice—like skin or eye color—as a given, unchangeable quality, changing voices in writing can in fact be no more difficult than changing clothes. In the same way that you might choose to express different aspects of your personality on different days by wearing different colors or styles, you can cultivate a variety of voices in your writing. When you're feeling funny, you can write like a comedian; when you're feeling profound, you can sound like a philosopher. You can also shout: "I am talking to you! Do you hear me?" You can whisper: "Ssh. Talk very quietly, so you don't wake the baby." You can cajole: "I just hate to go out by myself at night. I get so scared. Won't you please walk me to the library? Please?" You can lecture: "All right, class, today we're going to discuss the causes of the Civil War." Or you can express an unlimited number of voices, tones of voice, or speakers in your writing.

There are also occasions when a particular voice can serve your purpose in writing. For example, if you're trying to show how unconvincing a gun lobbyist sounds defending the sale of Saturday night specials to anyone who wants them, you could try writing in the lobbyist's voice. If you want to convince readers that the Soviet Union is full of people who want peace as much as we do, you could write as if you were a Soviet citizen trying to persuade Americans to control the spread of arms.

If you think of using different voices as acting or role-playing in your writing, the possibilities multiply. You are restricted only by your ability to create a given role convincingly. In order to sound like a scholar, for example, you have to understand what characterizes a scholar and how to write to convince readers that a scholar is the author. If you sound like a student trying to imitate a scholar, you give yourself away. It's a good idea to write about what you know about, and it is equally advisable to cultivate voices you know well. If your readers happen to be more familiar with the voice you're attempting to capture than you are, you run a big risk of alienating them. Even the various voices you own, however, offer you more of a selection than you may have realized you had.

For practice, try capturing a variety of voices by writing a few sentences for each. See if you can sound like

> a student asking a professor a question
> a person undergoing a job interview
> a psychiatrist talking with a patient
> a grandparent talking to a grandchild
> a sportswriter
> a movie or music critic
> a salesperson

Show your paragraphs to friends and see if they recognize the voices. What makes a voice convincing? What ruins a voice's credibility?

As a resource for your writing, make a list of all the roles you play in daily life. For example, you might be

> a son or daughter
> a brother or sister
> a friend
> a student
> an athlete
> a cook
> a roommate
> a club member
> a Catholic, Muslim, or Jew
> a black, white, or brown American
> an Italian, a Pole, or an Asian-American

a southerner, northerner, westerner
a person from the city or country
a jogger
an optimist

The list could go on and on. Looking over your own list, perhaps similar to this one but undoubtedly much longer, how many distinctive voices can you affiliate with your various roles? These voices include not just your own voice, when you are playing that role, but other voices that role brings to your attention. For example, if your parents or grandparents were immigrants, are you familiar with the sound of their accented English? If you're an athlete, can you convey the sound of a coach's voice? For every role you play, you probably could recognize and express several distinct voices. Go down your list and record all the voices you can think of that are associated with your various roles.

Of all these voices, you might only select a dozen or two dozen with which you feel comfortable and to which you are confident you could do justice in writing. That still leaves you as a writer with many options every time you sit down to write. Instead of simply writing as yourself at that particular moment, whoever that may be, you can write as any number of selves if you believe that a particular voice will assist you in accomplishing your purpose in writing. For example, if you're writing an essay on hostilities between black and Vietnamese students in a city high school, the fact that you are Vietnamese and from a city yourself could prove to be a great resource. Instead of writing in the voice of any college student, you might want to write as a Vietnamese-American and include firsthand experiences to show readers how the data looks when someone from your background presents it.

On the other hand, there are times when you will want to conceal elements of your identity. You may, for example, want to assume a role as an objective observer even though you have strong opinions on the subject you are writing about and can speak with the voice of experience. If you want to claim that a certain theory in sociology fails to explain why some minorities have succeeded more easily than others in reaping the benefits of mainstream American culture, your personal experience will carry little weight. You might even turn your readers against you if you reveal your biases by speaking in a voice which clearly represents its own self-interest. In a case like this, you will want to restrict yourself to your scholar-researcher role and speak with the authority that accrues to you as a representative of an academic discipline. When you choose an appropriate voice for a given writing assignment, you need to consider the ramifications of your choice.

Obviously, the more voices you command, the more versatility you have as a writer. You can convey your message by using the logic of your argument to influence your readers, or by relying on the credibility of your chosen voice, or by doing both. Not infrequently, establishing the credibility of a voice is the writer's primary purpose in writing. Convincing us that this person who sounds like a crook also speaks with the authority of a senator is just what a political columnist wants to accomplish. Even when voice plays more of a supportive role in your writing, however, it can contribute greatly to or detract from your overall effectiveness. In your effort to represent yourself as a serious writer on a variety of subjects, the voices you control can provide an additional and often hidden resource for your writing.

Using the Resources of Language

We all know that word choice can substantially affect the meaning of a sentence and that the misplacement of a modifier can prevent readers from understanding the writer's intention. If we read "The children ran all the way down the hill covered with snow," we have no way of knowing for sure whether the writer intends us to understand that it was the hill or the children who were covered with snow. Changing "the hill covered with snow" to "the snow-covered hill" makes the intended meaning of the sentence clearer. Substituting "embankment" for "hill" differentiates this slope from others, adding an element of precision to the sentence which signals readers that the writer takes the job of description seriously. Serious writers clearly want to present themselves as people attentive to language and language structures. Anyone can think of hill, but only a writer recognizes hill as too generic a term and seeks out an alternative like embankment.

Much of what you convey to readers about yourself comes through language and language structures. If you use slang, you sound like a teenager: "I thought that was awesome." If you use lots of three-syllable words, you sound like a pseudointellectual: "I will not condescend to pay attention to the incoherent ramblings of those imbeciles any longer." If you write much the way many of your peers may write, using a modest vocabulary and a small variety of sentence and paragraph structures, you sound just like everyone else: "I wouldn't listen to them again." How can you distinguish yourself as a writer?

Many nonwriters believe that the quality of writers' ideas distinguishes them, once they establish control over the basic elements of writing. Certainly ideas matter a great deal, but command of the language matters also. Much of the most profound, beautiful, and influential writing we read addresses ideas that have intrigued people for centuries and reflects little new thinking. When the poet Robert Frost invites us to stop by woods on a snowy evening or consider the value of fences, we heed his voice not because his message startles us, but because his choice and arrangement of words impresses us. The same is true of a rhetorician like Martin Luther King, Jr. The cadences of his prose affect readers at least as forcefully as his ideas and readily distinguish him from other writers on the same subjects.

To establish a unique personality in writing, develop an intimate and rewarding relationship with language. Become familiar with many different words and many different ways of using those words in interesting combinations. Review the variety of acceptable sentence structures, recognizing ways in which you can enrich your writing by employing different sentence structures in random order to create a specific design or rhythm in your writing. For example, begin with a simple declaratory sentence: "I saw the cat." Then add a question: "Did you?" Follow these two sentences with one that's more complex: "I wondered at the time where it was going, but I didn't think to ask." Then go back to a simpler form: "I'm sorry now."

For a different effect, try repeating similar sentence structures: "Although I came early, no one asked for my help. Even if I had brought my tools, they wouldn't have trusted me. Almost a year ago, I tried the same approach." Then add something different for emphasis: "They just don't like me."

Paragraphs also merit the same kind of attention. Alternating long and short paragraphs helps keep the reader from becoming tired or bored. In addition, breaking up a paper with paragraphs that perform different functions helps add variety and interest to your writing. For example, paragraphs can assert a position and then offer examples: "In the last decade, the Supreme Court has decided in favor of individual rights in almost all cases in which the rights of individuals were at issue. For example, in. . . ." Paragraphs can elaborate on an idea: "Let's look at this problem from two distinct angles. First. . . ." Paragraphs can describe events: "Christianity was pronounced a legal religion by Constantine in A.D. 312. However, it was not until the eighth century A.D. that the Catholic faith had penetrated all areas of what had once been the Roman Empire." The list of possible types of paragraphs could go on at some length.

In order to enliven your vocabulary and discover ideas for sentence and paragraph structures other than the ordinary ones you use and read every day, you need to start attending to language as a writer. Listen to people speaking the way you listen to music. When you hear a word or phrase that strikes you, write it down. Keep a writer's notebook in which you can record language you want to remember and practice imitating language you hear or read and admire. Examine it carefully and try to identify its unique characteristics. What stands out—the nouns, the verbs, the adjectives, the sentence structure, the subject matter? Read writing out loud, so that you can hear the sound of it more clearly; notice the sustained phrases that leave you breathless, the pauses for emphasis, the paragraph breaks that, like the silence between movements of a sonata, give you a chance to stop for a moment and reflect.

When you read a sentence or paragraph that impresses you, examine its structure. Does a sentence begin with an introductory phrase, set apart by a comma ("Arriving at our destination, we piled out of the car"), or does it simply state its subject, verb, object in that order ("They ate fish")? Does a paragraph begin by presenting its main idea in the first sentence and then offering evidence, or does it just survey a scene, describing the appearance of sky, trees, water, as it strikes the writer?

Language expresses ideas, but it also affects readers in discernible ways. A word like *mushy* used in place of *soft* creates a more specific picture in the reader's mind and also influences the reader's attitude. A vivid description of a handicapped person overcoming obstacles might move the reader to want to work with handicapped people:

> The young boy reached out of his wheelchair and grabbed the ball from the air. The wheelchair swayed precariously, but the boy paid no attention. He was determined to catch the ball, and he did. At what risk to his person was an insignificant concern. As the onlookers cheered, the boy suddenly became self-conscious. He looked sheepishly around for someone with whom he could share his satisfaction in private.

Take a piece of writing you consider effective and examine what the sentences and paragraphs do to create their effect. What particular words or arrangement of words influences you? If you change the words around, do they lose their effect? Is it the sound of the words, their meanings, or how they interact with each other that affects you?

Every time you write a sentence or paragraph, all of these considerations vie for your attention. You want the words to say precisely what you mean, but you also want them to appeal to the reader's aesthetic sense as well as influence the reader in specific ways. If you are a no-nonsense writer, then you probably concentrate on saying what you mean, which can be a challenge in itself when you have complex thoughts to express. Many writers, however, recognizing that the pure logic of their arguments may not be enough to influence recalcitrant readers, strive to arouse their readers' interest. Such writers use words the way a weaver uses yarns and threads. Seeking both to communicate and to please and satisfy, the writer as craftsperson acknowledges another separate and entirely different dimension to writing. In comparison to the no-nonsense writer, these writers march to different drummers.

Cultivating a Personal Style

Although everyone has a personal style—a way of dressing, of walking, of communicating oneself that goes beyond voice—some styles do more for the person than others. Cultivate a style in writing that expresses your individuality and communicates something special to others. You don't want people to remember you for being bland or boring or colorless; you want to distinguish yourself for your mastery over language, your sense of timing, your ability to tell a good story, the clarity of your prose, the coherence of your arguments, the control you exercise over readers. Although you may want to change your style to suit different occasions, you want to achieve a sense of yourself that allows you to take best advantage of your style at all times. To do this, you have to cultivate your natural talents and work hard at acquiring additional skills. Style does not leap fully formed from your pen; you have to earn it the same way you earn other desirable distinctions. And it communicates itself, not from the thought down, but from the individual word up.

EXPERIMENTING WITH LANGUAGE

Before you make any decisions about style, learn what's possible. Take some time and experiment with using language to achieve interesting effects. To stimulate your imagination, notice the characteristics of other writers and try incorporating the ones you admire in your own writing without actually copying the writer's style. Look at how different writers describe or argue or put words together. What effects do they achieve with many complex sentences or with prose that is spare and unadorned? Even more importantly, how do they sound, and how do you want to sound? Unless you're an accomplished economist and political scientist, you don't want to write as assertively and with the scope of John Kenneth Galbraith. You can sound like an expert when you write about growing up in your community, but not on America's economic ills, unless you have special expertise or knowledge. Sound like someone you feel you can adequately represent, not like a child pretending to be grown-up.

TRYING OUT DIFFERENT STYLES

Try writing in different styles. Begin by ridding your prose of adjectives or other modifiers, reducing it to its basic components. Use very simple sentences: "I went down the street. I got on the bus. I arrived in town." The sparsity of description in these sentences is striking but not really interesting. Without adding much description, however, you can enliven the prose by using more descriptive verbs and nouns and varying the sentence structure: "I hurried down the pavement. I leaped onto the bus. An hour later, City Hall stood in front of me." The first group of sentences sounds bland; the second has more personality. It might not represent the personality you want to express, but this kind of self-conscious experimentation can help you determine which of your traits you want to express.

Write a paragraph and then go through it methodically and change all the verbs to more active, expressive ones. Every time you use *is*, substitute a verb that conveys action instead of just being. See if you can make your verbs more interesting by stretching your imagination and looking for less common ones. Refer to a file of interesting verbs that you have compiled from your reading, use a thesaurus, or ask friends who have good vocabularies to help you. Be careful about using words inappropriately, but try to add a new verb to your vocabulary every few weeks. Do the same for nouns and adjectives and adverbs. Train yourself to reach for the most expressive word for the job every time you write a word down, if not when you draft, at least when you revise. Never, however, use a word you're not sure of unless you have a reader who will help you by correcting such faults. Almost nothing—except possibly a spelling mistake—undermines your credibility more quickly than a misused word. Don't leave yourself open for attack at the word level. Force your readers to respond to the purity of your logic by leaving them no mistakes to laugh at or to busy themselves correcting.

IDENTIFYING YOUR PERSONAL TRAITS

Examine your writing for tics or for tendencies to overuse certain words or sentence structures. When you write in a hurry, for example, you may rely unconsciously on a small group of expressions. A computer program can help you determine how often you begin your sentences the same way, such as with an introductory prepositional phrase; it can also give you a printout of the first word in every sentence. Check the average length of your sentences as well and make sure you use a variety of sentence lengths as well as sentence structures. A paragraph like: "He got up. He washed his face. He ate breakfast. He went to work. He stayed there all day." would make any reader drift off. Keep readers alert by alternating sentences and paragraphs of different lengths.

COLLECTING RESOURCES FOR THE FUTURE

When you confront unfamiliar words in your reading, write them down, look them up in the dictionary, and store them in a file for future reference. Do the same with phrases that you might like to use sometime or substitute for the tried and true ones you use too much. When you're looking for a good verb, check your verb file. Do the same with interesting nouns, modifiers, sentence structures, and unusual ways of presenting a topic, such as through a dialogue or by adopting the persona of a famous historical figure. Remember that your personality can change, that you can grow under the influence of models or as a result of strong personal motivation. You want to do more than express yourself at the moment; you want to provide for your future. As your ideas and goals develop, you want to ensure that you have the resources to satisfy your expectations.

Working at improving your grasp of language may seem tedious, but the results are worth the effort. If you read a lot and can remember a lot of details, you might not need to write down the new words, phrases, and ideas that strike you, but few people have such a prodigious mental capacity. You can try storing this information in a file in your head, but it's quite simple to open an actual file and to increase your chances of remembering a particular tidbit by writing it down. Creating opportunities to experiment with different styles and voices falls into the same category. If you wait to practice writing sentences and paragraphs until you have mastered the style you want, how do you expect to achieve that style at all? You'll never know the writer you might become if you don't take yourself seriously enough to work at it.

Investing in Your Writing

Many currently popular style books encourage writers to use active verbs, eschew the passive voice, and reduce the number of modifiers in their prose. Although this is generally sound advice, it oversimplifies the concept of style. The process of working on your writing style consists more of achieving understanding, self-awareness, and confidence than it does of following rules. You want to write correctly and in conformity with what your peers, teachers, and members of your audience consider desirable practice, but you also want to write comfortably and to express yourself.

To encourage the emergence of your own sense of style, practice writing about subjects and for purposes and people you care about. The more you involve yourself in the activity of writing, and the more you experience writing as self-expression, the easier you will find it to recognize your style when you read it. Stop worrying about what your English teachers, parents, professors, and friends think you ought to write, and write what you think. Every time you hear a voice other than your own whispering, "Your writing is too wordy," ignore it. Judge your writing on the merits you establish for it. Does it effectively communicate what you want to say to your readers? Does it please you? Does it do justice to your thinking and to your aesthetic sensibilities? Does it adequately represent you as a person?

Create a writer's journal and use it to rehearse your style in private. You can try on different personalities without fear of consequences and see how you come across. You can try writing lengthy, ponderous, academic paragraphs and concise, staccato, journalistic ones. Choose a subject which captures your attention—one related to sex, love, politics, religion, or your future, for example—and then write about it, first subjectively and then more objectively. How does your style change as you become more objective? When you establish more distance between yourself and your subject, do you still recognize yourself in your writing? Whenever you find yourself separating from your writing, writing as if you were someone other than yourself (the typical student, for example), stop and ask yourself what *I* would say. Try inserting a few sentences using *I* as the subject on the order of "I believe" or "I want to say that. . . ." Keeping yourself honest while attempting to sound like an objective observer can prove challenging, but if you want to live up to your standards, you must keep a tight rein on your learned behaviors. Automatic writing does not automatically express you; it probably expresses a style you were taught and readily internalized. Expressing yourself requires more considered effort than you may care to contemplate making. If you want to be a serious writer, however, such effort is mandatory.

When you can choose what you write about, choose subjects that interest you and that you know well. When you feel comfortable with what you have to communicate, you will inevitably communicate more effectively and more naturally. If you find yourself feeling uncomfortable with what you're writing or struggling to manage it, stop writing and do more research. You might have to struggle over which information to include or what angle to take, but you should feel confident about your knowledge of the subject when you start writing. Your relationship to your material should allow you to assume a comfortable writing posture. You may present yourself as an expert, an informed source, an interested lay person, or a newcomer, but whatever posture you assume, the state of your knowledge should warrant it. Your self-assurance will transmit itself in your voice and style, and your readers will defer to your authority as a writer. They may not agree with the position you take, but they will recognize an author when they read one.

When you can choose your audience, write for readers you know and whom you consider your peers. Writing to superiors, although necessary in some situations, rarely puts a writer at ease, and treating support staff as peers usually brings better results than talking down to them, unless you're trying to be funny. When you write for people with whom you have natural relationships, you can be yourself, and your style will reflect how comfortable you feel with the audience you are addressing. You can dare to be bold or put yourself in your readers' hands because you trust them to respond in the way you want.

Most decisions about stylistic details will follow from your decisions about self-presentation. When you control the language and your subject well enough to command the attention of your chosen audience, your readers will respect your choices. Even when you attempt something extraordinary—an old word in a new and unusual context, for example— they will give you the benefit of the doubt. Once you have earned your reputation as a writer, you can venture where you will. Your readers will not always approve or follow you, but they will recognize your right to lead.

Finding a Comfortable Academic Voice

Not infrequently, writers are called on to play roles with which they have difficulty identifying and to speak in voices they do not recognize as their own. For many college students, the academic voice poses such a challenge. Relatively few college students aspire to become academics, and many have difficulty, as students, imitating the voices they read and hear in textbooks and lectures. When students are required to produce academic prose, their writing often reflects their discomfort with the role assigned to them.

If you find yourself in this position, don't try to fake it. Try, instead, to discover a role with which you feel comfortable and which will allow you to speak frankly and with authority. Be a student, someone studying the subject for the first time but someone with basically strong academic and intellectual skills. (If you don't feel your academic and intellectual skills are strong, work on those first.) Often the thinking students have to express gets lost in the rhetoric of academic prose, and you don't want that to happen. You want your ideas to emerge clearly; you don't want to bury them under layers of jargon, which you feel compelled to use whether or not it fits your personality as a writer. Your instructors will expect you to master at least some of the vocabulary of the disciplines you study, but as you become more knowledgeable about the subject matter, you should have no difficulty sounding convincing. You want, however, to avoid feeling forced into a position in which you have to pretend to speak with authority that you don't honestly feel you possess. To avoid this kind of pretense, accept the validity of your role as student.

How does a convincing student voice sound? It sounds:

1. Comfortable and in control. You demonstrate your mastery of the material by your ability to sound at home in the rhetoric of the discipline. For example:

   > Although the dialect and style were com-
   > pletely alien to me, this book was completely
   > American, written entirely by people whose
   > families had been in the New World for genera-
   > tions. Yet, something was missing. The cul-
   > tural displacement these writers expressed
   > seemed different from any other sort I encoun-
   > tered in studying the period. I came to wonder
   > whether I was capable of categorizing the
   > work, and also if I had a right to pass judg-

ment on literature so foreign to my
experience.

You want to sound knowledgeable and up to the intellectual demands the assignment imposes. You do not want to sound as if you're in over your head:

> Indeed, we are self-indulgent and individualistic, but we are also part of the whole of society. So, when the economy was in its recessive state during 1982, many were affected not only as individuals, but as an entirety. It is the combination of the aforementioned social and economic factors which have generated the keen interest on the part of the public. The success of the book may be attributed to the fact that we are human beings with certain inherent characteristics.

This student is struggling to sound like an authority but doesn't have sufficient control of the subject matter to sound convincing. As a result, the general form of the paragraph seems suitable, but the writing lacks substance. The writer needs to come down to a level more appropriate to his expertise.

2. Authoritative. You don't have to be an expert in the field to feel comfortable presenting yourself as an authority on your chosen or assigned topic:

> The three assigned studies, which investigate the causes of pathology, reach different conclusions. Two of the papers argue that social factors determine whether or not a person will require treatment; the third study claims the opposite, citing genetic factors as the cause of abnormality, and concluding that social factors have almost no significance.

You don't want to sound insecure, or as if you don't really understand what you're saying:

> Throughout history, certain traits inevita-
> bly become associated with either men or women.
> Although not always accurate, these social
> formuli help to determine how people properly
> conduct their lives. Shakespeare contrasts Mac-
> beth's view of masculinity and Macduff's view
> of masculinity to illustrate the vices and vir-
> tues of their different characters.

A paragraph like this one, which fails to make its meaning clear,
undermines the writer's authority. The writer's tendency to make
sweeping general statements makes him seem as if he's hunting for
things to say to take up space in his essay. If the writer has a point to
make, it should be clearly stated. If it isn't, readers lose patience
and assume that the writer has nothing to say.

3. Interested. Although much of the compulsory writing you do may
   not interest you at all on the surface, you want to sound interested
   when you write so that you can interest readers:

   > Over the past one hundred years, leaps
   > and bounds have been made in the field of medi-
   > cal science, and, consequently, more people
   > are living longer now than ever before. But
   > are the wonders of medicine actually increas-
   > ing the limit of our life span, or are they
   > just helping us to reach a maximum age which
   > cannot be surpassed? Hayflick's experiments
   > with human tissue cells support the theory of
   > a maximum life span.

   The writer at least sounds alert and interested in her subject. In
   contrast, many student writers sound flat and bored:

   > Symbolic death and rebirth into new form
   > is a point explored by both authors through

```
"regressus ad uterum." This return to uterus
is integral to Eliade's theory of mystical
cosmogonic rebirth. He gives an example of men
symbolically swallowed by a monster, similar
to Campbell's "Belly of the Whale" chapter.
For both authors, the symbolic "regressus ad
uterum" is followed by emergence into a new
level of existence.
```

This writer sounds in control and authoritative, but she doesn't sound interested. She has taken an uninspired assignment, which required her to compare two books, and mechanically performed her duty. Although her writing demonstrates competence, it does not create interest on the reader's part. Probably few people, possibly not even the professor who gave the assignment, would enjoy reading this paper.

Even when instructors inhibit you from writing well by handing out boring assignments, respond with imagination and energy. Choose an approach to your assignment that will permit you to play a role you can play well and to speak in a voice you will recognize as your own when you read it back. If the assignment doesn't interest you no matter how you interpret it, think of one that would and talk it over with your instructor. Explain your concerns and request permission to express yourself instead of pretending to be someone foreign to your experience and expertise. Many instructors have little sense of how some assignments can deaden student writing. If you seem conscientious and eager to learn, surely they will have the heart to let your writing live. It's certainly worth a try.

This Chapter in Brief

Whenever you write, you express yourself. Sometimes expressing yourself dominates your effort, and sometimes expressing your subject takes precedence over self-expression, but you inevitably convey your personality to your readers. Personality communicates itself in writing primarily through voice. Readers cannot see how you look, but they can hear how you sound, and on the basis of your voice, they draw conclusions about you as a person.

For this reason, as well as others, be yourself when you write. Enlarge your sense of self to include all the roles you play, but don't pretend to be someone you're not. Concentrate on using your experience as a reader and all the resources of language to establish your own voice. In addition:

1. Have confidence in yourself as a writer.
2. Care about what you write.
3. Care about your readers.
4. Identify yourself with your writing.
5. Write with courage and conviction.

APPENDIX

Some Information about Using and Documenting Sources

Although you may occasionally write purely from your imagination, much of the routine writing you do will involve information gleaned from sources. In academic writing, sources are often library books, but they can also include articles in magazines and journals, newspaper articles, interviews, data gathered by yourself or someone else, recordings, television and radio programs, movies, videotapes, slide programs, performances, musical compositions, and cartoons, to name a few of the more obvious possible sources. Sources usually become important in college when you write research papers, but journalists write from sources also, as do writers of magazines articles, report writers, and book reviewers. In fact, almost all nonfiction writing refers to sources.

Much of your credibility as a writer depends on the credibility of your sources. When Jonathan Swift in his satiric "A Modest Proposal" refers to "a very knowing American of my acquaintance in London" to substantiate his claim that "a young healthy child well nursed is at a year old a most delicious, nourishing, and wholesome food, whether stewed, roasted, baked, or boiled," we might well suspect the reliability of his source. If he referred us to a pamphlet from the Food and Drug Administration, we might give his idea more credence. On the other hand, in this case it would take powerful evidence to overcome our natural distaste for such a suggestion.

Reason and common sense play an important role in using and documenting sources. If you're not sure how credible your sources are or how many sources you need, consider your readers. How much do they know about this subject? How familiar are they likely to be with your sources? Is what you are writing about new to them, or are you trying to change their minds about a subject they know well? What type of evidence is likely to influence them most? What sources could you use that they would respect?

The credibility of your sources often depends on how thoroughly and accurately you document them. Simply citing an interview is less convincing than citing a specific date on which an actual interview with a particular individual took place. In some instances, quoting a source is more effective than paraphrasing, especially if the source is someone readers will recognize. Documentation which allows readers to verify your sources makes the sources—as well as your own writing—seem more trustworthy. Readers want to know that if they turn to the page given in the work cited in your paper, they will find the exact words you have quoted or they will acquire the same information you have conveyed.

In addition to using common sense and reason and knowing your readers, you need to follow an appropriate set of guidelines whenever you document sources for a paper. The guidelines you choose should be those respected or required by your audience. If you're writing for publication, every journal and magazine provides guidelines for submissions in each issue. For example, *College English,* a journal published by the National Council of Teachers of English, has a paragraph about editorial policy in the front of each issue requiring that essays conform to the Guidelines for Nonsexist Use of Language in NCTE Publications. Writers are instructed to follow the current edition of the *MLA* (Modern Language Association) *Handbook,* to "Use parenthetical references and a list of 'Works Cited,' " and to "avoid discursive footnotes."

In academic writing, nearly every discipline has customs writers should observe in documenting sources. If you're not sure about those customs, ask a professor or graduate student in the field. If you're writing for a course, ask your instructor to specify which method of documentation is preferred. Some instructors don't care which guidelines you use as long as you're consistent. The style guides most commonly used by students, the *MLA Handbook for Writers of Research Papers* (Third Edition, 1988)— usually for writing in the humanities, in subjects such as languages, literature, and history—and the *Publication Manual of the American Psychological Association* (Third Edition, 1983)—used mostly in the social sciences, in sociology and psychology, for example, and in some of the sciences— provide information on precisely how to document in nearly every imaginable situation. In addition, they offer advice about style and conventions relating to punctuation, abbreviations, headings, quotations, tables and figures, formats, margins, page numbers, and almost anything else you might need to know. Once you declare a major, or if you plan to go on to graduate or professional school, you will want to buy a copy of the appropriate guidebook for your discipline.

Students generally use guidebooks for instruction in how to cite references within a paper and in bibliographical format. Each discipline (and each guidebook) has slightly different customs in these areas. In recent years, these differences have become less noticeable. They often involve different customs for parenthetical references (MLA does not ordinarily list the date of publication in parenthetical references, while APA does); a different name for the same item, such as "Works Cited" (MLA) versus "Reference List" (APA); or slightly different punctuation or different arrangement of information (MLA puts the date of publication at the end of the entry, while APA puts it in parentheses right after the author's name). To some extent, these differences make sense when you consider the type of evidence each discipline requires. For example, when writing about literature, it seems appropriate to cite the author and page number of a text; when citing social science research, the date of a study would be as relevant as the page number.

References within a Paper (MLA and APA)

Both MLA and APA guidelines endorse parenthetical references within a paper over the older method of placing a number in the text and providing a footnote at the bottom of the page or endnotes at the end of the paper. However, because parenthetical references interfere with the flow of the writing, they should be kept short, and footnotes should be used instead if references are unavoidably long or when a "content note"—usually an explanation or amplification of material in the text—is indicated.

For references to a book with a single author, MLA recommends that you simply put the author's name and the relevant page number in parentheses:

His whole family had tended for generations
to choose imagination over action (James 99).

This reference refers to Henry James's *Autobiography*, which in this case would be the only book by James listed in Works Cited at the end of the paper. Instead of the author-page number format used by the MLA, the APA uses the author-date format:

> At least one researcher has connected lan-
> guage with social class (Bernstein 1971).

The page number would follow the date if it were needed.

Common sense plays a major role in making decisions about parenthetical citations. If you name the author in the sentence, you don't need to repeat the name in parentheses:

> James's family had tended for generations to
> prefer the life of the imagination over action
> (99).

If you use two works by the same author, you can cite the name of the relevant work in the sentence or, following APA guidelines, give the date of publication in parentheses, or both:

> Writing for Social Scientists provides much
> sound advice for graduate students (Becker 1986).

MLA distinguishes two works by the same author by citing the title of the relevant work in parentheses, while APA distinguishes by date of publication. For more extensive information about most situations you will encounter, consult the appropriate style book.

List of References at the End of a Paper (MLA and APA)

The list of references at the end of a paper should complement the parenthetical references in the body of the paper. In other words, entries should be listed alphabetically by the author's last name because your references in the text refer to the author's last name. (Bibliographies which serve a purpose other than providing information the reader needs to identify and locate sources cited in the text may follow a different format. When writing for courses, be sure to find out whether your professor wants a list of references or a bibliography, which might include background readings or suggestions for further reading. Journals will provide such information in their guidelines for submissions or description of editorial policy.)

APA and MLA styles differ in several respects in the way they advise

writers to present their lists of Works Cited or References. MLA divides
the citation into three parts—author, title, and publication information—
and separates those parts by using a period followed by two spaces. A
citation of a book would look like this:

```
Katz, Michael J.  Elements of the Scientific Pa-
    per.  New Haven: Yale UP, 1985.
```

The comparable APA version of this citation follows:

```
Katz, M. J.  (1985).  Elements of the scientific
    paper.  New Haven: Yale University Press.
```

Note that in APA style only the author's initials are used, the date follows
the author's name, and only the first letter of the title is capitalized. The
MLA guidebook suggests using UP instead of writing out University Press,
but the APA manual does not. It does, however, suggest listing the publisher's name in as brief a form as possible. A sample citation for a journal
article shows similar differences. The MLA version would look like this:

```
Berlin, James.  "Rhetoric and Ideology in the
    Writing Class."  College English 50 (1988):
    477-94.
```

The comparable APA version varies somewhat:

```
Berlin, J.  (1988) Rhetoric and ideology in the
    writing class. College English, 50, 477-94.
```

For information on how to list other sources as well as how to deal with
more complicated situations such as when you're using translations, edited
works, works by multiple authors, books in several editions, and unpub-
lished manuscripts, among others, consult the appropriate style book.

Other Systems of Documentation

In addition to the author-page system and the author-date system for
parenthetical references, some fields, especially in the sciences, use a
number system. In the number system, references are numbered at the end

of the paper, and the appropriate number appears in the text in parentheses, followed by a comma and a page reference when needed:

    Extensive research (5) supports these conclu-
    sions.

Some writers use superscript numbers instead of parentheses:

    Extensive research[5] supports these conclusions.

To indicate more than one source, multiple numbers are used:

    Extensive research (5, 11) supports these conclu-
    sions.

In some cases, the references are listed in the order in which they appear in the text; in other instances, the references are listed alphabetically and a number is assigned to each one that identifies the citation in the text. Listing references alphabetically keeps all works by the same author together, but then the numbers in the text don't follow sequentially. Listing references in the order in which they appear in the text makes it easier for the reader to locate information, but makes it more difficult to see at a glance which authors are cited and how many works by a single author are used.

There is no authority on documentation for science writers comparable to the MLA or APA style books. Some instructors may recommend the *CBE Style Manual* published by the Council of Biology Editors, which endorses alphabetical listing of references or literature cited. The *CBE Style Manual* refers writers to guidelines issued by the American National Standards Institute in New York for precise instructions. It suggests the following format for a bibliographic citation for a book:

    Adams, J. L. Conceptual blockbusting. New York:
        W. W. Norton; 1979.

A standard journal article would be listed as follows:

    Berlin, J. Rhetoric and ideology in the writing
        class. College English. 50: 477–94; 1988.

In upper-division college courses, instructors often advise students to target a paper for a specific journal and follow the guidelines provided by that journal. *The American Journal of Medicine*, for example, instructs authors to follow the Uniform Requirements for Manuscripts Submitted to Biomedical Journals. It endorses the number system of documentation with references listed at the end in the order in which they are cited in the text. Instructions for authors in scientific journals, which are often at the back of the journals, also give guidelines about presentation of tables and figures, length of abstract, and the appearance of the title page.

The Literature Cited section or list of references in scientific papers follows a format similar to that recommended by the APA, placing the date at the beginning of the reference, but the punctuation and exact format vary. For more information about how to document sources and list references in scientific and technical writing consult the *CBE Style Manual*, guidelines published by professional organizations in your field, a field-specific guidebook, such as Herbert B. Michaelson's *How to Write and Publish Engineering Papers and Reports*, or instructions in specific journals.

Acknowledgments (continued from p. iv)

H. L. Mencken, "Capital Punishment," from *Prejudices, Fifth Series*. Copyright © Octagon Books, a division of Hippocrene Books. Reprinted by permission of the publisher.

From "On Warts," *The Medusa and the Snail* by Lewis Thomas. Copyright © 1979 by Lewis Thomas. Reprinted by permission of Viking Press, Inc.

From "On Natural Death," *The Medusa and the Snail* by Lewis Thomas. Copyright © 1979 by Lewis Thomas. Reprinted by permission of Viking Press, Inc.

Barbara Tuchman, *History as Mirror*. Reprinted by permission of Russel & Volkening as agents for the author. Copyright © 1973 by Barbara Tuchman.

Joseph Weizenbaum, "Contextual Understanding by Computers," *Communications of the ACM*, August 1967. Copyright © 1967, Association for Computing Machinery, Inc. Reprinted by permission.

Eudora Welty, "The Little Store," from *The Eye of the Story*. Copyright © 1979, Random House, Publishers, Inc. Reprinted by permission of Random House, Publishers, Inc.

200 words from "Once More to the Lake," from *Essays of E. B. White*. Copyright © 1941 by E. B. White. Reprinted by permission of Harper & Row, Publishers, Inc.

William Carlos Williams, *Collected Poems, Volume 1: 1909–1939*. Copyright, 1938 by New Directions Publishing Corp.

PICTURE CREDITS

Marc Chagall, *Lovers under Lilies*. Philadelphia Museum of Art: Private Collection.

James Ensor, *Self Portrait*. Philadelphia Museum of Art: The Louis E. Stern Collection.

Jacob Lawrence. *The Libraries Are Appreciated*. Philadelphia Museum of Art: Louis E. Stern Collection.

Auguste Rodin, *The Thinker*. Philadelphia Museum of Art: Gift of Jules E. Mastbaum.

Ben Shahn, *Nearly Everybody Reads the Bulletin*. Philadelphia Museum of Art: The Louis E. Stern Collection.

Fumio Yoshimura, *Typewriter*. Philadelphia Museum of Art: Given by Mr. Benjamin D. Bernstein.

INDEX